Also by Brian Meadley.

CW01498045

An RAF Anthology

From Blue to Grey
Woodfield Publishing (2005) ISBN: 9781903953723
(with F D Hoskins and R H Robson)

Novels

A Question of Duty
New Millennium (1997) ISBN: 9781858451190

The Trial of Charlie Windsor
(The sequel to *A Question of Duty*)
Trafford Publishing (2004) ISBN: 9781412024365

The Contingency Plan
Moyhill Publishing (2007) ISBN: 9781905597116

Boasting is 'shooting a line' in the RAF and is frowned upon.
An example might be: *There I was, upside down....*

There I Was...

Memories of an old Aviator

Second and Enlarged Edition.

by

Brian ('General') Meadley

Moyhill Publishing

This revised and updated edition published in 2024
A CIP catalogue record for this book is available
from the British Library.
ISBN 978-1-913529-23-9

First published in 2012 by Moyhill Publishing.
ISBN 978-1-905597-36-9
Printed in UK.

Moyhill Publishing.
Unit 135393, PO Box 7169, Poole, BH15 9EL, UK

I dedicate this book to the most wonderful
group of People in the World:

THE AVIATORS

Contents

PREAMBLE

I have been flying aeroplanes for over sixty years, and have had some interesting, challenging, exciting, and frightening experiences, and met some wonderful people. These memories are about some of the episodes and people I met along the way.

Over the years I have met so many splendid people that if I were to mention them all, this book would be the size of a telephone directory. So I have included only a few of them, picked more or less at random, and I earnestly hope that I have not offended anyone who feels 'left out'.

There is nothing here about my personal or family life or of family friends – that would be of no interest to other aviators, but might one day be the subject of another set of memories.

The Grossmith Brothers wrote a wonderfully funny book entitled 'The Diary of a Nobody' in which nothing of any significance ever happens to the diarist, Mr Pooter, though he regards the most trivial incident as of earth shattering importance.

The difference between Mr Pooter and me is that I know that nothing important ever happened to me. I did not sink the Bismark, or shoot down any German aircraft – I never even fired on the Queen's enemies.

But if you have been in the Services, or have been an aviator, or know someone who has, I think you will find some of my ramblings evocative – they will remind you of episodes and experiences of your own, they will raise a smile or a laugh, occasionally offer food for thought, and here and there, might make you wipe your eye.

Chapter 1

WANABE PILOT

When I was ten years old, the Germans tried hard to kill me. It was 1940, and I was a scholarship boy at the splendid King Edward VI School, Southampton, evacuated for the war to Poole. There was less enemy activity at Poole, but still enough to excite us schoolboys. The Battle of Britain had started and Germans in bombers came over every day and tried to kill us. They were not aiming specifically at me (as far as I know) – they were trying to kill as many of us as they could, and I was, and am, proud to be one of us. They missed me, but succeeded in killing many thousands of us, and maiming many thousands more.

I well remember the wail of the air raid sirens, and the foreboding they caused, and can still recall the sight of large formations of enemy bombers in the skies. If they were high enough (I now know) they produced short exhaust trails. Then came the deep menacing thump of exploding bombs and the rather lighter but more intense anti-aircraft fire. Then there was the roar of RAF fighters diving to the attack, and the rattle of machine gun fire. Several times I saw aircraft diving down trailing smoke, and a few times men hanging on parachutes.

We boys did not see as much of this as we would have liked, because the adults – the spoilsports! – made us go to the air raid shelters. I can still smell the creosoted wood and concrete of them.

Sometimes one the boys at school would announce that an aircraft had crashed at so and so. We would jump on our bikes and race over to see it.

Not far from my school was a large brick factory, which had a large area where the bricks were laid out to dry. It had a roof, but no sides. One day, one of the boys said that a German airman had crashed through the roof. We got on our bikes again and got there as soon as we could. There was the hole in the roof, where the man had come through, presumably with a failed parachute. And there was the place where all the bricks had been flattened, leaving a distinct dent in the ground. The body had been removed, but there was still a large red stain.

Although I did not have any profound knowledge of what was going on, it was clear to me that the larger aircraft with the black crosses were the ones trying to kill us, and the smaller ones with roundels were the RAF fighters who were doing their utmost to stop them. I do not recall trying to rationalise the situation, but I do remember that I desperately wanted to grow up as soon as possible, become a fighter pilot, and help them.

Of course, the war did not last long enough for me to do that, though had it not been for the atomic bombs, I might well have been involved in the invasion of Japan. Had that happened, it may well be that this book would never have been written.

One day, we were at the railway station to meet someone when an Air Force pilot strode by – the first one I had ever seen. I could already recognize RAF pilot wings. I looked at him in awe, marvelling at the fact that I was standing near a man who could actually fly an aeroplane.

'One day', I remember thinking, 'One day, I will, too'. He made me more than ever determined to become an RAF pilot.

The first book I ever bought with my own pocket money was the Penguin book on aircraft recognition. That was early in 1941, and it cost 6d. It contained silhouettes, photographs, and details of all the significant aircraft of the day, and I soon learned it all, cover to cover. I noticed the other day in a bookshop that it is now in reprint. But I did not need to buy it – I still have the original on my book-shelf, and it is one of my treasured possessions.

The Germans stopped their daylight bomber campaign because (I now know) they could not sustain the losses that the RAF was inflicting on them. They turned to night bombing instead. The RAF, (I now know) had virtually no night fighter capability, and the gunners were literally shooting in the dark. So the Germans could roam over Britain at night as they wished. The result was that the air raids were more frequent and longer lasting, and sometimes we spent all night in the air raid shelter. Sometimes we took blankets and pillows with the intention of doing just that.

That situation lasted throughout the winter of 1940–41 until the Germans called it off in the spring. This was not because (I now know) they had been defeated at night by the RAF, but because they had decided to 'tidy up' their Eastern front by eliminating the Russian threat before finally annihilating Great Britain. We all know how that turned out.

The war continued overseas, and we schoolboys no longer had a front line seat. We could still sometimes see some of the training that the services were doing – training aircraft, army manoeuvres, ships coming into harbour and so forth.

One day, during a French lesson, we could see through the classroom windows a DC3 flying around with a man suspended underneath. He was a paratrooper under training, and when he jumped, (I now know) the static line and parachute pack should have stayed with the aircraft, the weak link between the pack and the parachute should have broken, and he and his parachute should have fallen clear. Evidently, the weak link had failed to break.

We were all looking out of the windows at this when the French master sternly called upon us to pay attention to the lesson.

"But sir! There is an aircraft with a man hanging underneath!"

Mr Fassnidge, who had finished his First War service as an infantry major, and who forever walked with a limp caused by his war wounds, looked out. He straightened his shoulders, turned and faced the class, and said: "Boys! That man is doing his duty. We will continue to do ours, which is the study of French verbs."

We heard later that they could not pull the man back on board and so had cut his line when they were flying low and slow over the sea near a rescue boat. But he did not survive.

Many years later, I was to do the parachute course myself.

When we were shown over the aircraft, still a DC3, the instructor showed us a winch near the jump door, and explained that in the unlikely event that a weak link failed to break, the winch can be unwound, the jumper can engage the hook into his harness, and one man can wind him back in. I was tempted to mention that I remembered the event that established the need for the winch. But then I thought that that was such an unlikely coincidence, that the instructor might think me some kind of nut, so I kept quiet about it.

And so the war went on. But now the Germans did not often try to kill us on the home front with explosives. But they still tried to kill us by starving us to death.

The Germans controlled the whole continent of Europe, thus cutting off most of our normal sources of supply. The Australians, New Zealanders and South Africans sent what extra they could, but the ships had to go a very long way through extremely hazardous waters, and many were lost in the attempt. The Canadians were not quite so far away, and they sent as much as they possibly could to help. To do so, they had to cross the Atlantic in which lurked German surface raiders and U-boats. Canadian and British merchant seamen risked their all and all too often gave their all to keep us fed.

But it was still not enough. Our weekly rations were reduced and reduced again. We were allowed tiny amounts of butter and cheese, small amounts of tea, a shilling's worth of meat, and one egg a week. Public parks were dug up to plant potatoes and cabbages, and everybody was urged to grow as much in their gardens as they could. People were eating swedes and mangel-wurzels, which before the war had been cattle food. We were all well aware that we were desperately short of food, but it was not so clear to the public that the country was getting precariously short of fuel, ammunition, weapons, machine tools, aircraft, guns, tanks and indeed of everything needed to fight the Germans.

The country (I now know) could not have survived without considerable help from somewhere, and it came, of course, from the Americans. They were constrained by the international laws of neutrality, but they broke those laws and sent us all they could. Much of the merchandise they sent, they really needed for themselves, but they sent it anyway. When we ran out of money, they invented 'lend-lease' by which we either paid nothing, or paid later. We finished paying off the debt only this century. And American merchant seamen joined the British and Canadians and all too often paid the ultimate price for doing so.

And so we survived.

For the next three years, the only British military action based in Britain was the bomber offensive. The bombers were based mainly in Lincolnshire and the east coast, so those of us on the South coast did not see much of it.

The supplies from the Canadians and Americans enabled us to avoid defeat, but by themselves could not bring victory. British forces were not strong enough to make an opposed landing on the coast of Europe and the Germans were not strong enough to come the other way. We could not beat the Germans without military help, and this too came from the same people. From 1943 onwards, the big build up of the army took place and an ever-increasing number of American soldiers together with many Canadians were to be seen, as well as soldiers, sailors and airmen of many other countries. Their equipment built up too, and eventually there were literally miles of tanks and guns and trucks crammed into the roads along the South coast. Then one day they had all gone, and D-day had come.

Now there was once more great air activity for us to see. Fighters and fighter-bombers in large numbers crossed the South coast to attack the enemy in Normandy. I was now fourteen years old and had a much better understanding of what was going on. How I wished I had been in one of those aeroplanes! I became keener than ever to be a fighter pilot.

The war moved east from Normandy, and the aerial activity in our neighbourhood decreased. But if we cycled to a military airfield, aircraft taking off and landing were still to be seen.

Then it was all over – the Germans had surrendered before I had had a chance to take part. Shortly after, the Japanese surrendered too.

This was a disappointment to me personally. But I had read in books about how, in years gone by, regular soldiers had gone from one war to another. I reasoned that these days, the same must surely apply to regular airmen. I decided not to abandon my ambition, but resolved to do my best to join the peace-time Air Force.

I sat the School Certificate at the early age of just fifteen and must have had easy questions, because I got a very good result. So I moved into the Sixth Form to prepare for the Higher School Certificate. At this time some of our regular teachers were coming home from the war. One of them, nice Mr Talbot, had been in the RAF, and I approached him and asked his advice about how to be accepted by the RAF. His reply surprised me, but was remarkably prescient. He suggested that I do as well as I possibly could at sport.

I was never very good at team games, and so was not very interested in them. I did like athletics, though, and I trained really hard and won the school mile race that year. It was a close run and exciting finish and I broke the school record. I did well in the other distances too, and the Sports master told me that I was Captain of Athletics, though there were no duties attached to the title.

Rowing was my other interest, and again I trained really hard and succeeded in stroking the senior eight to victory. The master in charge of rowing was pleased with me and told me to consider myself Captain of Boats, though again, there were no responsibilities involved.

I was sure that the nice Mr Talbot had had a hand in these quasi 'appointments'.

Two years passed quickly and it was time for Highers. Once again, I was lucky with the questions, and got a very good result. I was awarded what was known in those days as an open scholarship, which meant that the county would pay the fees of whatever university I went to.

At that time, candidates for Cranwell, Sandhurst or Dartmouth had to take the common Civil Service Exam. I never understood why the Civil Service ran it. But if a candidate had high enough marks in the right subjects in School Certificate and Higher School Certificate, (English, maths and physics) he was excused the exam.

This did not happen very often, but I was lucky enough to have the right grades.

Everybody urged me to take the scholarship up, but as the nice Mr Talbot knew, my heart was elsewhere. I was by then nearly old enough to join the RAF so I sent in my application.

In those days, one could apply to go to an FTS for a one year course leading to a short service commission, or the much tougher three year course at the RAF College at Cranwell leading to a permanent commission. With the nice Mr Talbot's advice and encouragement, I applied for Cranwell.

While I was waiting for a reply, I received a letter from the army calling me up for National Service, and ordering me to report to the army barracks at Bulford on a specified day and time. This put me in a quandary. How could I go to an interview with the RAF if I were stuck somewhere on Salisbury Plain? I went to the local army recruiting office and explained that I was unable to comply with their request.

The Recruiting Sergeant was a big, impressive man. He told me that he had heard all the excuses why people should not do their National Service, but that there was no way out.

"But Sergeant", I pleaded, "I simply can not risk missing the interview."

"Listen to me, my lad. If you fail to report as ordered, you will be arrested, brought before the court and probably sent to prison. Do you think that the RAF would accept you if you had a prison record?"

His argument was convincing, and anyway there was no certainty that I would be granted an interview. So I decided to do as I was told, and cross the next bridge when I came to it.

Many of my fellow conscripts hated the army. I didn't, even though it was not where I wanted to be. I liked the order and discipline and the way that everything worked so efficiently and smartly. After my basic training, in which I was proud to earn the marksman badge, the Army decided that it could use my limited talents best in the Royal Army Education Corps. This carried an automatic minimum rank of sergeant, which was some consolation for not having a more exciting job, such as driving tanks or firing big guns. I completed the training course and took up my duties teaching simple subjects – mainly the three Rs – to serving soldiers, a significant percentage of whom were illiterate.

I was just settling down to my duties when, at last, I received an invitation to attend the RAF Selection Board. I went to see the Adjutant, who very kindly gave me enough time off to go.

The selection procedure comprised interviews, discussion groups, reaction testing contraptions, and problem solving such as crossing an imaginary chasm on a plank that was just too short.

Though I do not remember the incident, Richard Robson in his excellent book 'An Airman of the Queen, my lads', describes a situation in which he and I were trying to get our team across a shark infested channel with a bit of rope, a barrel and an iron bar. At the critical point our structure collapsed in a heap, and we collapsed in laughter. Robbie opines that the selectors were impressed by the fact that we could laugh in the face of adversity.

My interview with the psychologist was a strange experience. He gazed at me steadily for a long time, than asked: "Are you happy?"

I replied that I was, and that I would be even happier if I passed the selection tests.

After another long pause he asked: "Could you kill?"

I replied that I was sure that I could kill the King's enemies if called upon to do so.

Yet another long pause, followed by: "Do you wet your bed?"

I replied that I had, once or twice, when I was little, but had not done so for many years.

Then he said that I could go. I do not know what he made of me, but I thought he was barmy.

Perhaps the Board was impressed by my dubious sports titles, or by my exemption from the exam, or by the fact that in the Boy Scouts I had made the grade to King's Scout or by my laughing in the face of adversity, but I must have somehow satisfied them, because I was awarded a cadetship, and I received a letter ordering me to report to Cranwell on the 27th April 1949.

How could I go wrong? That was my birthday and what a marvellous birthday present!

I went to see the Adjutant again. He admitted that he did

not know what to do in this situation, so he decided that I had better see the Colonel. The Sergeant Major marched me in. The Colonel was an impressive man. He had a waxed moustache and decorations and campaign ribbons from both World Wars and other campaigns too. Perhaps he had endured too much gun-fire over the years because he was rather deaf.

He asked what I wanted, and I respectfully replied.

"What? What do you want to do?"

The Adjutant leaned over and I thought I heard him say: "He wants to join the RAF, Sir."

"What's that, what's that?"

The Adjutant must have misunderstood him, because he leaned over again and I thought I heard him say: "It's a new-fangled body which seems to have taken over some of the duties of the cavalry, Sir."

The Colonel glared at the papers again and then again at me. Then he said: "You will serve your King and Country in the Army for two years as required by the law of the land. You can then go and join whatever organisation that you please. Dismiss!"

I considered that if I failed to present myself at the appointed time to take up my cadetship, I might very well lose it. So I had to go. And if I could not go with permission, then I would have to go without it. I would have to go absent without leave until the RAF could sort it out. I knew that a soldier could be charged with the more serious crime of desertion if he abandons his kit or 'casts off his uniform'.

On the day, therefore, I put on my uniform, packed all my kit and took it with me to Cranwell.

On the train, I met Richard Robson again. He too had won a cadetship, so perhaps he was right about our shark infested channel fiasco.

Thus it was that I arrived at Cranwell in army uniform. Within minutes I was nicknamed 'General', by which I am known to this day by my Cranwell colleagues.

My contemporaries and I, about thirty of us, were to form Number 54 Entry of the Royal Air Force College. The cadet wing comprised three squadrons and Robbie and I were allocated to B Squadron, whose commander was the formidable Bob Weighill.

11

He welcomed us to the College and explained what we would be doing over the next few days. Then he asked if any one had any questions or problems. I diffidently stood up and said that I had, because I was absent without leave from the army.

"Leave it with me and don't worry about it."

I received by post an honourable discharge from the army some weeks later.

That night I went to bed between new blankets in a new room among new colleagues. As I dozed off, I remembered myself as a small boy watching the Battle of Britain and wanting to be an RAF pilot. Now, I was a member of the Royal Air Force, and starting a course which, if I made the grade, would get me my pilot's wings. How proud and pleased I was!

Where it all began, the RAF College, Cranwell

'54 Entry just before graduation.

'54 Entry 40 years on. **Back Row**: *Don Cooper, Paddy King, Bobby Hutchinson, Colin Foale.*
Centre Row: *Fred Hoskins, Ted Peters, Bob Fox, Phil Farmer-Wright, Sandy Innes-Smith, Norman Glass.*
Front Row: *Tony Dawes, Jock Christie, BM, Dave Keats, Cecil Jonklaas.*

Chapter 2

CADET PILOT

We spent the first two terms living in a barrack block because the RAF wanted its future officers to be familiar with the conditions under which the airmen lived.

(I had assumed that the word 'airman' would be used for those who actually flew. I was surprised to learn that it was the title of the lowest rank – the equivalent of the army 'private')

So it was that my first home in the RAF was a barrack room containing about twenty-four beds. We all quickly made friends with each other, especially those in the adjacent beds, who were, in my case, Bill Nuthall on one side (who was destined to be killed on operations in Cyprus) and Barry Mills on the other (who was to die of a medical condition after he left the Service)

It must have been the cleanest block in the Service because every day we polished the floors, cleaned the windows, and made the ablutions sparkle. We also had to clean and polish our boots and buttons, blanco our webbing, and clean our rifles. Every day our kit was laid out in a precise pattern ready for inspection at any time. Once a day we had a strenuous period of PT, and every morning we did an hour of drilling on the parade ground. When we were considered smart enough, we joined the main Cadet Wing parades, which many visiting army officers considered unmatched, even by the Brigade of Guards.

There was a great deal of class-room time too, studying a wide variety of subjects. Over the next three years we would study aerodynamics in the class room and at the wind tunnel, aircraft structures, engines, both in the classroom and in the workshop, meteorology, navigation, radio communications and navigation aids, radar, English and Service writing, Air Force law and administration. There were classes in government and how the Service ministries worked, and not only did we learn about Fighter, Bomber, and the other Commands, we also studied the organisation and functions of the army and Royal Navy. We learned about imperial history, and studied in detail several campaigns of WW2. We had to learn about all types of aircraft weaponry, not only the nuts and bolts, but the theory of its use. In the Cadets' Instructional Workshops, we learned to strip, re-assemble, run and tune aero engines, and took an aircraft apart and rebuilt it, and learned to make repairs to metal and fabric. On the range, we were taught how to maintain, clean and fire a variety of small arms, and in ground combat training we learned basic infantry skills. Dinner was a parade for which we wore best blue and answered a roll call. On Wednesday and Saturday afternoons there was compulsory sport and Sunday morning, Church Parade. We would not start flying training proper till our third term. Now we would fly in Ansons once a week to learn the rudiments of navigation. The only time in which we were not told what to do was about an hour before dinner and Sunday afternoon.

This time was used to give our boots an extra shine, review the academics we were studying or get a haircut. Gliding, in very low performance gliders, was available on a voluntary basis on Sunday afternoons. I enthusiastically took it up. In hindsight, I was wrong to take on yet another activity, but I did so enjoy it. I achieved my British Empire A and B Gliding Certificates. I deeply regret the passing of that great institution, but I still have the Certificates! So our days were full, and just keeping up required all our efforts.

It did not take long to be most impressed by everything at the College. The senior cadets were so smart, and so fit. Everything was so well organised, and only the best would do. The class room syllabus was huge and amounted to degree standard in several subjects, and it was said that in flying there were no scrape passes – you either got a good pass or no pass. How could I possibly reach the standards required? I resolved that if I did not, it would certainly not be for the want of trying.

Each cadet had his own chore in the barrack room. Mine was keeping the showers clean. Dave de la Harpe's was to weed and water the flower bed outside the front door. We were all doing

Cadet glider. The first a/c I ever soloed.

our stuff early one morning when the Sergeant said: "de la Harpe! Why aren't you watering the flowers?"

"Because it's raining, Sergeant. "Well, you have been issued with a cape, haven't you?"

Dave was an extremely nice fellow from Ceylon. Some years later he was killed in a Vampire in Germany when he pulled out from a ground attack manoeuvre a little too late.

On Friday mornings there was a ceremonial parade. Not only did the Sergeant and the Under Officer inspect our turn out, but the Squadron Commander too. Squadron Leader Weighhill, who could spot a dirty button from two miles away, was very strict. Almost everyone would be criticised – 'coming up to a haircut' or 'trouser creases could be sharper' or 'boots could shine a little more'. If he passed without a word, that was praise indeed! The smartest man in 54B was my good friend Tony Dawes, who did not even seem to try – it just came naturally to him. When the Squadron Commander came to him, he often said: "Good turn-out, Dawes!" To which the only possible reply was: "SAH!"

No one else ever received that compliment. I saw Tony at the Cranwell reunion last year. He is still remarkably fit and smart and looks many years younger than he is.

After the inspection we would march to the main parade ground where we would await the Reviewing Officer, standing to attention for up to ten minutes.

Shortly before the end of term, the Entry had to undergo First Term Boxing. All the senior cadets attended together with most of the instruction staff, including the Commandant. We were paired off and each pair had to box three rounds. No one mentioned it, but you did not have to be a rocket scientist to realize that anyone who showed weakness would not be invited back the following term. Apart from some recent training during PT, I had never boxed before, and would not have done then had I had any choice in the matter. I was paired off with Mike Dark. He was a little bigger and heavier than me, but worse, he had boxed for Public Schools. I decided that the only way I could beat him would be to knock him out in the first second. So as soon as the bell sounded, I went straight for him to do that. Before my fist made contact, however, I felt a pole-axe like blow on my head, followed by another and another. I was told later that HE had knocked ME down in the first second. Apparently I got up and went for him again only to be knocked down again. And Again. And Again. And Again. I cannot claim any credit for stamina or bravery, because I remembered nothing between the first few blows and standing in the shower feeling my battered face.

We all must have done well enough because no one was told not to come back next term.

I did not enjoy it, and I never boxed again. Unless you count the two occasions when I recovered my wife's handbags after Spanish thieves had made off with them. Or the altercation with the Rome airport baggage handler who was on strike.

The long arduous term came to an end, and the Senior Entry, Number 47, graduated. The guest of honour and reviewing officer was none other than Marshall of the Royal Air Force Lord Trenchard, the 'Father of the RAF'. He inspected us, and I had the opportunity to look the great man in the eye. Then, of course, I was there when he addressed the cadet wing.

A wide variety of vacation activities were available, and we were expected to take part. On this first vacation, I opted to

19

join the group going to RAF Upper Heyford to undertake a short parachute course. We were taught how to jump and how to land in various conditions, and then did two practice jumps from a cage suspended under a tethered balloon, then two jumps from a DC3.

They explained that it was quite natural to feel fear. (They could say that again – I was terrified!). The school had developed a training technique of getting the students to react to the word 'GO'! We stood on low benches and jumped a few inches to the floor on the command 'GO'! We did this dozens of times, with the benches getting ever higher. We reached a point where if someone shouted 'GO' we could not stand still even if we wanted to. When we came to 'the fan', which was a fearful device that enabled us to jump off the hangar roof, we found that the 'GO' certainly helped us to overcome our fear. It was the same with 'the tower', which was an even more ghastly contraption.

Came the day for our first balloon jump. I was fairly confident that all my courage coupled with the 'GO' reaction would just see me through. Five of us under the command of Sergeant S... went up. As we ascended, Sergeant S.... pulled out some photographs of a parachutist who had had the misfortune to have a 'roman candle', the Parachute School's jargon for a parachute that sticks together and so fails to open. There were two pictures of the man descending very fast, one of him striking the ground, and a close up of his mangled body.

"Here, pass these round", he said cheerfully. We looked at them, but with rather less cheer.

We reached the 800 feet, and Sergeant S.... quietly said: "Now gentlemen. I am sure that you potential officers do not need a 'go' from me. In your own time, step up to the door and make your exit."

I was wondering if I could ever do it without the Pavlov dog routine, when John Price stood up without a word, went to the door, paused for a moment, and jumped. One of the others did the same. I think I was third, followed by the others.

We all found the experience most exhilarating and looked forward to our next balloon jump, although our longing was tinged with a touch of anxiety.

The jumps from the aircraft were even more exciting. We stood in line as close as possible to the man in front and jumped as soon as he had departed so as not to be too spread out on landing. My second aircraft jump was even more exciting for me because I was made lead parachutist, and had to 'stand in the door' with no one in front of me, and when the dispatcher shouted: "Go!" be first out.

We had learned the important lesson that our fear of not measuring up in front of our comrades was greater than our fear of breaking our necks. I later realized that this was a factor in many really brave and noble deeds performed by servicemen.

Another vacation activity was visiting army and navy establishments. On one visit to the army we were shown over a military prison. The regime there is very strict, even harsh, though, of course, there is no cruelty. The principle is to make the prisoners endure a time that they never want to repeat, and so will never do anything that will incur a risk of going back. It is a very effective system and very few prisoners do go back again. It is a method that should be adopted by the civilian prison system, which is ineffective in that many inmates go back time and again. At one point in the tour, one of the cadets remarked that such and such was hard on the prisoners. The Warrant Officer in charge replied: "Yes it is, but remember that they are all volunteers!"

On a visit to the Royal Navy we were being shown something, I think to do with flag hoisting, and one of the cadets remarked that it was done differently in the RAF.

"And why is that, sir?" asked the Chief Petty Officer.

"I don't really know", answered the cadet, "Tradition, I suppose."

The CPO sniffed: "The RAF is not old enough to have traditions, sir. All it's got is a few 'abits'."

The new term started. We had a new Senior Entry and so a new Under Officer, and we were now the senior of the two Junior entries. Our activities were much the same, though we were a bit smarter at drill and a bit fitter at PT, and our ground studies a bit more advanced.

I cannot say that I ever enjoyed drill and parades, but I would give almost anything to march again with 54 Entry on the College parade ground to the College Band playing the Royal Air Force March-Past.

Just before the end of term I must have said something or done something to upset the Under Officer, though I never found out what it was. He sentenced me to three days restrictions. This involved reporting to him at six p.m. in best blue. He would then examine my turnout in minute detail and any short-coming would result in further restrictions. He would then dismiss me with orders to report back in a different dress, say, combat fatigues, at six fifteen, then another dress, say mess dress, at six thirty and so on till seven o'clock. It was an exhausting process, especially when added on to an already tough day. My good friend Barry helped immensely. He would have all my kit ready and clean as a new pin, and would rapidly get me prepared for the next round.

On the third day, the Under Officer said that my brasses were not shiny enough and awarded me another three days. On the third day of that, two days before the end of term, he said that my shoes were not shiny enough, and gave me yet another three days.

Next day at six, he did not do the normal inspection, but looked at me and asked how I proposed to complete the punishment bearing in mind that there was only one more day of term to go.

"Sir, I will stay behind to do it, or complete it next term, as you order, Sir!"

The suggestion of a smile crossed his face, and he said that he had expected me to cave in and ask to relinquish my cadetship.

"I was wrong about you", he continued, "You are excused your restrictions as of now." Then he added: "Well done! And good luck next term!"

Back at the block, Barry was jubilant. "I knew you would beat him!"

I had not thought of it as a contest between us, but in hindsight, I suppose it was.

Then Barry with a broad grin added: "I knew you wouldn't quit, but I nearly did!" Good old Barry. Thanks again, my friend, wherever you are.

After the Christmas vacation, our lives changed. We ceased to be 'cadets' and became 'flight cadets'. We moved out of the barrack block and into rooms of our own in the College. Ted Peters, Robbie Robson and Malcome Cowper and I were in adjacent rooms, and we became great chums. Malcome was destined to go onto Meteor 10s. One day while he was making a single engine approach, another aircraft blocked the runway. Malcome attempted to go around on one engine, but he was below the minimum speed and height for that to be possible. The aircraft rolled into the ground and he was killed instantly. I still think of him on occasions. For me, he will always be 21 years old.

But the big thing was that we started our basic flying training on the Prentice. The instructors had two students on each group, and I was paired up with Robbie – he of the shark infested channel debacle. Our instructor was Harry Dryhurst, who was a very good pilot and an extremely good instructor. He had been shot down on his first trip in Bomber Command, which was to Berlin, and he hated the Germans with a passion, not because of the misery and privations of life as a POW, but because they had frustrated his ambition to become the best pilot in Bomber Command. He always strove for perfection and wanted and expected us to do the same.

My first three trips ended in failure, because I became airsick and we had to return to base.

HD briefed me for the fourth trip, which was level turning, and added that this was the day when we cured my airsickness. When we got airborne, he demonstrated an aspect of turning and invited me to try. Then another demo followed by my attempt. This went on until the wretched feeling came back again. I said: "I'm sorry, Sir, but I must get my bag out."

"No time for that", he said, as he pulled the nose up till it was nearly vertical. "You have control. You can either recover the aircraft, or we can end up in a smouldering heap. Your choice." Then he folded his arms.

I got the aircraft back to some sort of level flight, when he immediately did the same again, only this time, nose down. Once again I recovered and again he put me into a difficult (for me) situation. We did this about a dozen times, then he asked me if I still felt sick. "Why, no Sir!"

He grinned: "I thought you wouldn't. Now let's get on with the lesson!" I was never air-sick again.

But then a medical problem showed itself. I had difficulty clearing my ears when descending from even the modest heights at which we operated. HD told me to see the MO, who referred me to a specialist, who opined that my nasal passages should be made wider, and I was sent to the RAF Hospital at Nocton Hall to have my head reamed out. They put me in the officers' ward where I was made very welcome.

The hospital worked like clockwork and everything was as clean as could be. No one ever picked up an illness in an RAF Hospital. It soon became clear that this was because of the discipline imposed by the most efficient and rather daunting Matron. On daily inspections, she insisted that those patients who could stand did so, at attention, at the foot of their beds. Those who could not had to sit upright and with their heels together. Those who could not get up had to lay to attention. It was strict, but how well everything ran! Most of the shortcomings of modern civilian hospitals could be rectified by the re-introduction of matrons.

In the evening, the Ward Sister checked that everything was ready for Matron's last visit of the day, and we waited, somewhat tensely, for her appearance. She came, accompanied by the Sister and one of the nurses. She adjusted a pillow here, a glass there, and moved a curtain slightly, then with a: "Good night gentlemen", which was answered by a chorus of "Good night Matron", she switched the lights off and swept out.

About ten minutes later, the door would open quietly and a dim light would show. The doctor would arrive with some important sustenance for his patients that Matron would not have permitted. It came in the form of a suitcase full of bottles of beer. There was one for everyone including me. When that had been consumed and the evidence disposed of, it was time for the evening expedition. Those who were mobile, albeit with arms in slings and legs in plaster, climbed through the window, went through some woods and over a fence and into a pub. They were kind enough to invite me along too. After a few drinks we went back the same way, taking something for the unfortunate bed ridden fellows. One of these was paralysed from the neck down, and had devised a code for his Samaritans. When he closed his left eye, they were to pour the drink into his open mouth. When he closed his right eye, they were to stop. No wonder we won the war – such people are unconquerable.

My operation went well and was completely effective. I never had a head clearing problem again except for the time when I was foolish enough to fly with a head cold.

After that, under HD's expert, patient guidance I began to make progress, and my confidence and ability slowly improved. I was certainly not a natural pilot, but then (I now know) such people are extremely rare.

A few flying hours later, Robbie and I were approaching first solo. Ken Bones was sent solo before we were. On his approach to land, his throttle linkage broke leaving him with no control over his engine. We listened at the runway caravan while his instructor talked him round the circuit by radio and then told him when to switch his engine right off. So Ken did his very first solo landing dead stick. It was a good effort. Some years later, Ken hit an obstruction while flying very low and very fast in a Meteor. He was killed instantly.

We were doing circuits and bumps when HD told me to taxi to the NAAFI wagon. (It was a grass field and possible to taxi anywhere.) He jumped out of the aircraft, went over to the wagon and came back with a doughnut.

"You're going on your own now!" He briefed me on what he wanted me to do, and added: "We are running late, and I'm afraid that you are going to miss your lunch. So while you are doing what I told you, eat this doughnut!"

First solo is the most memorable trip of any aviator's life, and over the years I have reminisced about it with many other pilots. But I never met anyone else who ate a doughnut whilst doing it. With that hurdle overcome, I really began to enjoy my flying, and started to make satisfactory progress.

We normally flew with our own instructors, but sometimes the programme required that we fly with one of the others. Thus it was that I flew with Arthur Kell, DFC and bar. He had served on

617 Squadron, the Dambusters. He used to say that his best trip was the one on which they sank the Tirpitz. He was a modest, very nice Australian. After surviving the rigours of Bomber Command, and teaching cadets to fly, he was to be killed in a light aircraft in peace-time.

On the first two ceremonial parades of that term, we were held at attention for even longer than usual, and on both occasions, one of the cadets fainted.

We were addressed by the Assistant Commandant, the redoubtable Group Captain 'Doggie' Oliver. He reminded us that before parade we should have a nice breakfast, but not too much, and that we should keep our circulation going by wriggling our toes and slowly and imperceptibly shifting our weight from heel to toe and back. He went on to say that any cadet who could not stand still for a few minutes without falling over could not be expected to fly an aeroplane at high g or in very high or very low temperatures or in the excitement of combat. Consequently, in future, any cadet who fainted on parade would have his cadetship terminated.

I had never had a problem in this regard, but on the very next parade, I did. I began to feel hot then cold, sweaty then clammy, and I longed to sit down. I was determined not to faint, but was aware that I was loosing my senses. I must have passed out momentarily, because the next thing I knew was that my head was level with my knees (which fortuitously had cured the problem). My heels were still together in the approved fashion, and I still held my rifle, though at a silly angle.

Very slowly, so as not to call attention to myself (some hope!) I resumed the attention position. Within a few seconds, I felt fine.

After the parade, the Under Officer slapped my arm in a friendly way and said: "Well done! I'm glad we have you in B Squadron."

A friendly word from the Under Officer! I felt that I had arrived. No one else mentioned it, so presumably I was forgiven.

I never felt faint again.

A guest night was held in lieu of a normal dinner night every two weeks. We wore our interim mess kit – best blue with white shirt, wing collar and black bow tie. The College band played in the minstrels' gallery and several instructors and senior officers would attend. They would sit at random among us, and we had the opportunity to talk informally with them.

They had all served in the war, and many had decorations for bravery, and we used to try to get them to tell us about it. But they all seemed to be obsessed with sport and would talk of little else. I would remember nice Mr Talbot's remark about the importance of sport to the Service.

After dinner on the first guest night of the term, the new entry was required to entertain the rest of the Cadet Wing in the main lecture room/theatre. The Senior Entry sat in the front rows and gave a thumbs up for a good show, which meant that the entertainers could take seats in the audience or thumbs down which meant that they would have to pay a forfeit, such as running across the parade ground while being sprayed by fire hoses, or being blindfolded and required to jump out of the high windows on to the flower bed.

Barry and I blacked our faces and did a minstrel act, telling feeble jokes such as:

"Say, Rastas, I have just visited North India."

"Really, Bones? What did you think of the Himalayas?"

"She was all right, but I didn't like him."

"Oi!"

Then: "Say Rastas, last leave I took my girl friend to the West Indies."

"Really Bones? Jamaica?"

"No, she wanted to go."

"Oi!"

It seemed to catch on, and produced much laughter and applause, and Barry and I were excused forfeits. Sometimes at parties we would be asked to repeat the act, and some of the awful jokes are still recalled at reunions. What wouldn't I give to do that again with dear old Barry. But I suppose it would be politically incorrect now. It is not everything that changes for the better.

On Sunday evenings, during the first term in College, the cadets were invited in small groups for dinner with the Commandant at the Lodge. Air Commodore George Beamish had been flying since the days of the Avro 504 and had, of course, served throughout the war. But he did not talk about it – his subject was, as always, sport. He had played for England in several sports and for in RAF in even more.

When I was invited, the annual College Run had just taken place. This was an event in which everybody on the station – officers, cadets, NCOs and airmen competed in a five mile cross country race.

The Commandant asked Dave; "Tell me, de la Harpe, where did you finish in the College run?"

Dave, whose abilities did not include athletics, replied miserably: "Three hundred and eighty seventh, Sir."

The Commandant, who was a little hard of hearing, answered: "Eighty seventh! That was not very good was it?"

Dave did not correct him.

Then he turned to Tony. "Tell me, Dawes, what games do you play?"

"Tennis, squash and fives, Sir."

"No, no. Dawes. What team games, of course?"

"I don't play many team games, Sir."

"Come, come, Dawes. Are you being fair to yourself?"

These quotes are trotted out at every reunion, and produce as much amusement as ever.

George Beamish was not married, yet he was wed – to the Service. He and his staff turned a disparate group of immature youths into RAF officers. What an achievement! We still talk of him, and them, fifty and more years later.

Vacation time came round again and it was time to choose an activity. At the parachute course the previous year, I had been disappointed with my own fear, though I had managed to conceal it from my instructors and colleagues. (In later years, the class-mates I discussed it with all admitted to exactly the same feelings)

So I asked to do the course again, in the hope that next time I would take it all easily in my stride.

To my chagrin, I found that I was just as frightened before a jump as last time, but to my relief, I did find it just that little bit easier to overcome the fear.

The next term passed with no problems. I was criticised less often on inspection, I could do more press-ups and pull-ups in the gym, I was coping with our ever more complex ground studies, and I found my flying training more relaxed and enjoyable.

I did have one problem that term – I was afflicted by mumps. They put me in Sick Quarters with instructions to lie still and move as little as possible. Twice a day, I heard rapid, determined-sounding footsteps coming down the hall, my door would be flung open, and Harry would be there. He encouraged me with remarks such as: "You'll never learn to fly by laying in bed!"

One time he said: "You'll never kill any Germans by laying in bed!"

I boldly replied: "But, Sir, the war is over!"

"It might seem like it to you at the moment, but they are bound to try again. And you must be ready for them when they do!"

(He was not being facetious. WW2, that had finished only five years before, was, of course, the Germans' third unsuccessful attempt to dominate Europe by force of arms, and Harry and many, if not most, of his vintage considered that it was only a matter of time before they tried again, and that it really was our duty to be ready to make their next try unsuccessful as well.

Now, many years later, I sometimes wonder if the Germans realized that we were then already training to beat them again if the need arose, and that they then decided on a change of strategy. Instead of using force, they would use guile – instead of blood and iron, they would use wining and dining, a cheque book and promises of unlimited prosperity. Instead of being clearly German, their next foray would be camouflaged as the European Common Market and they would inveigle their neighbours to simply sign away their freedom. Our continental partners would succumb to either technique, but they must have been surprised to find that British politicians had become so decadent and gullible that they would sign too.

Our forebears had the courage and determination to do whatever was necessary, and accept any sacrifice to protect their freedom. No sacrifice need be made today to regain ours – all that is required is for the modern counterpart of British statesmen to write the required words on a piece of paper. It is a sad reflection of our times that they lack the resolve to do that.)

His tone always softened before he left when he asked if he could get anything for me.

Fortunately it was a mild attack, and after a few days I was back with Harry getting ready to meet the Germans when they tried again.

The third and last term of basic flying training, however, brought me a major disappointment. Harry Dryhurst was no longer to be my instructor. It seems that one of the other chaps 'could do better' and so the Flight Commander re-allocated him to his best instructor, who was, of course, HD.

I was re-allocated to Flight Lieutenant XXXX. He was everything that Harry was not. He was curt, bad tempered and bad mannered. He had no sense of humour and gave me no encouragement. My rate of progress slowed right down, but because of HD's expert foundation, I was just able to cope. He did do one useful thing for me though. I had already decided that if ever I were to become a flying instructor myself, I would do my best to model myself on Harry. Now I resolved that in that event I would also do my utmost not to be like XXXX.

Some years later, I did become an instructor, and I did try hard to follow those examples, but with what degree of success, I must leave for others to judge.

At a Hunter reunion a year or two ago, I ran into Brian Walton. Brian was one of my best students when I was instructing on Vampires. So good, in fact, that when he graduated, instead of going off to fly fighters or bombers, he went straight to CFS to become a flying instructor himself.

After chatting for a while, he said that there was something he had always wanted to tell me – that when he became an instructor, he had modelled himself on me. I was more moved than I could say. But I did manage to say that I had modelled myself on Harry Dryhurst, who had done the same with his best instructor and that knowing Brian, I expected that his own students, in their turn would do the same.

And that is how a Great Service is built.

Harry, after a fine record in the RAF, left the Service, and became an examiner with the Civil Aviation Authority with the job of testing candidates for their civil pilot licences. One day, he had an engine failure on take off in an HS125. The device that automatically applies rudder in that case also failed. This was a situation beyond even Harry's ability. He crashed and was killed.

But he still lives in my mind. If I do one of my rare good landings, I think how Harry would approve. If I am faced with a difficult situation, I wonder how Harry would handle it. A Great Aviator, and a Great Man. Rest In Peace.

We started our final year and our first term of advanced flying training on the Harvard. Compared to the Prentice, it was a fearsome beast. The cockpit was higher off the ground, and it had a much more powerful engine which gave it a much stronger swing when changing power or speed. This was most noticeable during take-off, but had to be controlled at all times if the aircraft was to be flown accurately and smoothly. It went faster and was much more manoeuvrable than the Prentice and was capable of much more effective turns and aerobatics. It was equipped with a gun-sight and towards the end of our course we learned the

The Harvard advanced trainer.

basics of air to air shooting with cine camera guns. It also had bomb racks and we were taught elementary dive bombing using small practice bombs.

My somewhat disappointing performance in my final term on the Prentice must have been noticed, because I was allocated once again to the best instructor on the Flight who was the Flight Commander himself, Tom Pearce. Unlike Harry, who was physically a big man, Tom was of average stature or perhaps a little smaller. In all other regards they were the same. Tom was just as good a pilot, just as good an instructor, just as dedicated to the RAF in general and his student in particular as Harry.

He applied his magic to me and by half term I had recovered my confidence and form, and started to make good progress.

That term, the eminent Douglas Bader visited the College. He was an old Cranwellian himself. We all knew that he had lost both legs in a flying accident before the war. Now we learned that he preferred to keep his balance by rocking gently from leg to leg and moving one or other foot. He could stand still, but that required him to work his stumps against his artificial legs, which was uncomfortable at first, then soon became very painful.

He attended the Friday ceremonial parade. Anyone on the parade side of the flag-pole is 'on parade', and must observe the orders and procedures that apply. 'Officers behind the flagpole' are AT the parade, but not ON it. They can come and go as they please, can stand at ease when they wish or even talk quietly to each other.

When we marched on to the main parade ground, Douglas Bader was already there behind the flagpole. He was physically incapable of standing at attention, but was at the 'stand at ease' position with his feet apart, and his hands clasped behind his back in the approved fashion.

Perhaps at his instigation, we were kept at attention even longer than usual. He stood there too, as long as we did, and was still there when we marched off. He did not appear to move, though his stumps must have been working overtime and causing him great pain. He did move his eyes though, and seemed to look at each of us in turn. He seemed to be sending the message: "If I can stand here without moving, you should be able to, too."

After the parade, he went into the College building and told the College Warrant Officer that he would like to meet a few cadets. The CWO quickly had about ten cadets who happened to be nearby formed into a line. For once in my life, I was in the right place at the right time, and I was one of them. The Great Man moved along the line and when my turn came, he shook my hand and looked steadily into my eyes. I thought that he could see all my weaknesses. His strong personality was evident and it was easy to see why he had been such an effective fighter leader in the war.

"What do you want to fly when you graduate?"

"Fighters, Sir."

"Good lad!"

I was proud to have shaken his hand. I was also delighted that he had said 'when' and not 'if'.

On the drill square, we progressed from taking orders to giving them. One of the drill sergeants gave us a lecture on what orders to give, how to give them and when to give them. He explained how to shout without straining the voice. He went on to explain that if it became necessary to give a non-standard order, it was necessary to

- (A) explain to the squad what the word of command would be
- (B) explain what was required of the squad when the command was given
- (C) give the word of command.

We then went to the square and practiced giving orders to each other.

The following week, he was drilling us and wanted to do a manoeuvre for which our rifles would be in the way. But there was no standard order for disposing of them. So he shouted: "Squad! When I give the order to fall out and put your rifles against the wall, I want you to fall out and put your rifles against wall. Squad! Fall out and put your rifles against the wall!" It was instructive to have a practical demonstration of the theory.

The start of the new term brought me another change. Tom Pearce decided that one of the other cadets needed his expertise and I was re-allocated. I was fearful that I might have to go through another XXXX experience, but I need not have worried. Flight Lieutenant Ely was as good a pilot, as good an instructor and as nice a man as any. I took to him at once, and he saw me through to my wings.

Many years later, when he was a group captain, he went to RAF Chivenor to learn to fly the Hunter. I was instructing there at the time and it was my great pleasure to return the compliment.

At the end of term, 53 Entry graduated. The reviewing officer was HRH Princess Elizabeth.

When we came back for our final term, we were the Senior Entry. There were no cadets senior to us, and our Under Officer, Paddy King, was one of us. All junior cadets address us as 'sir'.

One of our privileges was to have our own ante-room, which contained the usual armchairs and large refectory table on which were newspapers, magazines and the inevitable Bradshaws railway timetable. Before we could use the room freely, we were required to enter, stand on our hands and walk on our hands around the table and back to the door. We were all very fit and we all did it after a few tries. Bob Fox was a hefty muscular chap. He could keep his balance, but could not hold his weight on his hands for long. He completed the test with his nose running along the carpet. Tony Dawes, on his first attempt, completed the circuit, then, still on his hands, got on a chair and then on to the table. He did a circuit of that, followed by a handspring and a somersault to land lightly on his feet. The last time I saw him, nearly sixty years later, he looked as if he could still do it.

That term we did our night flying. The Harvard had the usual undercarriage lights – green for locked down, red for unlocked and out for locked up. Because of their importance, they were quite bright. That made them much too bright for night operation so there was a device to dim them. On the second night, we got into the aircraft and found that the dimmer device was not working, and the lights were extremely bright. My instructor said that this would ruin my night vision and make it impossible to see the instruments. So the aircraft was not fit to fly at night, especially solo. (Ah! He plans to send me solo tonight!)

But we were behind schedule because of the weather and there was no spare aircraft. So he asked me if I thought I could cope. Two years of cadet training replied: "Of course, Sir!"

We did a session of circuits and bumps, and to my great delight he sent me solo. I completed the hour of circuits as briefed then turned off the runway to taxi back to the hangar.

I had been up early as usual that morning, had done drill, PT, ground studies and day flying. It was now nearly midnight and I was getting tired. (at least that's my story and I am sticking to it!). Instead of raising the flaps, I foolishly pulled the undercarriage lever. A very bright green light changed to a very bright red light. I immediately pushed the lever back again, and the light went green. I told 'Chiefy' and he looked at the gear and pronounced that no harm at all had been done, and that there was no need to report it. It may well have been that had the lights been properly dimmed, I would not have been quick enough, and the Harvard would have collapsed on to its belly. I learned the lesson that sometimes bolder is safer.

End of term was a few days away. During the course, some cadets had been suspended for not quite making the grade in flying, or in ground studies or in what were termed 'personal qualities'. Those of us who remained had now passed our final flying tests, and our final ground exams, and it no longer seemed a financial risk to order our new uniforms.

We had completed a very tough, lengthy and demanding course successfully, and we were all very proud of that. The staff of the College – the officers and NCOs of the cadet wing, the flying instructors, and the class room lecturers – were all of a very high calibre, and their dedication and conscientiousness knew no bounds. And in our keenness to reach and maintain the required standard, we had all worked as hard as we could, and that also kept the standards up. And though we did not talk about it much, we had all developed a great pride in the Royal Air Force in general, and the Royal Air Force College in particular. No one told us that we should, it just soaked in from the environment and the splendid people who were our mentors.

The efforts and endeavours that we made over that time together created a strong bond between us. It is sixty years since we graduated, but we still have links between us, and still have reunions together, though regrettably, our duties and the toll of the years have reduced us to half our former number. As Fred Hoskins writes in one of his pieces in 'From Blue to Grey' (the 54 Entry book of reminiscences), he joined a wonderful company of young men who have become a wonderful company of old men. Thank you Fred, I feel the same about all of you too.

It was, probably, the finest training for military aviators that money could buy, and the King, which is to say the taxpayers, had spared no expense on us. The nation had spent every dollar and every pound it had on World War II, and was broke at the end of it. It had been over for barely four years, and the country was still broke, and living on loans from America, which it has only recently finished paying back. In spite of this, huge sums of money were lavished on us. Again, we did not talk about it much, but we were all well aware of the investment and trust that had been invested in us, and we were determined that we would do our duties, especially those against the King's enemies, in a manner that was worthy of our forebears and the taxpayers. Only others can be the judge as to how well we succeeded.

We had been invited to choose between fighters (Vampire or Meteor), bombers, coastal, and transport. I put my name down for Meteors, and was overjoyed to be lucky enough to get it. In hindsight though, I wish I had gone with Fred Hoskins, Ted Peters, and 'Chico' Cooper. They did the Mosquito course and thence to the Hornet – perhaps the best piston engine aircraft ever built – and then to the Far East. They were not flying jets, but they did see active service in Malaya and that was ten times better.

Our Graduation Parade went without a hitch, and some visiting army officers opined that it was the only parade they had ever seen that outsmarted the Brigade of Guards.

Daedalus House, in the College grounds, used to be a private house, and is used as an annex. On graduation ball nights it is used to accommodate single lady guests. My guest was my school-boy sweetheart, Sylvia, and she had a room there. After the ball, I escorted her back. Sitting at a desk in the hallway, just inside the door, was large, formidable, sergeant policewoman.

"Good evening, sir", she said. "Good evening, Sergeant", I replied, "I'm just going to see my lady to her room."

"You're not!"

I learned the lesson that rank does not bring limitless authority.

The ball was a most memorable occasion and I shall never forget it. I had S at my side, I had the braid of a pilot officer on my sleeves, but so much more important than the braid, I wore on my chest the fulfilment of my greatest ambition – my RAF pilot wings.

Chapter 3

METEOR PILOT

With a few others from 54 Entry, I joined No. 203 Advanced Flying School at RAF Driffield to learn to fly the Meteor.

We did no drill, no PT, no compulsory sports, meals were informal affairs and after duty we exchanged our uniforms for lounge suits. Our time was devoted only to the study of the Meteor and its operation. Life was agreeable.

I must confess to being a little apprehensive about my first trip in the two-seat Meteor 7, but I had a super instructor who put me at my ease, and I found my first trip both awesome and wonderful. After only three trips, he sent me solo in the single seat Meteor 4. Every instructor I subsequently flew with was first class. The airfield was very busy, and the scream of jet engines filled the air as aircraft arrived and departed in a steady stream. It was an exciting place to be.

In each squadron the flying was supervised by the duty instructor, who moved from instructors' crew room to students' then to the aircraft line and to the hangar, with his portable board showing the programme for the day.

One day, one of the students was doing a solo exercise, and for reasons that I forget, landed at high speed in a field. One wing was torn off by a tree, then the other. The tail come off next, followed by the nose cone and shortly after that, all the fuselage behind the cockpit. G... came to rest, quite unhurt, sitting in the cockpit. He walked to the nearest road and thumbed a lift with a very nice man who took him back to Driffield. He walked from the guard-room to the hangar and flopped down in an armchair in the students' crew room. The duty instructor came in and said: "Ah! G.... I see that you are back. Has your instructor debriefed you?"

"No, sir. I haven't seen him yet."

"Okay. Let's run through it now. Any problems? How was your landing?"

"Well, Sir, as a matter of fact........."

And that was the first that the RAF knew of the incident!

The Meteor was much more advanced than the Harvard in every way. I don't think we ever went faster than say, 160 knots in the Harvard, while the Meteor would do over 600. And while the maximum altitude we reached in the Harvard was around 8,000 feet, in the Meteor we went to 40,000. One could go as fast as possible in the Harvard, pull the stick back and zoom to perhaps 1,200 feet; in the Meteor one could zoom to 12,000 feet. The Harvard could maintain sufficient g to cause a 'black-out' for a few seconds, but in a descending turn from 40,000 feet, the g could be held for several minutes. The Harvard could not get anywhere near the speed of sound (though the propeller tips did – producing that distinctive noise) whereas we were taught to fly the Meteor to Mach 0.84, at which speed it became uncontrollable. This was a little disconcerting the first time, but we soon learned to regain control, either by using the airbrakes to slow down, or by allowing the aircraft to roll over and descend to a warmer altitude where the airspeed would be equal to a lower Mach Number.

Engines were less reliable in those days, and just as single engine pilots practiced forced landings, we were trained in flying on one engine. If one engine was running at high power and the other shut down, there was a speed below which the rudder was not effective enough to keep the aircraft straight and it would (not might, would!) roll over out of control. If there was sufficient altitude, the aircraft could be dived to gain that speed. If there was not, the live engine must be throttled back. So on an approach to landing on one engine, there was a height and speed below which the pilot was committed to land because a 'go-around' was not possible. My good friend Malcome Cowper of 54 Entry was to be killed attempting to do so.

We practiced all this with our instructors with one engine shut down. To re-light a shut down engine takes several seconds, so it was not available in the case of a mishandled approach. And the result of that could be fatal. When our instructors considered us competent, we were sent off to practice it solo. We would take off on two engines, shut one down, and land. Then we would turn off the runway, relight the shut down engine, taxi back to the take-off point and do it again. We did this many times and became quite confident in it.

Nowadays, instructors are not allowed to shut an engine down below 5,000 feet, and students do single engine approaches with the engine simply throttled back. It is not everything that changes for the better.

A student who practices with the engine only throttled back or with an instructor might show that he has some manual ability, but he has not demonstrated that he has the 'right stuff' to do it for real, when a mistake might leave him in a smouldering heap. A student who does it solo with the engine shut down HAS demonstrated that he can do it for real because he HAS done it for real.

A similar argument can be made in the case of the modern day use of flight simulators. Simulators are useful training aids, but no more than that. A pilot who shows an ability to master difficult situations when he knows full well that whatever happens, he will go home for his tea, has not shown the same qualities as a pilot who demonstrates control of a real aeroplane in a difficult situation when he knows that if he goofs, he will end up in the morgue.

The asymmetric qualities of a twin at low speed make it impossible to take off on one engine. This does not matter because there is never a requirement to do so. Some students at RAF Middleton St George discussed this one day and one of them asserted that though it would be difficult, a very good pilot (like himself) would be able to. His colleagues assured him that it simply could not be done. In the morning he determined to prove that he was right. He taxied out to the runway on two engines, then shut one down before commencing his take-off run. As he staggered into the air, the aircraft started an uncontrollable turn. At a few feet above the ground the aircraft crossed the airfield and hit a bedroom in the officers' mess. But he caused no inconvenience to the room's owner – he had hit his own room!

In ground school, we studied, among other things, aviation medicine and the effects of altitude on the human frame. Then we had practical instruction in the decompression chamber. This was a large steel cylinder with seats for about twenty students. We would go in, accompanied by an RAF doctor, and the air would be pumped out till the air pressure was the same as that at 40,000 feet. We breathed oxygen through the same type of mask as we used in the aircraft, and we did this until we were familiar with it and confident.

Then the pressure was increased to the air pressure at say 15,000 feet, which is the same as in a pressurised aircraft at 40,000 feet. The chamber was connected to another adjacent one by a valve. The air in this was pumped out leaving almost a vacuum, and when the valve was suddenly opened, the air on the training tank rushed out and the pressure dropped very rapidly. This 'explosive decompression' would happen for real if, for example, the canopy came off. When this happens, the air in the body cavities in the head, chest and abdomen swell up like a balloon. This was unpleasant but hardly painful, and was rather alarming the first time, but after a few such experiences we took it in our stride.

Another device was the ejector seat trainer. The seat normally goes up a rail not much higher than itself. On the trainer it went up a rail about 50 feet high, and at its highest point, a ratchet device would prevent it falling back down, and the technician would wind it down with a winch.

We were all, I am sure, apprehensive about 'pulling the blind', but were standing around taking it in turns and watching each other, so we all had to put on a nonchalant air. After a few times, we did not have to put it on – the contraption gave us confidence in our equipment, and I would never have hesitated to use it if the need had arisen.

Further research by the aviation medicos showed that the effects of the 22g punch were cumulative, and some pilots suffered back problems, so the training was discontinued.

During the course, HM The King passed away. We all observed the Court mourning period – no social functions, black arm bands et al. But the intensity of the flying did not slacken at all.

After three months, the very intensive and very enjoyable course was completed. We could now fly the Meteor. The next step was to learn to operate it as fighter pilots. For this purpose, we all moved to No. 226 Operational Conversion Unit at RAF Stradishall.

The Chief Flying Instructor there was a formidable fighter pilot, if somewhat eccentric. During one dog fight in the war he had run out of ammunition so had successfully rammed his opponent.

I was reminded of his welcoming (well, sort of) address to the course by one of Don Cooper's pieces in 'From Blue to Grey'. (a book of reminiscences by members of 54 Entry – and a good read)

"Stand up the National Service pilots."

The few we had on the course stood.

"The RAF is making a big mistake wasting time on you lot! You are wasters, and if you do not measure up, it will be my pleasure to sack you!"

"Stand up the Old Cranwellians."

The few of us stood.

"The RAF is making a big mistake running that place. You are wasters, and if you do not measure up, it will be my pleasure to sack you!"

"Stand up the short service commission chaps."

Most of the class stood.

"You chaps are the salt of the Earth. I and my staff will do all we can to help you. My door is always open to you. Good luck!"

None of us had even met him at that point. Goodness knew what he would think of us when we did.

Next day he was in the Mess at lunch-time and noticed one of the students dozing in an armchair in the ante-room.

He picked up the Bradshaw (the heavy book of railway timetables) and very accurately hurled it at the sleeper. It hit him, as intended, square in the face, making copious quantities of blood flow.

He stormed: "Night fighter pilots should sleep during the day. Day fighter pilots should sleep during the night!"

This was another very busy station, and another one with some very fine instructors. Here we would learn to fly battle formation, fighter manoeuvres and tactics, tail chases and dog fighting, and it all needed us to pull high 'G' for long periods. We also learned to fire our cannon at towed targets over the sea. We now flew the Meteor 8, the front line fighter, which was noticeably superior to the Mk 4. We had a great deal to learn, but with the guidance of the splendid staff, we learned our stuff.

We were all being trained to join day fighter squadrons in UK, Germany, or the Middle or Far East, whose prime function is the interception of enemy aircraft.

Of the very many fighter squadrons in the RAF, only three were fighter-recce squadrons, which had the additional role of low-level tactical visual and photographic reconnaissance. This involved lots of low flying. Low flying in the Harvard at 150 knots was fun, but in the Meteor at 360 knots was even better! They picked only one or two students per course to do this further training and there was much competition for the slots. Not very hopefully, I put my name down.

There must have been fewer applicants than usual on my course, for I was awarded one of the two places.

Bill Liddell and I started the FR course conducted by a super chap called Derek Maddox. His painstaking briefings, and meticulous demonstrations in the air taught us the basics of the role.

As part of the course, Bill and I went to the Army School of Artillery on Salisbury plain to learn to do 'ARTY/R'. This consists of spotting for the guns and correcting their aim. This is normally done by a gunner in a high place like a tree or church steeple, or from an Army light aircraft that can fly at 60 knots and turn inside a field. With training and practice it can be done in a jet at 250 knots and low level. Our instructor had been a gunner in WW1 and had been one ever since, and was steeped in gunners' lore and tradition.

He concluded his first lecture to us: "We gunners have used yards as the unit of distance since long before Napoleon invented the metre. It is now my unpleasant duty to inform you that we now use metres, in order to please some foreign wallahs. Please make a note of the conversion factor. One yard equals one metre."

Two of the FR squadrons were based in the 2nd Tactical Air Force at RAF Gutersloh in Germany, and we both went there – Bill to No. 79 and me to No. 2.

Before I went to Germany, Sylvia and I were married. My very good friend Bill Nuthall of 54 Entry was my Best Man.

He was very pleased and proud to have been posted to No. 1 Squadron – the right of the line. But I used to remind him that when the first five founder member squadrons of The Royal Flying Corps were formed out of the old Air Battalion of the Royal Engineers, they inherited the RE balloons. When the first aeroplanes came along, they went first to No. 2. As the last verse of the squadron song goes, to the tune of 'Green grow the rushes O'

"Two, Two, the Shiny Two,
Dress them all in Air Force Blue,
One is One who fly balloons,
And ever more should do so."

So Bill and I enjoyed a wonderful friendly rivalry – he of the most senior Squadron in the Service, and me of the oldest aeroplane Squadron in the Service, in fact in the world.

He gave me a very large cup and saucer covered in amusing writings. It has always held pride of place in my bar. And his wedding present to us was a pair of silver napkin rings on which he had had our initials engraved.

These days, it is my chore to lay the table for dinner, for which we always use Bill's napkin rings, and when I handle them, I think of him. It is many years since he was killed on operations in Cyprus, but in my thoughts, I can still see his smiling face as clearly as ever. And sometimes, hoping that no one is looking, I have to wipe my eye.

At last, I was a member of a squadron, which, it has often been said, is the greatest flying club in the World. We flew every day, practicing combat tactics, formation, cine gunnery, navigation, and lots of low flying.

The 'Boss' was Bob Pugh who ran the show most efficiently without having to give many orders. A suggestion from him was an order to us. He took the time and trouble to help and encourage new pilots like me.

I was allocated to A Flight, which was commanded by Mike Cole. He had flown Typhoons in the war and had won the DFC for his exploits. He was a very experienced fighter pilot and he too was a very good guide and mentor, and I learned a great deal from him. He was good company at table, and a bundle of fun at a party. When the RAF equipped with the North American F-86 Sabre, Mike left us to join the operation to ferry them across the Atlantic via Labrador, Greenland, Iceland and Scotland. He took off from Greenland on one trip and failed to arrive in Iceland. Neither he nor his aircraft were ever found.

There were few rules and regulations in the fifties and so there were many accidents. Most aircrew, certainly all the middle and higher rank officers, had served in the war, and regarded the loss of pilots to be inevitable, routine, and acceptable. We new boys were not much concerned about it either. Of course, we all thought that we were such superb pilots that we would never prang. Only the other fellow, who was not such a good pilot, would. This certainty of our own excellence led us to make black jokes about the 'lesser' breed who, we thought, were in constant jeopardy. I well remember, when I was still a new boy, being in the crew room when the crash alarm sounded. Roy Smith was there, and he asked me if I knew the appropriate prayer for the occasion. I admitted that I did not. So he told me to repeat after him: "Our Father, we pray that the pilot in trouble will not spear in, but if it be Thy will that he must, please have the Grace to let me be there to watch."

In hindsight, I am sure that one needed both skill and luck, and I now consider myself lucky to still be here. Even the pilots who really were good needed a stroke of luck from time to time, while luck would sometimes save an inferior pilot from the consequences of his inability, at least for a time. The fighter force (fighter, fighter/ground attack and fighter recce) suffered about two hundred 'fatals' a year, which, if you think about it, means that there were more days when a fighter pilot was killed than days when one was not.

One or two politicians and newspapers were beginning to express disquiet about the accident rate, so the Air Ministry made some attempt to lower it.

Soon after my joining the Squadron, a major exercise with the army was held, that involved plenty of low flying. The Wing Commander briefed us on our tasks, and added: "Air Ministry seems to think that in recent exercises, there have been too many accidents, and we must try to reduce them. So, throughout this exercise, I don't want anyone flying below twenty feet."

Boss Pugh immediately stood up: "I take it, sir, that that does not apply to the FR chaps?"

"Of course not, Bob. No limits for your chaps."

Nowadays, I understand, the limit is two hundred and fifty feet and that only in approved areas. It is not everything that changes for the better.

I was on a low level cross-country exercise and the weather was getting worse and worse. I was as low as I could get and the cloud base was just above me. The visibility was deteriorating and it began to drizzle, which made it difficult to see through the windscreen. I realized that I was uncertain of my position, (the RAF euphemism for lost) and as my fuel was getting low, I decided to call base for a 'steer'. This is a public admission of incompetence, and done only when really necessary. Then I found out that my radio was dead. I did not get the 'steer', but at least no one knew that I needed one!

I continued towards where the airfield ought to have been, but saw nothing that I recognised. The cloud base got even lower, the visibility got worse and the drizzle got thicker, and the fuel was getting lower. My watch told me that I should be at the airfield by now, so I started a square search to look for it, or at least somewhere I recognised, but I had not been at Gutersloh very long, and failed to see anything I knew. The fuel was running very low now, and I had to get down in the next few minutes, or climb and eject. If I ejected there was no knowing where the aircraft would land or who it would hit. And if I did a good forced landing, perhaps the aircraft could be repaired. So I decided to land in a field, undercarriage up.

I approached the next field and closed my throttles. Just as I was about to touch down, I saw through the murk and drizzle a line of tall trees that I would have to hit if I continued. And that, as they say, would have been that. So as I touched down, I applied full power, slid on the belly for a few yards and took off. The full power had taken up nearly all the fuel so the next attempt would have to be the last. I cleared the trees, closed the throttles again, and landed in the next field. There were no trees in this one. I was lucky (again!).

As soon as the aircraft came to rest, I jumped out, ran a few yards and threw myself down and awaited the explosion. It did not explode, but I did hear the sound of jet engines and wondered if the boys were out looking for me already. Then I realized that in my haste to get out, I had not closed the engines down. I went back to do so, but one of them ran out of fuel before I could.

The farmer arrived and took me to his house where I telephoned base, which turned out to be not far away. He then produced two beers for us, and then two more. Then he ran out of beer and poured us some schnapps. Now schnapps is an acquired taste. I acquired it. Boss Pugh arrived to take me back to base, and judging by the relish with which he put away the schnapps, he had already acquired it! Back at base, the boys were waiting for us and we had a very nice party to celebrate my continued existence. Next day I put in my written report. The Boss was satisfied that I was not to blame. He and the Wing Commander discussed it on the telephone, and I never heard any more about it.

These days, there would be a board of enquiry and the legal people would try to 'apportion blame', and 'award punishment' and destroy a reputation or a career. It is not everything that changes for the better.

The squadron ground crews were first class. It is a cliché in Air Force writing to say that, but the fact is that they always were. And they had that aircraft fit to fly again in about three weeks.

The Meteor air frame was extremely strong, which was why a wheels-up landing in a rough field did not destroy it. Not long after that incident, one of the chaps on 79 had a double flame out and was gliding towards base. He nearly made it, but when he was less than 1,000 feet, he judged that he would not make the runway, so decided to eject. He was either too low, or had some seat malfunction, because his parachute did not open and he was killed on impact. The unmanned aircraft landed by itself on some fairly level ground, and in a few weeks the ground crew had it flying again. It was speculated that if the pilot had, instead of ejecting, simply folded his arms, he might well have survived.

The Korean War was in progress at that time. The army and RN were honourably represented, but to our shame, there were no RAF fighter squadrons there because the government took the view that our best aircraft, the Meteor, was not good enough, even though the Australians were doing a fine job there with them. The only way that an RAF pilot could see action there was to volunteer to go on secondment to the Americans flying the F-86 or the Australians flying the Meteor. Of course we all volunteered, but there was a long waiting list. Only two pilots per month from Fighter Command, 2nd TAF, MEAF, and FEAF were lucky enough to go.

The first pilot from our Squadron to go was Roy Smith, who was a dedicated fighter pilot and possibly the best one we had. He had just missed seeing action at the end of WW2, a fact that forever caused him great regret. When he received his orders to go, he was absolutely delighted. He completed a successful tour of duty, and was then sent to the Central Gunnery School to teach candidate gunnery instructors. He was to die there in a mid air collision.

Another good friend on the Squadron was John West, ex 52 Entry. He had a friend on the personnel staff at Command Headquarters, and he told me one day that he had heard that he and I were pencilled in to go to Korea in two months time. The war ended the following month. That was a bitter disappointment. Now I understood how Roy had felt about missing WW2.

John West was a very good pilot and a most amusing fellow. At Saturday night parties he could render us helpless with laughter.

No. 2 Squadron. I am third from right, centre row.

For one of his tricks he had learned the first eight notes (bars?) of a Tchaikovski piano concerto, and he would play it with much flourish on the mess piano. On the seventh note, one of us, (often me) had to rush in shouting: "John! You're wanted on the phone", in the hope that no one would find out that he did not know any more. Of course, everyone knew, and the jape caused great merriment. Another of his party tricks was to contort his face into the most extraordinary shapes. One afternoon we had completed a high level cine exercise, and I was leading us back down through thick and very bumpy cloud. Every time I glanced round, there he was close in to my wing tip. We went through a particularly turbulent stretch that would have made some pilots break off. But not John; when I looked round, he had undone his oxygen mask, and was making a face at me like a chimpanzee. And he was still sticking like glue to my wing tip.

At this time the French were fighting in Indo-China (as it still was) and the Battle of Dien Bien Phu was soon to be fought. I wrote a paper to higher authority suggesting that it would be a good idea if it could be arranged for an RAF fighter pilot to be seconded to one of the French squadrons and operate with them. I suggested that it was possible that we might learn something of their tactics, and if we did not learn how the campaign should be fought we might at least learn how it should not. Either way, it could be useful. And to save the personnel staff the trouble of finding a volunteer, I added that I was ready, willing, able and available.

I never received a reply.

Don landed one day and said that he had had an encounter with a 'flying saucer', or UFO. It had manoeuvred around him and he had tried unsuccessfully to get on its tail to take cine pictures. Then it vanished. Most of us were sceptical, but he seemed to be in no doubt about it. The flight commander sent him to see the Station Intelligence Officer who immediately sent him to RAF Wildenwrath to catch the daily transport flight to London to be debriefed that day at the Air Ministry (as it then was). When he returned to the Squadron, he was under orders not to discuss the incident or the debriefing with anyone. So someone in high places took it very seriously. And that is the closest I ever got to a UFO.

When our aircraft had flown a high number of hours (was it 1,000?) we would fly them to the Maintenance Unit at RAF High Ercall in Shropshire where they would completely refurbish them. We would fly back one that they had already completed. One day in late autumn, Alan Middleton and I were doing this. We arrived at the MU without incident, the fresh aircraft were ready and after checking the weather we took off. Half way back across the water, I was in radio range to contact base to re-check the weather. In barely an hour, not only had base completely fogged in, but so had all the other stations in Germany. They suggested that we return to High Ercall and wait for the weather to improve.

I turned around, set course, and called High Ercall to check their latest weather. It had been clear an hour before, but now it too was 'clamped', and air traffic centre advised us that every station in UK was also 'clamped'. It looked as if we would have to point the aircraft out to sea and eject. The fog was forming over the cold ground, but there was none over the warmer sea and from our height we could clearly see the shape of England and the continent outlined in cloud. Then I saw, on the North east corner of Kent, a tiny patch of land sticking out of the fog, and on the patch was the first two hundred yards or so of the runway at RAF Manston. If we were quick, we might just get in before it too closed. I started a steep descent towards it with Alan tucked in on my wing tip, got the Manston frequency from centre and called them up and reported that we were diverting to them due weather, were getting short of fuel and asked clearance for a straight-in approach. Legally, it was an RAF Station, but in fact was operated by the American Air Force. An American voice said that the cloud base and visibility were 'sky obscured', (very thick fog) so a visual landing was impossible, but if I was in distress I could attempt a GCA (ground controlled approach). I replied that I did not have sufficient fuel for that and was coming in visual. We were now on a long final approach and I was too busy to discuss it further. We landed in formation, as usual on the main wheels, and as our nose wheels came down and touched the ground we went into the fog. It was so thick that we needed a vehicle to show us where to taxi.

After finding rooms in the mess (now called the 'club') we went to the bar and ordered two very large beers. We were still in our flying suits which were the only clothes we had. A group of Americans were nearby, and we overheard one say: "Say, did you guys hear about those two crazy limeys who landed visually in this fog just now? You've got to hand it to the RAF, they sure know their stuff!"

Then they recognised who we were and there was much hand shaking, back-slapping and beer buying. As their guests, I thought it would be churlish to tell them that they had got it all wrong, so I did not mention the tiny clear patch. For once in my life I was looked upon with awe.

For some exercises, the Squadron would move to the far side of the airfield and live in tents and trucks for a few days, to make sure that we were self sufficient. To make doubly certain, the mess was out of bounds. We were doing this during an exercise with the army, and were visited by a very smart major of the Brigade of Guards. We showed him over an aeroplane and he asked where the rest of the crew sat. We explained that it was a single seater and that there was no other crew.

"What! How do you manage without your NCOs to pass on your orders?"

"We have no orders to pass on."

He looked as if he thought that officers with no orders to pass on were not real officers.

He said that he would like to look at his unit from the air to see how effective its camouflage was. The boss told me to take him in the T7. He declined the offer of a flying suit and flew in his immaculate uniform. He seemed to enjoy the trip though there was one period of silence from the back seat. After landing, he climbed out of the aircraft as immaculate as ever as if he had just come off parade. I invited him to the mess tent for tea or coffee, but he said that he would like to go to the real mess. I explained that that was out of bounds, but he said that he really would prefer to go there. Since he was a guest, I could hardly refuse. Once there, he asked if he could have a shower, so I organised that and found a towel and soap and what not. Then he started to undress and I understood why there had been a period of silence. He had been airsick and had undone his tunic and shirt buttons and had vomited inside them. I asked why he had done that.

"Wouldn't it have been better to have been sick on the outside rather than the inside?"

"What? And allow my driver to see that I had been weak? We do not do such things in the Guards!"

I was most impressed with his determination to do the right thing, even while being sick, and my respect for the Brigade of Guards went up several points. But when I see the Brigade at Trooping The Colour, I sometimes wonder what is underneath those immaculate tunics!

Bob Pugh's tour came to an end, and we were all sorry to see that much liked and much respected Boss leave. His replacement was none other than Squadron Leader Weighill, who had been my Squadron Commander when I was a cadet. I was apprehensive about his coming, fearing that we would revert to College type discipline. This would have affected me especially, because Boss Pugh had made me the Squadron Adjutant, a secondary job that involved getting all the paperwork ready for the Boss.

I need not have worried. On his first day he made a point of saying to me: "Don't worry, Brian. We are not at Cranwell now!" He turned out to be a very good boss indeed.

One morning he sent for me and told me that the Commander-in-Chief had personally just telephoned him and ordered him to select a pilot for a special mission. "I have chosen you. You are to take off at once and fly to Buckeburg (the Headquarters of the 2 TAF) where the C-in-C himself will meet you and brief you on the mission."

As I taxied on to the Station Flight apron at Buckeburg, I could see the large black car with the flag on the front. I marched up and gave my best salute.

"You must be Meadley?"

"Yes, Sir."

"I'm told that you are reliable."

"I try to be, Sir!"

He signalled to his ADC who handed me a package about the size and shape of a shoe-box. "You are to take this box to Wildenrath. Do not hand it to anyone but my son who will be there waiting for you."

"Yes, Sir!"

At Wildenrath, I taxied in and R.... (whom I knew slightly) greeted me. He took the package and looked inside. I found out why it was the size and shape of a shoe-box. It was a shoe-box. And it contained his carpet slippers. He had spent the weekend with his parents and had forgotten to pack them.

It is an amusing little anti-climax, but I reflected that neither the Boss nor I knew what the mission would involve or how difficult or dangerous it might have been. But the Boss did as he was told without hesitation or question, and I did the same, twice. As it turned out the 'mission' was frivolous, but if the box had been, say, a miniaturized nuclear bomb that I was to crash into the Kremlin, I suppose I would have done that instead.

Every day we practiced one or more of our skills. Every two or three weeks it was our turn on the air to ground range, and we fired our guns at dummy ground targets. It was not as satisfying as firing at the Queen's enemies, but it was exciting and fun. About every nine or ten months, the whole Squadron would move to RAF Sylt (on an island off the coast) for concentrated air-to-air firing over the sea. This was even more exciting and every one enjoyed it immensely.

The targets were drogues towed by pilots of the Target Towing Squadron in Tempest aircraft. The Tempest was, perhaps, the finest propeller fighter ever built. Now it was towing targets, like an old racehorse put out to grass. The chaps had rather a boring life, flying backwards and forwards for other people to have the fun, and if someone offered to do a stint for them, they were very amenable!

One of the big regrets of my life was (and still is) that I never had an opportunity to fly a Spitfire. Here might be a chance to fly the next best thing.

I went over to the target towers and had a chat with one of the Flight Commanders, and mentioned that I would be happy to do a few tows, but had not flown the type for some time and would need a couple of re-familiarisation trips first. He pretended to believe me, and got one of his chaps to come out to the aircraft with me to 'remind' me of the cockpit layout.

After briefly explaining it all, he started the engine for me, jumped off the wing and with a cheery wave departed. I gingerly taxied out. It was quite a hand-full. The huge engine was controlled by a single throttle lever, the propeller pitch control and the mixture and supercharger being controlled automatically by the most complex pieces of machinery, and the propeller gearing was so high that at low rpm you could see the individual blades going round. But it was not good practice to keep the rpm low, because that caused the plugs to oil up, and make the engine run rough. So a higher rpm had to be maintained making taxiing even more tricky. I got to the runway and was cleared for takeoff. As I opened the throttle, the swing started, and I applied rudder to keep straight. As I had been briefed, when I reached about half throttle, I had full rudder applied, so had to delay further throttle till I had more speed. Only when in the air could I apply full power. A small change of pitch or power or speed, and that gigantic engine and propeller would yaw the aircraft madly to one side. For accurate shooting it is essential that the aircraft is not slipping or skidding, so the 'needle', or 'ball' must be kept on the centre mark. I found that I simply could not keep it there, and in a loop, I could not keep if off the stops! My respect for the war-time chaps who had hit their targets flying these beasts went up even more. Jets were easy to fly compared with this! I did a few trips and the more I flew it, the more I liked it. Then I started doing tows, and found out why the full time towers were glad of a relief.

There were usually four squadrons at Sylt at one time. Most of us had friends on the other squadrons, and we had many parties together. At one of these I arranged to fly one of the visiting Vampires. There were no two seaters then, so my first trip was solo. There never were two seat Venoms, so my first trip on that was also solo. Now, I suppose that the clerks in MoD would fall off their stools at the thought of someone taking someone else's unfamiliar aircraft for a trip. It is not everything that changes for the better.

On the Gutersloh Communication Flight there was a Tiger Moth, though no one knew why it was there, what it was for, or where it came from. I always regretted that I had missed being trained on the Tiger, and thought that I could at least have a trip in one. So I bullied, cajoled, and bought beer for 'Com. Flight Steve' until he agreed to check me out in it. We flew together for about half an hour, then he sent me off on my own for another half hour. It was as nice flying it as I always thought it would be.

The Coronation of HM Queen Elizabeth was getting closer and plans were being made for the fly-pasts.

Fighter Command in UK was to fly one over the Palace, we were to fly one over the High Commission in Bonn, and others were to take place in MEAF and FEAF.

2nd TAF in those days was a very large force. There were eleven or twelve wings, each of three or four squadrons. Each squadron was to put up twelve aircraft, so there were to be well over four hundred aircraft in the formation.

Naturally, every one wanted a place, so the Boss said that it would be done on seniority. I had not been on the Squadron long enough to have a slot, but I did have enough seniority to be a reserve, which entailed starting a spare aircraft, and being ready to fill in for anyone who failed to start.

There were several wing rehearsals for which I started but was not needed. Then came the day when the Squadron redeployed to RAF Wahn for two more practices of the whole formation and the actual fly-past. One of our chaps had a faulty engine, and I was instructed to take his place. I was sorry for the other fellow, but delighted to be able to take part in the biggest formation I have ever been in. We went to RAF Wahn because it was closer to Bonn where the High Commission was based.

To form up, the leader flew a many sided figure and at each turning point, another wing would join at the rear. In the first rehearsal, my wing joined, and at the next turning point, another wing came in behind us. Their leader had slightly misjudged, and its lead aircraft overlapped our rear aircraft in the turn. Of course, only the squadron leaders keep a look out – in close formation you do not take your eyes off the leader for a second. Boss Weighill's firm voice came over: "Tuck in tight, and keep your eyes on your leader!" We were already doing that! Out of the corner of my eye I saw an aircraft pass close above me, and a second later, another one below. One collision would have lead to another and so on, and we could have entered the Guinness book of Records for the largest number of mid-air collisions at one time. But we were lucky (again!).

As we approached the saluting base, the squadron leaders could see ahead a light aircraft towing a banner displaying an advertisement. I would like to have seen the expression on the towing pilot's face when he saw that over four hundred fighters were approaching fast! He dived rapidly and so we avoided another collision.

We were all flying with under fuselage and under wing drop tanks because at low level we were using fuel at a very great rate. The Venoms had only recently got their drop tanks and some of the pilots were unfamiliar with them and their effect on aircraft performance.

On take-off for the second rehearsal, one of the Venom pilots pulled up too steeply. The aircraft flick-rolled on to its back, hit the ground and burst into flames. There was no chance of survival.

The leader of the next four, on the runway waiting their turn to go, called the formation leader: "Leader from Green 9, Green 6 has crashed on take off, runway clear!"

The Wing Leader considered the situation for a full second. Then replied: "Continue the take-off as briefed. Green 8 become Green 6, Reserve 1 become Green 8, Reserve 2 become Reserve 1. Acknowledge with your new call signs."

There followed a crisp: "Green 6".

"Green 8."

"Reserve 1."

I was reminded that I was no longer a cadet, but had joined the mans' Air Force.

On the day, everything went according to plan, and the formation leader crossed the saluting base on time to the second.

That evening, the Coronation Ball was held in the mess. It was a splendid occasion. We had all contributed half a day's pay per month for three months to make it the best ever ball.

There was a good orchestra with no amplifiers or loud speakers so that the music was enjoyable and conversation easy. And in those days we danced waltzes, foxtrots and the like. It is true that most of us needed to be fortified by a little sustenance from the bar before we had the nerve or co-ordination to try.

RAF summer balls had a reputation for serving the very best of running buffets, but this one surpassed them all. There was a profusion of every type of hot meat, cold meat, poultry, fish, seafood, salads and cheeses and a huge variety of sweets and puddings. At four in the morning, I recall, I went for another lobster; there were still plenty left.

The ball ended with eggs and bacon at seven am. There was still plenty of champagne and other good things available.

Not long ago, we were invited to a modern RAF Summer Ball at RAF Shawbury. There was no orchestra and the taped dreadful modern music was fed through amplifiers to gigantic speakers which made the noise painful and talking impossible. Dancing had long since given way to a series of demented muscular spasms in roughly the same vicinity as one's partner. So instead of speaking softly into his lady's ear as we used to, a youngster today has to bawl, if and when he gets within hailing distance. It is not everything that changes for the better. We sought consolation at the buffet. Alas there was none. It seems that one of the unelected corrupt foreigners who now govern us from Brussels had some sort of phobia about salmonella caused by salad dressing that had been in the open air too long. Instead of deciding never to eat it himself, he issued a proclamation that the hundreds of millions of people of Europe would not have salad dressing that had been laid out for more than fifteen minutes, or some such. This made legal buffets impracticable. This was an extraordinary thing for him to do, but what was much more extraordinary was that anyone took any notice of him. It seems that the British government regards itself as responsible to these corrupt unelected foreign people rather than to the British electorate, and so meekly agreed. And so the RAF has no option but to comply.

It would be amusing, if we could arrange a time warp, to see what would have happened to the chap if he had issued his proclamation at the Coronation Ball. No doubt he would have been smothered in mayonnaise and laughed off the station.

It is not everything that changes for the better.

Shortly after the Coronation, the Squadron was moved permanently from RAF Gutersloh to RAF Wahn (now Cologne/Bonn Airport). We were thus separated from our sister FR Squadron (No. 79) and joined two night fighter squadrons – 68 and 87.

We had not been there long before Charlie xxxx was killed in a low flying accident. The Boss detailed me to take care of the arrangements.

I made out a list of things to do (low loader for the hearse, blank ammo for the firing party, army buglers and so on) and went to see the station adjutant to arrange it all.

"I've done this so many times, old boy, it's automatic for me. Leave all this to me, and you take care of Charlie's kit and personal matters, and the squadron drill."

It did not take me long to sort out Charlie's RAF issue kit and his personal effects. And the airmen did not need much drill because they had had plenty of practice. (Charlie was about the fourth fatal we had had that year).

We were to slow-march with Charlie from the station morgue through the station to the guard room where we were to board buses to take us to Cologne cemetery. Before we set off, I decided to check the location of the plot with the Station Adjutant rather than wait and check with the cemetery clerk in case he was not there.

"I never get involved with the cemetery arrangements, old boy. I always leave that to the squadron."

We were just about to set off and there was no grave! The Squadron was ready, the parents and girl friend and some senior officers were waiting. For me to go to Boss Weighill and say that we would have to postpone was simply not an option.

A wing of the RAF Regiment was also based at Wahn, and I mused that their stock-in-trade is digging-in. I was friendly with one the flight commanders, John Strickland, so I telephoned him and explained the situation.

"Leave it to me – and give me as much time as you can!"

Five minutes later, two RAF Regiment Land Rovers containing John and about ten of his chaps with shovels raced through the gates.

I led the slow march from the morgue, slightly slower than usual and with shorter steps than usual. It was a long way to slow-march, so I let the men fall out to stretch their legs. When we fell in, I inspected them very thoroughly. I sat next to the leading bus driver and made him go very slowly. Another thorough inspection at the cemetery was followed by another very slow march. As I turned the last corner I caught a glimpse of the last two diggers taking a header over the low hedge, where they remained during the ceremony, and there was Charlie's last resting place all ready for him. Thank you again John and if you should read this – my warmest regards.

I learned the lesson that if you want to be sure that a job is done properly, you should do it yourself.

Charlie was a great chap, and I cannot help thinking that he was looking down on all this and laughing his socks off.

At that time, the RAF started to present the squadrons with their squadron standards. Of course, it was done in order of seniority and No. 1, in Fighter Command, received theirs first. We were the second in the Service and the first in 2TAF to be so honoured.

John West, very good pilot and very good chap, was also very smart, and the Boss selected him to receive it. He and the appointed escorts went off to the RAF Drill School at Uxbridge to learn colour drill. The officers were to wear swords for the ceremony, and it was John's task to lead us in sword drill. Unlike soldiers and sailors, air force men do not own swords, so a stock of swords was kept at Command HQ and lent out as required. The Boss ordered me to fly up to Buckeburg and get them in the T7. This was our two seat training Meteor, and there was room for the swords on the back seat.

Morale on the Squadron had always been high, and the presentation of the Standard made it even higher. The Parade was most impressive – the airmen were keen and smart, the officers' sword drill immaculate, and John's drill and deportment in taking and parading the Standard perfect, as we all knew it would be.

The day ended with a splendid banquet. There were to be more guests than usual and the PMC (President of the Mess Committee) considered that we did not have enough waiters. I asked for volunteers among the ground crew, and told them that the squadron officers would ensure that they did not go thirsty. So, many of these highly skilled fitters and riggers and radio and instrument technicians became waiters for the evening. But it did not go quite as the PMC intended. Our chaps would be waiters, but only to Squadron officers. So we all had a waiter each, while every else had rather a slow service. We gave our 'waiters' their own party later. Squadron morale is a wonderful thing.

Next day, the Boss told me to take the twenty swords back. I strapped them into the back seat of the T7, as before, and took off.

In those days, it was quite normal when one fighter saw another to set up an attack pattern and get it in the gun-sight. It was just as normal for the other to take evasive action, and so an impromptu dog-fight would start. Frequently other aircraft would join in. It was all very good training and very good fun. I was half way to Buckeburg when I saw a Venom starting a curve of pursuit to get on my tail. I immediately turned towards him to prevent him from doing so. He could not (or did not) turn steep enough and 'flew through' (to use the jargon) my six o'clock. When he had gone far enough out the other side, I rapidly reversed my turn to try to get on his tail. He then started to dive away. I pushed the stick forward to follow him. The next thing I knew was that there were swords everywhere – left and right, up and down. I could hardly move my hands on the controls for them. If one had jammed the controls, I would have been poorly placed, so I gingerly resumed level flight, and very carefully resumed course to Buckeberg. I was lucky (again!) and the controls were not affected.

I learned the lesson that it is unwise to engage in dummy dog-fights if there are twenty swords on the back seat.

When there was a serious accident, the RAF held a court of enquiry (nowadays called a board of enquiry). If it was a fatal, the president had to be a GD (General Duties, ie pilot) wing commander, the senior member a GD flight lieutenant, and the junior member a technical officer. Those appointed had to come from some other station to avoid conflicts of interest or prejudice.

A fatal occurred at RAF Celle, and the President was to be none other than Wing Commander Alan Deere, DSO, OBE, DFC and bar, AFC, American DFC, C de G. I was appointed as his senior member.

We all knew about this very famous fighter pilot – how he had shot down over 20 Germans, crashed landed four times, and baled out several times including twice in one day. He was no slouch in peace-time either – before the war he had been middle-weight RAF boxing champion, and had played rugger for the RAF.

How ever could I be of any assistance to this great, unconquerable New Zealander?

He turned out to be one of the most modest, considerate, and kind men I ever met. He explained that as I had studied air force law and procedures more recently than he had, he would rely on me to remind him of anything that he could not remember. He treated me as an absolute equal and would ask me if it was convenient for me to, say, adjourn for lunch, or to resume at 2 o'clock.

The engineer and I worked with him for about three days gathering the evidence, coming to conclusions, and writing the report.

It was a very great pleasure and privilege to get to know him a little.

One of my secondary duties was Squadron Flight Safety Officer. It was not a demanding job – making sure that accident reports were available for the pilots to study, reporting accidents, incidents, and potentially dangerous situations, and assisting at enquiries.

The Flying Wing Adjutant was also the Wing Flight Safety Officer, and he was about to go on leave, so he asked me to stand in for him. His secretary would contact me if any action were required.

83 Group HQ was on the same station. The Group Flight Safety Officer was a full time job for a staff officer, though I never knew what he did all day. He too was going on leave,

and asked me to stand in for him. I agreed to call in and see his secretary once or twice a week and to be available to him if I were needed.

Station Flight operated a variety of aircraft – they had an Oxford, an Anson, a Prentice, and a Devon(I think). They were not very exciting, but they were different, and I did the occasional trip for them. One day I flew two staff officers from 83 Group to Wildenrath in the Prentice. I delivered them safely and returned to Wahn. As I taxied towards the Station Flight apron, the brakes failed. I was going down a slight slope towards a line of aircraft with no way to stop. The Prentice was a tail wheel aircraft, and there was only one thing to do; I opened up the engine and applied full rudder. It swung round smartly and I went back up the slope and I switched the engine off and stopped it on the grass. I had not quite made it; the wing tip hit the hangar frame-work that holds the doors when open. The turned-up part of the wing tip was torn right off.

In those days, accidents were reported on RAF Form 765c. It had a space at the top for the pilot's report, and below that were spaces for the comments of the squadron, wing and group flight safety officers.

As Squadron FSO it was my duty to see that the pilot filed a report, comment on it, and forward it to higher authority.

The ground crew had found the cause of the brake failure (I now forget what it was), and I included that in my pilot's report on what had happened. As Squadron FSO, I added the comment that the pilot had handled the situation extremely well. As Wing FSO, I added that the pilot rapidly appreciated the situation and took precisely the correct action. As Group FSO, I commented that the pilot was to be commended for handling a potentially dangerous situation in an exemplary fashion.

I never heard any more about it!

My tour on the Squadron came to an end, and it was time to move on. They gave me a wonderful farewell dinner and a silver beer mug that is one of my most valued possessions. I had met some superb people, had some new and exciting experiences, and had enjoyed every minute of it.

Chapter 4

VAMPIRE PILOT

In those days, officers returning from an overseas tour of duty had to report to Air Ministry to be detailed for their next appointment. I duly reported. The Hawker Hunter was just about to come into service and I had high hopes that I would be sent to one of the new Hunter squadrons just forming.

So I was somewhat dismayed to be told that I had been selected to be an ADC. I explained that I would much rather help introduce the Hunter to the Service than open car doors for senior officers.

They cancelled that posting, and took me off the list of officers considered suitable for such posts. Instead, they proposed to send me to RAF Gaydon. At that time, the V Force was coming into being. The Valiant had already arrived and the Victor and the Vulcan were not far behind. The V Force ground school was at RAF Gayden, and they wanted me to go there as aerodynamics instructor.

I pleaded that I was too young to go to Bomber Command, and much too young to become a ground school instructor.

So they sent me off on my disembarkation leave and said that they would let me know my posting later. And for the third try, there would be no argument!

The posting note came. The good news was that I was to stay on fighters. The bad news was that I was to become the regular adjutant of an auxiliary squadron. So we travelled north to RAF Thornaby, the home of No. 608 (North Riding) Squadron, RAuxAF. I considered it bad news because it was not equipped with Hunters, and because the auxiliary squadrons lacked the zest and dash and discipline of the regulars.

I replaced a chap called Mike Bxxxxx. He was sent to the ADC job that I had wriggled out of. He later retired as an air marshal and I sometimes wondered what if…

The squadron was equipped with Vampires. I was not sent on a Vampire course first, but told to go up there and get on with it. As it happened I had had one trip in one in 2TAF, but anyway it was a simple aircraft and presented no difficulties.

The 'week-end warriors' came in on the week-ends for flying training and on Thursday evenings for ground training. On Saturday nights, many of the Auxiliaries would stay in the mess, and so that evening was a social gathering and usually a party. That was good for squadron cohesion and morale, but the next day was our most intensive flying day – the very opposite of regular air force practice. We did all the usual fighter training – tactics and dog fights, cine gun attacks, high and low level navigation, formation flying, and P.I.s (practice interceptions in which the Fighter Command radar defence system guided us on to our targets).

The regulars' week-end was on Tuesday and Wednesday. On Mondays and Fridays we caught up with the paperwork and made preparations for the weekend and evening training, but I cannot pretend that this was a very strenuous job. I could, on these days, take a Vampire for a trip any time I liked, and it was rather like having my own aircraft.

Once a month we would do live firing over the North Sea.

There were no target towing squadrons available, so we did our own towing. The Vampire was not equipped for this, so we used to borrow a Meteor that was.

I was flying the tow one day in late autumn, when the tower called and said that the 'haar' was coming in fast. This was the local name for a sea fog which rolls in over the land in that part of the world at that time of year. It moves in very quickly and can make the airfield unusable in minutes. We had no navigation or landing aids then so it was necessary to land before the airfield 'went out'. The four Vampires firing on my flag immediately broke off and headed for home at high speed. The maximum speed for towing the flag was (if I recall correctly) two hundred and fifty knots. It was likely to break off at higher speeds. So I set course for base at two hundred and forty nine knots. Of course, I could have dropped the flag in the sea and chased the others, but pilots who have fired are so keen to get their results that I would not have been very popular had I done so. There was a rule that we were not supposed to fly over built-up areas when towing, in case it did come off – there was a sixty-pound weight on the bottom of the spreader bar to keep the flag vertical. On this occasion however, I considered that I simply did not have the time to go the long way round. The thing came off when I was over the centre of West Hartlepool, fell through a roof then through the ceiling and ended up in a bedroom where a man was in the company of a lady. For a time it looked as if they were going to make a big fuss about it, but we invited them for drinks on Saturday evening and all was forgiven.

During a Fighter Command exercise, 603 Squadron deployed to Thornaby. We were all up one day looking for 'enemy' bombers, and the fighter controller gave me a course and height to make an interception. This entailed flying through a thick layer of cloud, and so I was concentrating on my instruments and not looking out. There was nothing to see but cloud anyway. Suddenly a shape appeared at the edge of my vision. I looked up and saw a Vampire flash past bearing the badge of No. 603. The cloud was quite thick and I would guess that the visibility in it was about 50 yards. So I was within milliseconds of a mid-air. He was gone long before I felt the adrenaline kick in. I was very lucky (again!). And yes, it is possible to feel the adrenaline if you are sufficiently alarmed – it feels like a jet of warm water under each kidney.

Fighter Command used to hold its major exercise every September. We used to take part with as many auxiliaries as could attend. During one of these I was way out over the North Sea at forty thousand feet to intercept some 'enemy' bombers when my engine failed. This caused a pressurisation failure, which though by no means an explosive decompression, was surprisingly rapid. This caused the air in my head, chest and stomach to expand. I was familiar with this through my training in the decompression chamber, It is unpleasant and uncomfortable but not very painful. But in the chamber, we were not strapped in. In the aircraft my straps were tight at my normal body size, but now they were inordinately tight and painful until I could slacken them off.

The engine was not even wind-milling. This was shown by the very rapid decompression and by the fact that the rpm and oil pressure were zero, and the generator was producing zero amps. So the engine had seized, and an attempt at a relight was worse than pointless – it would use up the battery for no good purpose.

I flew at the best gliding speed and set course due west for the nearest land. The Vampire would glide about two miles per thousand feet, so there was a good chance of reaching it. If I could not reach it, I would get as close to it as I could because the closer I was, the sooner I would be picked up. I did not want to be in the sea too long, because the North Sea is cold, and if they did not recover me in about half an hour it would probably be too late. An hour certainly would be, because this was before the days of immersion suits.

I transmitted my 'mayday', then switched off the electrics to save my battery. Without the engine the cabin heater also failed. The heater is not just a comfort as in a car. The outside air temperature was 30°–40° below zero and the inside temperature started to drop to the same level. I was wearing only my thin flying suit, and soon my teeth were chattering and I was in a state of non-stop shivering all over. Of course I could have done a rapid descent to warmer air, but that would have meant landing further out to sea, so I had to stick it out. The weather was good, and I could see for miles in every direction and there was no land, or indeed anything else in sight. I felt lonely and cold and miserable.

Then I saw land, and it looked as if I would make it with height to spare. A few minutes later, the land turned out to be a bank of cloud. A few more minutes went by and again I could see land. This time it was real, and I altered course just a few degrees to head for the nearest point of it. It still looked as if I would have enough height to reach it, and soon I could see where I was, and made another small alteration of course and headed for Thornaby which is not far from the coast, and happened to be the nearest airfield anyway. I reached it with about two thousand feet to spare and set up my pattern to land dead-stick (Landing without power is known in aviation circles as landing 'dead-stick'. I do not know where the phrase came from – it always seemed to me that 'dead-throttle' would be a more accurate term)

So far, so good, and I thought I had handled things rather well. But not well enough! I knew, of course, that I would have to lower the gear and flaps with the hand pump, and allowed for the fact that that process is much slower than the engine driven pump. But I did not allow enough extra time. I could not allow as much as I would have liked as I dare not lower the gear until I was certain to make the runway. The result was that I crossed the hedge with the gear down, but with very little flap, and still pumping as fast as I could. So I was too fast, and had poor deceleration. The only way to avoid going off the end of the runway and into the various obstacles was to force the aircraft onto the ground so that I could use the brakes. This I did. I had to be 'firm' with the controls to get it down, and that caused the nose wheel leg to break. The nose wheel rolled across the airfield, and the stub of the leg caused (I was told later) a huge shower of sparks behind me, making me look like a firework. I wish I could have seen it myself.

Also based at Thornaby was No. 275 Squadron, one of the first helicopter squadrons in the Service, equipped with Sycamores. Its role was air/sea rescue, which is a tedious job unless there is someone to rescue. Here was a real emergency and right on the doorstep!

As I came to a stop, there was a Sycamore hovering a few feet away. A man swinging an enormous axe was hanging from it on a wire. It looked as if he planned to smash the canopy. I quickly opened the hood and put two thumbs up. Then I quickly withdrew them, in case in his enthusiasm he had a swing anyway. He didn't, and that was my second piece of luck that day.

That evening we celebrated my continued existence in an appropriate fashion.

About this time our son Francis was born. He was born in Yorkshire, and so is entitled to play cricket for the county, but so far he has not shown any interest in doing so. The motto of No. 2 Squadron is Hereward, and the centre-piece of the badge is a Wake Knot. Francis' second name is Hereward, the same as all the first-born sons of my contemporaries on the Squadron.

The highlight of the year was Summer Camp. The auxiliaries would come in for two weeks continuous training, and the Squadron would deploy to another station so that they could not slip off home if they had some free time.

There were some 'old sweats' among the ground crew who liked to tell the story of how the Squadron had been at Summer Camp when WW2 started, and was immediately placed on active service. They had left home for two weeks and a few of them did not get home again till six years later.

That year we were to deploy to RAF Gibraltar. We would fly our Vampires, and Transport Command would ferry the ground crew and equipment.

Our routing would be to RAF Tangmere on the South coast to refuel, then on to the French Air Force base at Istres in the South of France for more fuel thence to Gibraltar The maximum average headwind component we could accept on the critical last leg was (if I remember) fifteen knots. A Canberra was to fly ahead of us and the navigator was to calculate the wind and let us know. The direct route would take us over Spanish territory which was forbidden, so we were told to fly a dog-leg out to sea. But because we were on limits for fuel, we decided to go direct – we considered that the Spanish Air Force would not even know, and if they did, there was nothing they could do about it.

That situation reminds me of a story told me by my friend Mike G.... He had been on a squadron in the Middle East, and they were redeploying from RAF El Adam in Libya, to some station further east (Amman?). They could not get diplomatic clearance to over fly Egypt so were told to avoid Egyptian air space by dog-legging out to sea. They too were tight on fuel and the Boss decided to go direct. In the hope of avoiding subsequent trouble, he called up Cairo Military to at least be polite.

Boss: "This is RAF Squadron xyz en route from El Adam to Amman(?) requesting clearance to over fly Cairo Military at 35,000 feet."

Cairo: " Have you got diplomatic clearance?"

Boss:	"Negative."
Cairo:	"In that case you are ordered to land at Cairo Military at once."
Boss:	"I take my orders from Her Majesty, and so cannot comply."
Cairo:	"If you do not land at once, the Egyptian Air Force will intercept you and shoot you down!"
Boss:	"Come on up!"
Cairo:	Nothing further heard.

We would have just enough fuel to make Gibraltar, but not enough for a possible diversion. Even if the Spanish would let us land in Spain there were no airfields there in those days suitable for jet fighters. The only possible alternates were Tangier and Tetuan in Morocco and they were beyond Gibraltar and therefore out of range.

I mentioned this to the Fighter Command Navigation Officer.

"Don't worry about it, old boy! Gibraltar never clamps! Their weather factor is 100%!"

We had a most enjoyable trip out – we flew in high level battle formation, two or three hundred yards apart. The Command Navigator seemed correct about the Gib weather – we could see the Rock from about a hundred miles out.

If I remember correctly, the lowest fuel state remaining was twelve gallons, and the highest about twenty five. Which was not enough to fly one more circuit.

Next day, we each did a 'sector recce'. This is standard air force procedure when at a new airfield – a pilot goes off by himself to get to know the airfield layout, taxi ways, local area, useful visual points, and a few circuits and bumps to learn the local runway. Seven or eight of us were up individually doing this at about the same time. I was just about to return to base for a few landings when the tower called up and said that there was now a 'levanter' over the field. That is the local name for a wind that blows in from the East and brings in low cloud and fog. The effect is very localised, but one cannot take chances there because there is a very large obstruction very close to the runway!

We all had to divert to Tangier.

If this weather had come in the day before, we would have lost the entire Squadron. But we were lucky, (again!).

We had two weeks of good, continuous, intensive training and the Squadron (nearly) reached the standards of a regular squadron.

Our accommodation and mess were in temporary buildings on the North side of the runway. We had heard that there was an agreeable hostelry on the other side of the runway at the Eastern end, so one evening after a few beers in our mess tent, some of us set out to walk to it. On the way, we came to the anemometer pole. This is a device with cups that are blown round by the wind to let the tower and the met man know the wind speed. That evening there was not a breath of wind and the cups were stationary. I considered that it would be a good jape to shin up the pole and spin the cups round so that the controllers would think a gale had appeared from nowhere. I was very fit in those days, and soon completed my mission.

We had a super chap on the Squadron called Arthur ...... He was the only man I ever met who wore an Air Gunner's brevet and among the medals below it was a Battle of Britain Clasp. He had been one of those brave men who had manned the turrets of the Boulton-Paul Defiant. That was not a successful aircraft and they had been shot down in large numbers. Arthur opined that it would be an even better jape if we did it twice – he shinned up the pole, got nearly to the top and fell off. He banged his head on the concrete and his face was soon covered in blood. For some reason that I could not understand, he could not stop laughing at this. We took him to the duty MO who was the army man.

"The man is clearly drunk and so are you all! Take him away and bring him back when you are all sober!"

So we took him to the RAF doctor. He said that he was off duty and had had a few gins. But we persuaded him to do his stuff anyway. The stitches were not very straight, but they did the job.

And the MO enjoyed the further gins that it was our pleasure to provide while he did his stuff.

I met two interesting fellows in the main mess one evening. They had flown in the RAF in the war and were now civilian airline pilots working for Gibraltar Airways and were honorary members of the mess.

They told me that theirs was one of the best jobs in civil flying – all they had to do was operate to Tangier and back twice a day. No all-night flying, home every night, no early starts or late finishes, and living in Gibraltar was most agreeable. They advised me that if I ever wanted to fly for an airline, this was the one to go for.

At that time, I had not even started to think about leaving the Service, and anyway, airline flying seemed to me to be nothing but straight and level flying, and that was all right only for old men.

Little did I know that many years later, when I WAS an old man, I would work for Gibraltar Airways, go to Tangier twice a day, and be an honorary member of the mess.

It was a great pleasure to meet up with Phil Jevons and Doug Wood, both of 54 Entry, who were stationed there on No. 224 Squadron flying the Shackleton. Better them than me, I thought, but it was what they had asked for.

I took them both for a ride in our Vampire T11 (the two seat version). They seemed uncomfortable in it, and I think they were glad to get down. Phil then took me along on a training trip. We did a couple of ASV runs (attack patterns on a dummy submarine by radar), and Phil let me fly it for while. Then back to base for a few circuits and bumps. Phil would not let me try a landing – he said that if I did a bad one, his crew would not like it much. Ah, the crew! I had never had one, and so had forgotten about them! The next thing they were to do was to navigate to Rockall, a tiny rock out in the Atlantic somewhere. Phil bragged that they would hit it on the nose and to the nearest second. But it was to take several hours each way, and so I got off. This time it was me who was glad to get down.

We had had a most enjoyable camp and it was time to go home. We landed at Istres according to plan, but the weather at Tangmere was below limits, so we had to stay the night. The French Air Force was very hospitable and looked after us very well. At lunch, we noticed several of their pilots taking wine with their meals.

After lunch, they gave us a tour of the line and hangars, and I noticed that in the hangars, most of the mechanics working on the aircraft were smoking. I casually mentioned that that was not allowed in our Air Force. Our guide smiled: "But our mechanics are not 'appy if they do not smoke, and if they are not 'appy they do not work."

Then I noticed on the wall in very large letters the sign 'DEFENCE DE FUME'.

"But what about the sign?" I asked.

"Ah! There is a rule that says we must have that sign."

"But you do not obey it?"

"Mais non! There is no rule which says that we must obey every rule!"

There are air forces and air forces.

RAF Thornaby held an 'At Home' on Battle of Britain Day. The public was allowed in and there were ground shows and stalls and static and flying displays.

I was to do a solo aerobatic routine. I worked out a sequence and practiced it at ever lower heights. It included a Derry turn, a manoeuvre invented by the famous de Havilland test pilot of that name. To change a steep turn one way into one the other way, it is normal to roll through the upright position. In the Derry, the aircraft is rolled further the same way through the upside down position. At an air show, it is an impressive way to change direction.

The Vampire, if not handled accurately, was to prone to flick, or as the Americans say, snap. This is a condition in which one wing stalls before the other, producing a very high rate of roll.

On the day, I completed the first two or three manoeuvres then started a steep turn round towards the crowd at about two hundred and fifty feet. Now for the Derry turn. It required a hard push on the stick to keep the nose up, full aileron to start the roll and just a little rudder to prevent skidding.

In spite of my practice, I must have applied a little too much rudder and the aircraft flicked, and since I was upside down and pushing, it was a negative flick. I instinctively relaxed the push, and the aircraft recovered instantly. Quite by chance, when it recovered, I happened to be at the bank angle that I had intended! I let the aircraft carry on the turn while I gathered my wits and was then able to carry on the rest of the sequence.

Most of the public, of course, do not know a flick roll from a clambering swerve, but to the pilots who were watching, it looked as if I had invented a new trick – a Derry turn with a negative flick roll! I had really fluffed it, but after landing several chaps congratulated me on a good show!

At the mess party that evening, while I was still being congratulated, Dougy Thomas beckoned me over to the bar and got me a beer. Dougy was a super fellow who had been a flight commander on 79 at Gutersloh when I was on 2 and used to do the solo aerobatics for visiting dignitaries. He used to have them seated in a row parallel with the taxi way and his most impressive trick was to fly low just above it, pull up into a loop, drop (raise?) his undercarriage at the top of the loop and at the bottom of the loop touch his wheels on the taxi way. I have never seen any one else do that, and I would not even consider trying it.

He raised his mug to me and said with a broad grin: "There are two people in this room who know what really happened this afternoon. I am the other one!"

"I wouldn't even try to fool you, Dougy!"

When Nasser seized the Suez Canal he started an international crisis. The politicians dithered, but war was at least a possibility; at last I might get my chance.

The Services began to prepare just in case – landing craft, tanks and guns were sent to Malta and Cyprus, and the RAF began moving a few squadrons out and sending some pilots out to reinforce squadrons already there.

Every day I telephoned the personnel officer at Fighter Command (I still remember his name) and asked for a posting out there. I telephoned and wrote letters to anyone whom I thought might be able to pull some strings. I wrote to the Commander in Chief of Fighter Command and pleaded that as I had just missed the Korean War, surely I should be head of the queue for this one?

Besides, I had experience on the Meteor, the Vampire, and had flown the Venom. I doubt that he ever saw the letter.

And so the war came and went and I stayed at Thornaby. It was my second great disappointment.

Shortly after that, the RAF announced its intention to disband the flying squadrons of the RAuxAF, retaining only the ground units.

The Fighter Command personnel man called me: "I really did want to get you out to Suez, old boy, but the disbandment was still secret, and I could not tell you that we wanted you here to disband the Squadron. Could hardly put in a new man to wrap it up – he would not know the ropes."

It was true that the disbandment process was a big job – all the personal records had to be brought up to date and sent to Central Records, all the accounts had to be reckoned to the penny and closed, all the equipment had to be returned to stores, and the inventories closed – but I deeply resented the fact that I had been robbed of my chance of going on active service for the sake of a load of paperwork.

Once the Squadron was completely shut down, I was sent on the OATS (Officers' Advanced Training School), and it was a pleasure to meet up with Bob Fox of 54 Entry. That was about the only pleasure. We were taught about accounts and stores procedures and law and administration and parade ground drill. No one mentioned flying or aeroplanes although several of the DS (directing staff) were highly decorated veterans of WW2.

We took turns at the various positions on the parade ground from parade commander to right marker. Of course there were not enough of us to form the rows and columns so the front left hand man and the front right hand man held a rope between them to simulate the front row.

I was taking the part of the front right hand man on one occasion, and when we 'left wheeled', the rope hung slack till the turn was complete. I found by experiment that by flicking my wrist, I could cause a loop of rope to run along it. I managed to get one such loop all the way to the front left marker, and to my great delight he stepped into it. A backward jerk was all that was needed to make him trip over, and lower the level of seriousness with which the parade was being treated. Of course it was more luck than judgement, but I was quite proud of my achievement.

In the hall of the officers' mess, there was a post horn mounted on a plaque that had been presented many years before. After a few beers (perhaps too many?) one evening, when we were for once free of 'homework', I was persuaded to take it off the wall and give a rendering of the 'Post Horn Gallop'. I did my best and some kind persons remarked that they could even recognise the tune. Then everyone went suddenly quiet, and upon looking behind me I realised why. The Commandant was standing there with a rather grim look on his face.

"Give that to me", he ordered without any preamble.

I sheepishly handed it over, wondering if I would simply be thrown off the course or court-martialed as well.

The Commandant played a perfect gallop, which drew applause from us all. He handed it back to me saying: "Here. I think you need more practice than I do. Put it back when you have finished, won't you?"

So I was not thrown off, and got a reasonably good pass and was told that I was suitable for Staff College.

Chapter 5

INSTRUCTOR PILOT

Once I had completed the OATS, I was available for a new appointment, and had high hopes that at last I would get to a Hunter outfit. Alas! Again that was not to be.

When I was a cadet, each squadron was commanded by a full time squadron leader, assisted by a part time flight lieutenant who spent the other half of his time as a flying instructor. It was now planned to replace the one part timer with two full timers, and so six new appointments had to be filled. I was available, and was posted in to be the Flight Commander of the junior half of A Squadron. My friend Tony Dawes of 54 was to take the equivalent post in B Squadron.

My duty was to supervise my cadets – help, guide and advise as required, discipline when necessary, and follow their progress. I attended their drill and PT sessions, and their sports activities. I would join them for dinner, not on the staff table, but finding a place among them, so that we could chat somewhat informally. The working time table allotted us only one hour per week for 'flight commander's period' in which I discussed customs of the Service, informal RAF history, and such subjects. This was popular with the cadets because there were no examinations or minimum pass marks. I accompanied them on the escape and evasion exercises and survival camp, but these were not held often.

The majority of their time was taken up with flying training or classroom work, and there was not much I could contribute to that, indeed I could not even be present. This allowed me time to go to Barkston Heath where the basic flying training was now based, and borrow a Piston Provost, which had replaced the Prentice, as often as I wanted. The advanced training was still based on the

South Airfield, and there a Vampire was sometimes available. I was checked out by my old friend Fred Hoskins of 54 Entry.

It did not take me long to realize that I was under-worked and not really earning my pay, so I wrote a paper to higher authority pointing this out and suggesting that the duties could be performed very well by a part time QFI (qualified flying instructor) as had been done in the past. It was not well received, though a few years later they did revert to that previous system.

My next paper pointed out that when the new system started, the six of us had been appointed at the same time, and if we did the normal two year tours, we would all depart together so that there would be a complete change of cadet wing officers every two years. This, I submitted, would be bad for cohesion and continuity (good jargon words!), and I proposed a schedule of staggered postings to obviate that problem. My name happened to be at the top of the list for departure the following term.

Shortly after that, I received a summons to go to the Central Flying School (CFS) to be interviewed. This was followed by my posting there to join Number 196 flying instructor course. I never found out if this was the result of my paper, or if there was a plan to get me back as a QFI, in case they went back to the old system.

Either way, I was going back to a flying job again!

The CFS ran an intense ground and flying course that lasted just over eight months. The ground school was concerned only with flying subjects – no law, or administration – and we not only revised these subjects but had to learn to lecture and brief on them too.

In those days, QFIs had to qualify as basic and advanced instructors. I did my basic, on the Piston Provost, with the excellent Bert Lane. First he insisted that I fly accurately. For example, if the circuit height was 1,000 feet, I used to consider anything between 900 and 1,100 to be satisfactory. Not anymore! Bert considered that 999 was too low and 1,001 too high. I was surprised to learn that if I worked at it hard enough, I could be that accurate, and then flying became even more satisfying. Bert also insisted on using the correct word, not a word with vaguely the same meaning. I well remember doing a practice lesson with him in which I had reduced power and was raising the nose and explaining that as this happened the airspeed fell off. He cupped his hands under the air speed indicator and said: "Don't worry. I'll catch it!" Then he grinned at me and asked if I meant that the airspeed would reduce. He was right, of course. Sloppy language leads to sloppy instruction, and a good instructor uses words and phrases that cannot be misunderstood.

He went on to teach me how to be a beginner basic flying instructor. Thank you, Bert, you greatly improved my flying, and I learned a lot from you. We then progressed to the advanced phase on the Vampire T11, and I had another very fine instructor – Captain John Smitherman of the USAF who was on an exchange posting – a very nice and a highly capable pilot.

We all had to know the emergency drills without reference to the checklist list and we all soon could repeat them accurately with no hesitation, Our instructors would frequently simulate an emergency and we students had to respond in the approved way. One day an instructor and his student had the engine fire warning light come on. The student immediately started the procedure: "throttle closed, fuel high pressure cock closed... He was interrupted by his instructor saying: "We haven't time for all that – this is a real emergency!"

An amusing tale but knowing the standards of the CFS staff it cannot be true.

There had recently been several spinning accidents, and so this subject was covered in detail.

The Vampire rotated very quickly and lost height very rapidly in a spin and it was considered that the lowest height at which a successful ejection could be made was 10,000 feet. So it was necessary to commence practice spins with plenty of height, and 25,000 feet was the figure laid down. Though higher was safer, it also meant (because of the IAS/TAS relationship) that the spin was faster.

One exercise that we all had to complete was an 8–turn spin with our instructor. This took us from 25,000 feet down to about 13,000 feet. If there was any problem with the recovery we would have to eject by 10,000 feet, which gave us less than 3 seconds to decide. Fortunately we had no problems.

A variation we all did was the partial control spin. This was a 'mutual' exercise, that is, we did not do it with our instructor but with another student. I clearly remember doing it with Ernie Constable. In a normal spin, the stick is pulled fully back and the rudder applied fully in the required direction of rotation. So one wing is stalled just before the other and the resulting differential lift causes auto-rotation, which is the essence of the spin. In the partial control spin, the stick is pulled back a tiny amount at a time, and the rudder applied in very small amounts. When it goes, one wing is only just stalled and the other is nowhere near the critical angle and so the lift differential is considerably greater than in a 'normal' spin, and this results in a very high rate of roll. No RAF man ever admits to being nervous, though from time to time one might acknowledge that his 'attention was gathered'. We were going round very fast indeed and my 'attention was gathered' so much that for a moment I was speechless. Ernie's attention was not 'gathered' as much, and he still retained the power of speech. He said: "GEEEEEEEEEEEEZ". We did it several more times as briefed – it did not get any slower, but we did get used to it. In spite of our comprehensive training, there were still a few accidents, and CFS came out with a supplementary action that was to recover using 'in-spin' (that is, against the 'natural' way) aileron. I did many spins with many students over the years but never had a problem in recovery.

There was a school of thought that held that there were more accidents in deliberate spinning for training purposes than there were in unintentional spinning, and that therefore spin training should be stopped. This argument misses the obvious point that if spin training were stopped, there would be more accidents caused by unintentional spins, because the pilot would not have been trained in how to recover from them. But whatever the statistics, I take the view that a pilot should be trained and experienced in every situation that can arise in an aeroplane, and that a pilot who is not trained in spinning is not completely trained and is therefore not a complete pilot. It follows that all pilots should receive this training, and if this results in a few accidents and the loss of a few pilots, then so be it. Anyone who considers that the risk is unacceptable should not be an aviator, but as it happens no real aviators do hold that view.

Anyway, the only way to avoid all accidents is to prohibit all flying. Taking a flimsy craft made of thin metal, plywood or fabric into the air and subjecting it to high speed or high g forces is inherently dangerous, and it has been said that any flight is an accident waiting to happen, and that the primary job of the aviator is to keep it waiting for as long as possible. I well remember my first day with Harry Dryhurst when he introduced me to the pre-flight inspection (or the 'walkround' in American parlance).

"Always do a thorough pre-flight, and always remember that when you go off duty, you might have a couple of beers, have dinner, read a book, play some sport, take some sleep or a dozen other things. The aircraft sits there all night doing only one thing, that is, trying to figure out a way to kill you, and it's your job to prevent it from succeeding." I have always remembered.

Before the war, CFS used to have a 'type Flight' – a variety of aircraft types that the student QFIs flew to broaden their experience. The sad news was that this flight had now been reduced to one type. The good news was that this was the Hunter. We were all programmed to fly it for three trips, but by begging and pleading, I found that it was possible to do more. What was even better was that the Mk T7 – the two seater – had not yet been introduced into the Service so my first trip was in the single seat Mk 4. To fly a new type for the first time in the single seat version is always an interesting and challenging experience. I had flown the Vampire and Venom this way. But the Hunter was positively thrilling, because not only was it much faster, but it had powered controls which gave it a very much higher rate of roll than anything I had flown before. The controls are so powerful that the new pilot finds it difficult to keep the wings level after take off because the slightest sideways movement of the stick will put the aircraft on its back. I think I had flown about seven or eight hours in it before I dared apply full aileron. It then did a complete roll in less than a second. Later, when I was on No.4 Squadron, we had No.19 (Lightning) Squadron on the same station. I asked a few times if

I could try one out. They would not let me go solo but did invite

My first students, Tony Ryle (L) and Guy Stephenson (R) just before their graduation.

Us again, at a reunion, 40 years on.

me to fly in the two seater. I always politely turned that down because once I had done that, I could never in the future fly it solo the first time if I got the chance. So I never did fly the Lightning. I suppose that these days for a pilot to fly a new type would need the approval of a committee of air marshals and MOD civil servants. It is not everything that changes for the better.

The other students were a most friendly crowd and we all got along well together. We worked hard through the week, and had some good parties on the week ends. We made several long lasting friends, but the one I got to know best was Ernie Constable, and he and his wife Pat are still great friends of ours, over fifty years later.

At the end of the course we were invited to say whether we wanted to go to a basic or an advanced Flying Training School (FTS) and which one. I got opinions and advice and requested to go to No. 5 FTS that was an advanced school. I was lucky and got my first choice, so together with Ernie and Brian Willis we made our way to RAF Oakington and joined E Flight of No. 3 Squadron.

The reason that we three new boys were allocated to one flight was that that flight was just about to start a new course and the Wing Commander wanted us to start with 'new' students – a very good idea.

My very first students were Tony Ryle and Guy Stephenson and I did my best to do a good job with them. After completing his short service commission, Guy left the Service and joined BA, and is now a retired 747 captain. Tony stayed in the Service and retired as a group captain, so I must have got something right! I still see them occasionally at reunions, and they are always polite to me and that confirms it!

I found that I quite enjoyed instructing. To take a student who could not do an exercise, and explain it and demonstrate it to him and analyse his mistakes and show him how to correct them and watch him slowly master the manoeuvre, I found of absorbing interest. It has been said that one's ambition should always be just beyond one's reach. Mine certainly was because it was to be as good as Harry Dryhurst. I could never do that, but it was a worthy aim.

Tony and Guy graduated and received their 'wings' and went off to their OCUs, and we started on a new course of students.

A week or two later, the Wing Commander sent for me and told me that he did not have a single qualified survival and rescue instructor on the staff, and that Group HQ had instructed him to have one so trained. He had selected me for this miserable job. I mentioned several reasons why I was not the man for the job, but he just smiled and told me to get on with it.

So I went to the Survival School at RAF Mountbatten near Plymouth to do the two week instructors course. We had to learn all types of dinghy, not just the one appropriate to our own aircraft type, so I had to learn to teach the one man, two man, eight man and sixteen man dinghy. We practised this in the demonstration room, then the pool, then out in the English Channel. It was late in the year and the water was COLD. Immersion suits were just coming into service then but the staff took the view that future instructors should be tough enough to do without them, so we did it in overalls. The RAF still had air/sea rescue boats in service then, and they took us out to sea in one and we had to jump into the water to do our practice teaching. It seemed to get colder every time.

Before going out onto Dartmoor for the escape and evasion phase, we had a class-room session. Among other things, they had a rubber chicken and we all had to learn how to kill a chicken (fairly) silently by holding it by the neck, and swinging it over the fore-arm to strangle it. This caused much amusement.

On Dartmoor, we walked all day and all night by compass course and map reading to a map reference. If we got to the right place at the right time we were to be given a live chicken in a sack. If we failed to get there, it would be another twenty-four hours without food. My group managed it, very hungry and tired, and I was voted in to do the execution. I grasped the poor thing as per the rubber one and swung it over my fore-arm in the approved manner. It continued to squawk. So I swung it round again. It still squawked, so I did yet again. And again. Its neck was now very long and thin, and it was certainly uncomfortable, but it was by no means dead. This produced more mirth than the class-room demo. We finally got it killed (with a big rock), and I cleaned it (more or less) with my dinghy knife. We got a fire going and I started to cook it. Dennis F... said he was so hungry that he could not wait for it to be cooked, so he tore off a raw piece and ate it. I don't think he liked it much, because he did not ask for any more.

I arrived back at Oakington as a fully qualified survival instructor, which meant that I would have to supervise the students' dinghy drills. My Wing Commander seemed pleased by this, but I hated the sight of a dinghy, and the mere thought of one made me shiver with cold!

When the course graduated, I left E Flight and was moved to F Flight as Flight Commander.

This was a most interesting job. I had my own two students and in addition I flew regularly with all of my instructors and each student. This was to check that the instructors were up to scratch and each student was making satisfactory progress. My task was easy because I had an excellent team of QFIs to work with. Not only were they all very good at their jobs, they were a bundle of fun. Tony Doyle and Frank Mitchell were always thinking up wheezes that would produce a laugh. On our ops desk, there was a pen on the end of a piece of string that went through a hole in the desk. There was a small weight on the end that gently pulled the pen back to its assigned resting place. Tony and Frank replaced the small weight with a ton, which pulled the pen back extremely rapidly, and anyone attempting to intercept it would suffer a broken wrist.

Peter Hull's laugh could be heard across the airfield. He had introduced two very funny books to the instructors crew room that were required reading – 'the Diary of a Nobody' and 'McGonnagal's Good Bad Verses'. F Flight members were expected to be able to quote at length from them. There was also a Line Book and a Bind Book. These are not uncommon in the Service, but the combined wit of the F Flight characters made them masterpieces.

Don Betts had a dry sense of humour, and was our best aerobatic pilot. He won the Training Command Aerobatic Contest, which was a difficult thing to do against a great deal of expert competition. We are still friends with him and his wife Josy.

Rod Woolfall also had a delightful sense of humour. There was a small engine in use in those days called a 'donkey engine'. It was a trade name, I suppose, and was used to power small compressors and pumps and the like. Fighter pilots had a habit of referring to their aircraft engine as the 'donkey' or just the 'donk'. Rod had an engine failure one day after take off at about 500 feet. The air traffic controller saw him start to descend and asked him if he had a problem.

"Yes," Rod replied. "I've got a wonkey donkey!"

There was a village not far from Oakington called Over. If the tower ever asked Rod for his position, it was his delight to report: "Over Over Over."

Bill Law was a forthright, downright Yorkshireman who said what he thought and did not know what tact was. He rarely said anything that did not produce a laugh. A few years before, I had completed the OATS Course and had the usual course photograph framed and hanging on my wall with my other certificates and mementos. One evening when my instructors were in our quarter for drinks, Bill asked what the OATS Course was all about. I explained it to him and added that I had decided that that keepsake of admin, punctuation and files was not really appropriate in a collection of flying memorabilia and that I had decided to get rid of it. Bill replied that he had nothing at all on his wall, and rather than throw the picture away perhaps I could give it to him for his wall. Thereafter, in Bill's quarter there was a solitary Course photograph on his otherwise blank wall. The fact that he was not in it worried him not one bit, and anyway, who would be so churlish as to notice such a thing? We were great friends with him and his wife Cathy, but I much regret that we have now lost touch.

Our working day started with Met. Briefing. One morning the met officer started his spiel with: "It's a red sky this morning, and you all know what that means!" At this, one of the F Flight wits jumped up and rushed out shouting: "I've got to get the sheep in!"

Each instructors' crew room had a row of lockers along one wall that contained the flying kit. In our crew room, we had pulled the lockers away from the wall and turned them round, so that from the sitting area we looked at the backs of them, while on the other side was a sort of changing area. Each locker had ventilation holes on its back.

Our Commander-in-Chief, the great Sir Gus Walker, carried out the annual C-in-C's inspection. After the ceremonial parade, he toured the station, and looked into all the crew rooms. My instructors and I were all required to be present in best blue and available to talk informally with Sir Gus. One of my bright sparks (I had better not mention his name because he is now a retired air officer) conceived the stunt of standing in his locker to observe proceedings through the ventilation holes.

The important personages came in, and I introduced my chaps. We all kept glancing at the locker, and the two eyes peering through the holes. They seemed to be trying to make faces in the hope that we would burst out laughing. But we kept straight faces until the visitors departed.

Of all the pranks perpetrated by the F Flight personnel, that one took the cake for the silliest.

We worked hard through the week and got together on the week-ends for dinners and parties. It was a most enjoyable time.

It was also my job to supervise the daily flying programme and to ensure that all the students completed all their training so that they were ready to graduate on the appointed day. I would review the progress at least twice a week, and sometimes daily if we were falling behind, and I knew exactly how many hours an instructor could fly, how many aircraft were needed, what percentage of the time would the weather permit solo flying, instructor only flying or no flying, and how quickly we could catch up if we flew on Saturdays or all the week-end. The numbers were so simple that I could figure it all out in my head.

One morning, I was called to a conference by the Wing Commander Flying, together with the Squadron Commanders (my boss was away, so I was acting squadron commander), the Flying

Wing Adjutant, the Wing Commander Tech and his Adjutant and the Chief Ground Instructor.

The Wing Commander announced that because of hitches in the Training Command Schedule, our senior course must graduate two weeks before the original planned date, so that the next course could start two weeks earlier than scheduled. He said he realized that it would be most complicated to work out the ramifications but that we would stay in session until we had worked it all out, however long that took.

I had thought that he and his Adjutant would be just as familiar with the Wing figures as I was with my Flight's, but apparently they had never considered it.

He looked round and asked if anyone would like to make a suggestion, and somewhat to my surprise, everyone seemed to be looking at me.

I said: "Well, Sir, if we work a normal week, we will need two extra instructors and three extra aircraft, and if we work weekends we will need one extra instructor and two extra aircraft," (or whatever the figures were).

"And that's all there is to it?"

"Well, yes, sir."

"Okay, thank you everybody."

And the meeting broke up. The WingCo Tech was a nice, efficient man and I got along with him very well. He invited himself to my office for a coffee. There, he told me that I had not done myself any favours by giving the answers so quickly.

"But my WingCo needed some info, and I gave it to him. What's wrong with that?"

"You should have agreed that it was a difficult situation and you should have taken an hour to figure it all out. The way you did it makes you look more efficient than he is, and you should never do that, even if you are!"

I suppose he was right, but I cannot be that devious.

After the next course, the opposite problem occurred. Our next course had been delayed at their basic flying school, and so we would have no students for a month. Those instructors with leave outstanding were required to take it then, and the others were invited to submit suggestions on how they could use the time profitably. Some went off on courses of one sort or another, some arranged to go back to their previous squadrons for refresher training.

In those days, flying instructors had to qualify as basic and advanced instructors. So I was qualified in the basic role and but had never had the opportunity of doing any basic instruction. This was my chance to develop my skills in that area, so I asked to spend the month at the Cambridge University Air Squadron, which was equipped with the Chipmunk basic trainer.

My request was granted. The CO and instructors made me very welcome, and after a few trips with the Chief Flying Instructor, I started flying with students.

One day, the CFI told me that they had a student who was making no progress. All the instructors had flown with him but none could get through to him. He said that if I really wanted to learn basic instructing, perhaps I should try to teach him something. I welcomed the idea, and after four trips with him in two days, I was, to everyone's surprise, making progress, and considered that one more trip and I would be able to send him solo. At cease flying, I said that I would see him in the morning, but the student told me that he would not be back at the UAS for about a month. In flying training, continuity is all important, and in a month he would have to start again from the beginning. I urged him to come in the morning, but he said that he simply could not make it. It is considered bad practice to tell a student that you expect to send him solo the next trip or the next day, because if he does not in fact reach the required standard, it might undermine his confidence, which (in most cases) should be carefully nurtured. But in this case, I decided to break the rule.

"If you can come back in the morning, I think I will be able to send you solo!"

"I have other things to do tomorrow."

"Like what?"

"In the morning, I have a chess tournament, and in the afternoon, a hockey match!"

"But couldn't you get out of them?"

"Oh yes, easily, but I don't want to."

I had never heard of such an attitude. In the regular RAF, a student would forego anything and everything for his first solo.

"But isn't your first solo important to you?"

"Yes, but no more so that my other activities!"

I had enjoyed the change of scene, and was delighted to have the chance to try my hand at basic instructing and to see how a UAS worked, and meet the other instructors, but I was glad to get back to the real air force.

The RAF had long taught students from foreign air forces, and the first course that I ran included one from Indonesia. The first time I flew with him I could see that he was finding it all rather difficult. A little later, his instructor told me that he was not making adequate progress. I changed his instructor. This sometimes works, not necessarily because the new one is better than the old. One QFI's style and approach might suit one student better than another. And the student can feel that he is making a fresh start, and that his previous difficulties are behind him. And of course, sometimes the new man IS better than the old.

The new QFI did his best for a few trips then came to me and said that he was getting nowhere and that in his view the student should be scrubbed.

The next move was for me to make a very thorough assessment myself. Two trips were enough to convince me that the chap simply did not have it in him, so with great regret I put him up for a 'scrub ride' with the Squadron Commander. He agreed and put him up to the Wing Commander. He also agreed, and would normally have authorised the suspension from training himself. But because the student was from another air force, there were diplomatic factors involved and the case had to be referred to Group HQ.

I heard later from a friend on the P staff that it went from there to Command, to Air Ministry, to the Foreign Office and to the Indonesian Embassy. They took offence, and the case went back to the Foreign Office and thence to the Cabinet. At that time, diplomatic relations were strained between the Indonesian Government and our own, and HM Government was anxious not to create further grounds for disagreement, so orders came back down the chain that the student was not to be suspended but MUST pass the course one way or another.

Of course a British service man must regard himself as subordinate to his superiors and hence to the elected government. So I was obliged to continue with the training. On the other hand, I was also obliged to carry out my duty of maintaining our standards. What to do?

In the RAF, every flight is 'authorised'. There is an official document in every operations room in which each flight is recorded with the name of the captain, the number of the aircraft, and the duty to be performed. It is 'authorised' in writing by an 'authorising officer' – the squadron or flight commander or his deputy. The pilot must counter sign to acknowledge that he understands his duty.

(Many years later when I became an airline pilot, I was surprised to learn that I could look at the schedule, then go out to an aeroplane full of people and fly it to another continent without authorisation from anybody!)

Our students had to complete so many dual hours and so many solo hours in order to graduate. I made out an entry for the student to do his first solo, and as my Boss was away, and I was acting Squadron Commander, I took the authorisation book into the Wing Commander. I explained that if the student was to graduate we had to start sending him solo, and that as I had forbidden any of my QFI's to authorise him and I certainly would not do so myself, perhaps he would.

"Is he safe to go?"

"He'll kill himself!"

Phone calls were made and the student was suspended.

It was not many months later that the 'strained relations' erupted into war, and the so-called 'confrontation' began. My friend Arthur Dodson of 54 Entry was killed in the conflict. I have sometimes pondered since that we should have graduated the student – the worse the enemy pilots are, the better! Perhaps we should pass all inferior foreign students and scrub the best, in case they subsequently become enemies of the Queen!

I had hoped that the 'confrontation' would provide an opportunity for some active service. But no extra fighter squadrons were sent, because the one squadron normally based there could handle all the set tasks. The personnel people told me that there was no chance of my being sent.

Tony Doyle, whom we have already mentioned, was an extremely good pilot, and a keen and thoughtful QFI, always trying to think of ways to improve our teaching. He was clever with his hands, and a terrific wit. I was sorry to lose him when he was posted to the staff of CFS – an eminently suitable appointment for him.

He called me one day from CFS and said that his Squadron was putting on an entertainment in the mess on Saturday, and that he had devised a sketch in which two gypsy violin players are doing their stuff when the violins explode and cover them with flour. Tony had made the violins and had not tested his trick because he did not want to have to make two more violins. So the explosives might have destroyed the whole building. No one at CFS was prepared to be the other violinist, but he was sure that I would agree to take the part.

So Sylvia and I and our son Francis, who was still a little boy, drove down to Little Rissington, Francis accompanied by his Teddy Bear.

The party was a great success, and the cardboard violins that Tony had made, and which did look like real violins, exploded on cue. It was great fun, but I could have done without all that flour.

After a nice lunch on the Sunday, we drove back to Oakington, and when Francis' bed time came, the Teddy Bear was absent without leave – we had left him at Tony's place. No other bear could take its place, and Francis was an unhappy little boy. We had to get the bear back somehow, and I decided to ask the 'Boss' if I could have an aircraft to fly to Little Rissington and collect the absentee. This turned out to be unnecessary, as on the Monday morning, after Met. Briefing for all the instructors and students, we were leaving the briefing room to go to our various flights, when a Jet Provost roared overhead. We watched an immaculate low-level aerobatic display, then the aircraft slowed down and flew past the tower with the canopy open, showing the unmistakable grinning face of Tony. Then a Teddy Bear jumped out in a made-to-measure parachute harness and parachute, and made a safe descent to the signal square. He was holding a note in one hand that said simply "Please take me to Francis Meadley." Francis was a happy little chap again, and the Teddy Bear had a smug look on his face that I had not noticed before.

On the wall of the students' crew room there was a squash ladder and a tennis ladder and each cadet had a card with his name on it somewhere on the ladder, and it was possible to see at a glance the order of merit in those games.

I added a Dullards' Ladder. When a student made a silly mistake, his card would go to the top of the ladder. The really good students stayed down at the bottom.

Forty years later, two regulars of the Seaplane Base were having dinner in a Florida restaurant and they were both wearing Seaplane Base T-shirts. A chap approached them and asked if they still had connections with the Base. They replied that they had. He then asked if I was still instructing there. They replied that I was and that they were scheduled to fly with me in the morning.

"Please give him my regards. My name is John Stansfield and I was a student in his Flight at Oakington. If he cannot remember me, tell him that I was often at the top of the Dullards' Ladder."

Of course I remembered him and how well he did and that his instructor was my old friend Bill Law.

What a small World!

Graduation day for the course was not far away, and I decided to ask the students who they would like to be their reviewing officer. Though they were sometimes asked, they nearly always were disappointed. The reviewing officer was normally a senior service officer or a prominent politician, or if they were very lucky a member of Royalty. So I was a little surprised when they said that they would like Bob Hope to do the honours.

But why not? I tracked down Bob Hope's telephone number in California and booked a call to it, as we had to do in those days. A man came on the line and said that Mr Hope never answered the telephone, but I could tell him what I was calling about. I explained.

"Did you say 'Royal Air Force'?"

"Yes I did."

"Mr Hope loves the Royal Air Force. He'll break his rule for you. I'll put you through."

Bob Hope himself came on the line and I gave him the invitation.

"Why I would do anything for the RAF. Of course I'll do it. I'll put you back to my man. Give him all the details. See you there!"

The 'man' came back on the line. "Let me have the details. First, what is the date of the event?

I told him.

"Yes, but which year?"

"This year."

"I am sorry. Every day of Mr Hope's engagement book is full for the next two years, and there are very few spaces for year after next. I am afraid that it is quite impossible."

So once again the students were disappointed.

Little did I know that years later, I would get to know his famous entertainments partner Bing Crosby.

One of the Flight students was a very good rugger player, so good that he had been selected to play for Flying Training Command. Orders came down from high level that he was to be made available for every game, every practice and every training session of the Command team. This meant that he was away more than he was present. Continuity is most important in flying training and his rugger was seriously interfering with his progress. The student had realized this and had asked to leave the team, but Command would not allow him to.

I raised the issue with my Boss and WingCo Flying, but both declined to question the orders of the Most Senior Officer. I certainly could not approach him myself, but I did call his ADC, whom I knew slightly, and pointed out that the student's primary job was surely to complete his training satisfactorily rather than play games, and asked if he could have a word with the Big Man and try to get the student excused games until he had won his wings.

The ADC assured me that there was no point in even trying, because the Big Man's devotion to rugger outweighed all other considerations. It was another example of the curious obsession with sport that seemed to cloud the judgement of many senior officers of that era, and led them to take the view that playing games was more important than flying aeroplanes. I was, and still am, of the opinion that in any serious air force, the opposite must be true. I am glad to report that we got the student through successfully with a great deal of effort on his part and on ours, but it was 'touch and go', which, in my view, it never should have been.

There was a Chipmunk based at Oakington mainly for giving air experience to ATC cadets. I had volunteered for that duty so that I could get my hands on the Chipmunk and I flew it whenever I had a free hour. Close to the airfield perimeter fence was a gypsy encampment, and there was some kind of altercation there one night and one of the gypsies was murdered. In the morning, several police cars arrived at the guardroom and the senior police-man said that they 'had reason to believe' that the felon had climbed the fence and was somewhere on the airfield. Of course the RAF Police cooperated with them but an airfield is a big area to search, and someone, I suppose the WingCo Flying, had the bright idea of an air search. A Vampire could not fly slowly enough for a good job, so I was asked to get airborne in the Chipmunk and look for the gypsy. I searched and searched but had no success. We heard later that he had been found hiding behind a false wall in one of the caravans. Although I failed to find the miscreant, I did get some satisfaction from the unusual entry in my log-book, which, in the 'duty' column was the one word "Manhunt!"

I had one engine failure at Oakington. It happened on take off which can be the worst time for it. But I was just airborne, and so was able to land back on the runway. I could not quite stop on the runway, and rather than going off the end into a variety of obstacles, I turned off onto the grass, which has greater drag than concrete. This caused no further damage to the aircraft. If the failure had occurred just a few seconds later, I would have been too high to land back on the runway and too low to eject. That would have meant landing on the rough ground which could have caused the aircraft to break up and the occupants' eyes to water. But I was lucky (again).

Battle of Britain Day was approaching, and several stations would have an 'open day'. RAF Oakington was asked to provide a four-ship formation to perform displays at some of them. I was detailed to select three other pilots and form the team. Because of our main training task, neither aircraft nor pilots could be spared for more than a couple of practice runs.

Our basic formation was the box, in which No. 2 and No. 3 were in echelon starboard and port of the leader and No. 4 was 'in the box', that is, in line astern of the leader, and a few feet lower to stay out of the slipstream. The standard way of achieving this was to take off in stream or pairs and join up in the air. This uses up time and fuel, so, as I had chosen three highly competent QFIs, I decided that we would take off in box. Of course, No. 4 could not take off straight behind me because that would put him right in my slipstream that would make his aircraft uncontrollable on lift off. So I positioned my right hand wheel about two feet to the left of the centre line. This put No. 3, on my left, in his normal flying position. No. 2, on the right, would position his right hand wheel as close to the edge of the runway as was prudent, and No. 4 would position himself between and behind us. After the front three lifted off, No. 4 would delay his lift off by a couple of seconds, then move a few feet left and No. 2 would close in so that we were in standard 'box' immediately.

On the day, we performed at two stations (I forget which) then did the show at RAF Benson, followed by landing there to refuel. After refuelling, we were to fly to another station for a show, then RTB (return to base).

We taxied out and I took up my normal position to the left of the centre line. The others seemed slower than usual to take their stations, and when they did they seemed much closer than usual. No. 3, whose wing tip should have been in line with mine, was overlapping by about six feet, and No. 2 was in the normal position. Then it dawned on me! I had not done my homework! The Benson runway was less than the RAF standard width. Who would have thought of that? (I always did after that trip!).

I considered changing the take off to stream or pairs, but I knew that the chaps would be offended by any suggestion of no-confidence in them.

So I said my usual: "Ready?"

There followed a very crisp: "Two!" "Three!" "Four!"

It was perhaps the most careful take off I had ever done, and the chaps were perfect. No. 4 must have had a most uncomfortable ride until I lifted off and went above him.

As I said, I had picked three highly capable pilots!

Graduates of CFS pass out as B2 QFIs, which means that they are under supervision and have limited authority – for example they may not send a student solo. After getting some experience, they go to the Standardisation Flight for a week of 'brushing up' fly with the Chief Flying Instructor, and are made up to B1. Any QFI who failed to make the grade to B1 would be sent to other duties.

After a year or more of experience, the B1 could opt to go to Standardisation Flight for further revision of flying and ground subjects and then go back to CFS to upgrade to A2. There was no obligation to do this, and it brought no reward except a feeling of pride in reaching 'above average' status. Ernie and Brian Willis and I all accomplished this step. There were few A1 QFIs in the Service, and most of them were on the staff of CFS. There were none at RAF Oakington.

My Station Commander at that time was the splendid Group Captain Charles Stewart, DSO. He had won his decoration as one of the stalwarts who had flown day fighters at night during the 'blitz' attempting to intercept the German bombers. They had no airborne radar then, so they had to rely on the Mark I eyeball. The optics of the Hurricane canopy made any small light reflect all round the cockpit making it impossible to see their targets. So they flew the unheated fighters at high altitude in mid winter with the canopies open. Many of them suffered frost-bite.

'Groupy' was a busy man, but he used to fly at least once a week, going to each flight in turn. Then I noticed that he was flying with me rather more often than with the other three flights. I asked him about this, and he said that he preferred to fly with me because I would point out anything he did wrong whereas the other flight commanders were too diffident (disciplined?) to offer any criticism. Of course, I could not teach him anything – I was a small boy gazing upwards when he was doing his stuff – but I could politely remind him of a few things.

After his trip he would come to our crew room and have a coffee and chat with the instructors. On one of these occasions he mentioned to me that he regretted that he did not have a single A1 on his staff.

"Don't you think we ought to have one?"

"Well, Sir, I suppose every FTS should."

"Quite so, and I want you to have a shot at it!"

I had already been toying with the idea, and this settled it. I went to Standardisation Flight whenever I could find the time, and worked with them on my flying and instructional technique, and all the ground school subjects, and studied the AP129 (the RAF flying manual) in my off time.

My test was held at CFS and was conducted by an A1. First, I had to give a prepared lecture to a group of staff members on a subject chosen from a short list. My lecture was on 'Aircraft Rocket Propulsion'. This had required a great deal of 'mugging up', but it seemed to go down well enough.

The whole of next day was spent in the classroom with my examiner and two other staff members giving me an oral examination on all aspects of flying. That seemed to go all right except when they asked me about the effect of density altitude on optimum gliding angle, which they said I had got all wrong. (Later, Standardisation Flight considered that I had been correct, but I forget exactly what the argument was.)

Next day I had to do two trips, the first being pure flying to assess my accuracy and precision in all manoeuvres. The examiner seemed happy with that. On the next trip, I was to treat him as a student and teach him an exercise (I forget which one) and finish off by teaching him to fly an accurate loop.

Everything seemed to be going well until the second loop, during which the 'doll's eye' went from black to white. This was a small warning indicator that showed that the inverter supplying AC current to certain instruments had failed. This meant that we would soon lose them. As the weather was marginal, we returned to base.

My examiner asked: "When did the MI (magnetic indicator – the proper name for the 'doll's eye') fail?"

"During the second loop. It was definitely black as we pulled up, and was white at the bottom."

"Yes. But where precisely in the loop?"

I had to admit that I did not know.

"It failed at about five eighths of the way round, just as the nose was coming down to the horizon."

I miserably repeated my failure to notice it.

"An A1 instructor should be able to notice little things like that!"

And of course he should. He told me that I was a very, very near miss. But as the saying goes, a miss is as good as a mile.

I had put in a great deal of work on this attempt, in addition to my normal full time job, so I was disappointed to fail it.

But I was just as sorry that my Group Captain, whom I much respected, did not get his one A1 on his station.

Junior officers had to pass a promotion exam before they could advance in rank. The A exam for promotion from pilot officer to flying officer had been abolished, leaving the B, for promotion to flight lieutenant, and C, for promotion to squadron leader. I had passed these and the next hurdle was the Q to qualify for entry to Staff College. This required a knowledge of army and navy organisation and operations, and government organisation, strategy, and international affairs. I studied for this in my off time, and was, I think, the first member of 54 Entry to pass it.

My Wing Commander congratulated me, but said that he could not recommend me for the next staff college course because he needed me to run the new course of students, which was about to start. When they were finished, he said, he would strongly recommend me, and considered that I had a very good chance of being selected. The new course was about half way through the training programme when the Wing Commander was posted, and replaced by a new man.

I never heard any more about going to Staff College.

RAF Oakington was now to have a change of role. It was to become the home of the Varsity, a big twin piston engine trainer that had replaced the old Wellington, and was to train those students not selected for 'fast jet' training. Those that were would still be trained on the Vampire, which would be relocated to RAF Swinderby.

There was a barroom joke being told at that time about the Irish changing from driving on the left to driving on the right. The plan was to change at 2 a.m. on Sunday morning, but because of the complications, it would be introduced in stages, with pedal cyclists the first week, motor cyclists the second week, and so on.

Someone in a high place must have heard the joke and thought it was a serious plan, because the change over of aircraft was done that way. The first month, a flight of Vampires was moved to Swinderby and a flight of Varsities moved in. The second month the same again, and so on.

The result was that we had student pilots in Vampires and Varsities flying solo (perhaps their first solo) in the same circuit, one at 180 knots and the other at 90 knots. The danger was increased by the fact that the view from the Varsity was very poor – only ahead and restricted sideways. The risk of mid air collisions was high, but we were lucky (again!).

As I was coming towards the end of my tour of instructing I was not sent to Swinderby, but stayed behind to run the last Vampire flight, which I contrived to be F Flight. Just before it was disbanded, I organised a reunion dinner in the mess for all former F Flight instructors. They came from far and wide, and were all kindred spirits. It was one of the most memorable parties I ever attended. We presented the Line Book and Bind Book to Peter Hull whose wit appeared on so many pages, and they were kind enough to present the 'Diary' and the McGonnagal to me. They are in pride of place on my bookshelf. The party went on till the early hours, and not long before dawn, those of us still standing ended the party in an RAF time-honoured way – we all went to my quarter for breakfast. Many civilian wives would take grave exception to being woken at six am with a request for eggs and bacon for twelve stalwarts. But Sylvia was an Air Force wife. She simply asked: "One egg or two?"

I must have got something right during my instructional tour because on its completion I was awarded a Queen's

Commendation for Valuable Service in the Air. I am touchingly proud of it and the parchment is in pride of place on the wall above my desk.

Then, when the last Vampire left, so did I. To, at last, Hunters!

Chapter 6

HUNTER PILOT

We went to RAF Chivenor where No. 229 OCU was based, to do the Hunter course. At CFS I had had a brief intro- duction to it – now I was to learn to operate it seriously and properly. Now I was to get a proper check out in the T7. I was glad to do that, but still glad that my first trip had been solo.

We first learned to handle the aircraft – high and low speed, through the sound barrier, turning, and the various types of circuit and landing. Then came formation, high and low level navigation, tactics, dog fighting and tail chasing, followed by live air to ground and air-to-air firing.

It was a very thorough course and I enjoyed every minute of it. Well, almost. We had to do the inevitable dinghy drill to get used to the Hunter's equipment. This was done out in the Bristol Channel in the very cold winter of 1962/63. It was so cold that ice floes coming down the River Torridge threatened the bridge at Bideford. The instructor (could I ever have been an ogre like him?) briefed us that we were to be in normal flying kit including life jacket, parachute and dinghy, and jump off the stern of the Instow life boat going at high speed. We were to do our drills, and because it was so cold, as soon as we had completed the last item, which was raising the antenna of the emergency radio, we would be winched out by helicopter. Winching out is a process by which a very cold person soaked in very cold water is subjected to a down draught of very cold air by a gigantic fan for a few minutes.

We jumped into the sea and started doing our drills. Just at that moment, the Chivenor aerobatic team, which was doing a practice run, had a mid air collision, and the two pilots ejected. They came down safely on dry land, but because they were a real emergency and we were only in training, they had priority. We saw the helicopter approaching us and were dismayed to see it fly overhead and continue on toward Hartland Point. They found the first pilot then the other and flew over us again on the way back to sick quarters. By the time they returned to pick us up, we had been in the water for about an hour. If we had not been wearing the new immersion suits, it would have been a very serious situation. I have had a dislike of cold water ever since, and at our home in Southern Spain, where the temperature sometimes goes over 100 degrees, the pool is heated!

Having completed the day fighter course, I did a refresher on fighter recce tactics and navigation prior to taking up my new appointment as Flight Commander (Operations) on No. 4 Squadron, based at RAF Gutersloh. Also on the course was Jock Beaton, an old friend from Oakington days. He was also to join No. 4. He and his wife Ulla have been friends of ours ever since.

It was great to be back on an operational squadron again. The fighter-recce world had improved since the fifties; there was now a big library of recce targets to practice on, and we briefed and debriefed in more detail than before. Our operational readiness was much improved – I think my record from in bed to airborne was 6 minutes. The Hunter enabled us to do our low flying at 420 or 480 knots, instead of the 240 or 300 as in the Meteor. (We planned to fly at a multiple of 60 because that gave us an exact number of miles per minute, and that simplified our mental navigation.)

We now had war targets, and in the safe in the ops room was an envelope for each one containing its details and a marked out route map and target map. One of my jobs was to keep these up to date. I also had to make sure that the take off time for each trip was not such as to take the aircraft through a planned nuclear strike. I figured out a better way of doing this, but though it is now history, I suppose I have said enough about it.

Nuclear war was taken seriously in NATO, and on exercises we all flew with a black eye patch on our foreheads like Long John Silver. The idea was that when the war 'went nuclear', we would lower the patch and if a 'nuke' melted the uncovered eye, we still had the other one to get us home. We were required to practice landing with the patch down using one eye every month. I had always been under the impression that depth perception using two eyes was indispensable for landing an aeroplane. I found that that is not so.

One of my jobs was to keep each pilot up to scratch in operational low flying and recce. I would set a target – a map reference – and then 'chase' him to make sure that he stayed low, and stayed on track. If I made an attack manoeuvre, he was required to take evasive action to shoot me down or at least 'lose' me, then resume his track and refigure his timing. Or I might radio him and say that his target had been 'nuked' and re-task him to check the activity at such and such a place. He was then required to find the place on the map, figure the heading and distance and time and set course – while maintaining 420 knots and on the deck.

It was impressive how proficient it was possible to become at this difficult role, given enough practice. We used to reckon that we needed about thirty hours per month to keep up to scratch. If we fell much below twenty five, we could feel that we were losing our edge.

These days the government prefers to spend the tax payers' money on welfare, or giving it away to corrupt foreigners in Africa, Asia or Brussels, rather than on the defence of the Realm, and I understand that now our fighter pilots are lucky to fly ten hours a month. It is not everything that changes for the better.

The Squadron's birthday came around again, this time the 50th. We had a grand banquet in the mess attended by many ex members including Marshal of the RAF MRAF Sir John Slessor – an ex squadron commander. Next morning I got together a four ship formation – me, Stanford Howard, Barry Stott and John Owen – and we flew over every other RAF station in Germany announcing that it was our big day. We finished with a display over base for visitors and VIPs.

People seemed to like it and we were asked to perform again several times, and so 'Four's Four' was born. I claim credit for the title, which was an adaptation of the Navy team 'Fred's Five'. We

At last! My own Hunter. (well, sort of).

became the official team and we all greatly enjoyed performing in a variety of places.

One day, we were on our way to a show at which several other air forces were to be represented, and I planned to arrive at the start of our allocated 'slot time'. The weather was very bad, and when I made radio contact with the airfield they told me that the American, German and French Air Forces had all cancelled due weather, and that I could start our show any time I liked. They then asked what time that would be. For once I thought of the right answer at the time instead of next day, and was proud to reply: "The Royal Air Force will come in on time!"

On another occasion we were returning to base short of fuel having done two shows in one trip. I checked in with the tower and said that we wanted to do a straight in approach and landing on runway 08. They replied that there was a very strong wind from the West, and they strongly advised we use runway 26 (the same runway but in the opposite direction). I already knew about the strong wind – I was using it to get us home! I said that we would still do a straight-in. The controller cleared us to do that but in a tone of voice that suggested that he realized we were very short of fuel. There was a barrier net at the end of the runway, to prevent an aircraft with an engine failure on take off from running off the end of the runway. It was raised or lowered as required by the controller. The visibility was very poor and so I was on short final before I saw that the barrier was still up. I called: "Barrier!" and it lowered just in time for me and the others to land. If the weather had been marginally worse I might not have seen it in time for the tower to lower it, and I did not have enough fuel to fly another circuit. That would have been awkward! But I was lucky (again!). The R/T is never used for idle chat, but as we taxied in, the Senior Air Traffic Control Officer (SATCO) said one word on the R/T: "Bar?" I replied: "Yep." It was beer time anyway, and when we came into the bar, the SATCO and three of his controllers were already there with our beers lined up. He said: "If I get you lots of beer, you won't put in a report about the barrier, will you?"

"That's a deal, but I wasn't going to anyway. And if I get you lots of beer, you won't put in a report about my low fuel state will you?"

"That's a deal, but I wasn't going to anyway."

Each of my chaps repeated the arrangement, and each of his too. And so on. They say that the best parties are the impromptu ones, and this one was no exception.

We used to deploy to the RNAF base at Leeuwarden every few months for air-to-air firing over the North Sea. During one of our attachments there, the Dutch held an open day, and asked if we could contribute something for the air display. Of course we offered 'Four's Four'. On the day, the weather was terrible, very low cloud and very bad visibility, and nobody was flying. But the crowds were still there and all they had to look at was the static display and the hamburger stand. The splendid Dutch Wing Commander (I regret that I cannot recall his name) came in to our crew room and said that it was out of the question for their

F104s to take off, but asked if we could possibly get a Hunter off, if only to make a noise. A Harvard was doing some low circuits, and I said that I thought I could. I planned to take off by myself and do a few circuits and land. The formation team was hanging about and I said: "I don't suppose you chaps would like to come, would you?"

"You're not going without us, are you?"

So we all went. I briefed that we would take off in box, stay in box, and land in box while I did three circuits. If we broke formation, the chaps would not be able to pick up their bearings in these weather conditions and find their way back to base. The first circuit went well, and we made a nice noise just in front of the crowd. The second one too. On the third time around, the weather thickened up even more, and John Owen in the box called: "Leader, my drop tanks are in the weeds, can you go up a bit?"

"Sorry, no. The top of my rudder is already in cloud. But don't worry, there aren't any hills in Holland."

"Hum! I hope you've got your eyes peeled for windmills!" We gave the crowd another flypast then went round for landing. John looked only at me till I called: "4 chop!" He then closed his throttle and looked ahead to make his landing. Two seconds later, I closed my throttle, followed by 2 and 3. The Dutch were impressed, and I was most impressed with the chaps. Any one of them could have done my job, but I doubt if I could have done theirs.

An important political event was to be held in Gutersloh town, attended by the President of the FGR, the President of Westphalia, and a number of other dignitaries. Several NATO armies were to provide military bands and soldiers marching about, and several air forces were to give displays, with 4's 4 representing the RAF.

A 'PR' man from command HQ arrived and announced that he was preparing a brochure to be distributed on the day. He wanted some photographs of Four's Four, both in the air and on the ground, and showed us examples of the sort of thing he was looking for. The examples showed young aviators with 'bone domes' under their arms, immaculate flying suits, clean white scarves, carefully combed hair and steely blue eyes gazing into the deep blue yonder. My chaps were certainly no poseurs, and considered that a different stance was required. So we had our pictures taken sitting on the Squadron tractor. What could be more down to earth?

Before the first of the two rehearsals, a senior officer came to the crew room and making sure that there were witnesses, asked me if I was aware of the provisions of Air Staff Instructions regarding air displays. I said that I was.

"What is your minimum height?"

"Five hundred feet, Sir."

"Good. Make sure that you obey the orders precisely!"

"Yes, Sir!"

The Americans and French and Germans did very nice displays, coming down very low, but I stuck to my orders because I knew that the Senior Officer would be watching.

After landing, the Senior Officer came back to the crew room. He said that our display and formation and positioning were very good, but we were very much higher than everyone else, and that did not look good.

"Can't you come lower?"

"Easily, sir, but we would be in breach of ASIs."

"Well, it's no good at that height, can you stretch it just a bit?"

"I probably would have, Sir, if you had not specifically ordered me to obey the rules."

"What can we do?"

"Well, Sir, you could give me an exemption from the rules, and I'll come as low as you authorise me."

"You know I can't do that!"

"Well, Sir, you could ask Group or Command for a dispensation."

"I can't tell them that I want to break the rules!"

"Then I'm afraid we are stuck with the 500 feet, Sir."

It was evident that the Senior Officer wanted witnesses to the fact that he was doing his utmost to enforce the rules, but in fact he wanted me to break the rules and give a good show. If we did well, it was to his credit, but if we had a 'nasty', it was not his fault.

As we walked out to our aircraft for the second rehearsal, Tony Richardson asked me what I was going to do.

"I'm going to do as ordered."

And I did, with the same result, followed by a similar conversation with the Senior Officer.

As we walked out on the day, Tony again asked what I would do.

"I'm going to obey orders. If he has not got what it takes to say what he means, then he must be shown up in front of all those people!"

"And stay at 500?"

"And stay at 500!"

"But, General, you can't!"

"Watch me!"

But Tony was right – I could not do it on the day. We came down to an 'appropriate' height and people were kind enough to say that we did a good show. The Senior Officer was delighted. He had had his cake and eaten it too.

Over coffee in the crew room, Tony said to me that he knew I would do the right thing in the end. Good old Tony – he knew me better than I knew myself.

I turned to Johnny Baines and Mike French: "You two did not have much to say about it!"

They grinned: "We did not think that we needed to – we knew that you would do a good show."

Splendid lads!

There are a few officers who will not make decisions, or discharge their responsibilities, lest they make a mistake. One would expect such people to seek a lower rank in order to reduce the stress. But on the contrary, some of them strive for and achieve higher rank, which carries even greater responsibility that needs even greater guile to avoid. I expect the psychologists have a long word for this peculiar mental condition.

We used to end our show with a 'thread the needle'. We would do a climbing vertical 'bomb-burst', and I would break right with No. 2 going to line astern behind me while No. 3 would break left with No. 4 going line astern behind him. We then completed the circuit with me and No. 2 going down one side of the runway as low and as fast as we could, while Nos 3 and 4 came down in the opposite direction but on the other side

4's 4 on duty, just before landing in box.

of the runway. We would cross right in front of the crowd. From the ground it looked most hazardous but in fact it was perfectly safe. Usually! It was easy for me to position, because that was my main job anyway. But No. 3, who looked only at me until we broke, had only seconds to orientate himself and set up for the manoeuvre. The first to see the other would transmit: "Contact" which also indicated that all was well. We did a show one day at an airfield that had two runways with only a small angle between them. No one said the vital word, and I was puzzled about the whereabouts of Nos 3 and 4. Then I saw them – they were coming down the wrong runway, and Stanford had, as usual, got his timing (though, alas, not his positioning) perfect and we were set up for a collision right in front of the crowd. The fact that he had not transmitted meant that he had not seen us. There was not time to change anything so I quickly transmitted: "3 and 4 go up a bit, 1 and 2 staying low." They went over us right in front of the crowd and this time the manoeuvre really was as dangerous as it looked! Later on, Stanford was kind enough to stand me a very large beer, which I was gracious enough to accept.

We did several shows at various German Aero Clubs, and we were usually invited to the 'gemütlichen abend' which followed our display and we made many friends in the clubs.

I thought it would be a nice wheeze to hold a fly-in of the clubs at Gutersloh, so that we could return their hospitality with our own 'friendly evening'. I got permission from the Station Commander and we went ahead. Several interesting aircraft arrived and many more people came by road.

One chap arrived in a Tiger Moth and I looked at it lovingly, not having seen one since my one trip in one about ten years before. Then I considered that faint heart never won fair aeroplane so I asked the owner if I could take it for a trip.

"How many hours have you got on Tigers?"

"Oh, less than a thousand."

"When did you last fly one?"

"Oh, at least a month ago."

"Take it!" And that's how I doubled my time on the Tiger.

4's 4 off duty, but still in box
Mike French, Tony Richardson, BM, Johnny Baines, Jock Beaton

Another chap, who was a low-time amateur pilot flew in a hot aerobatic ship, (was it a Zlin?) and treated us to a low level aerobatic display. It seemed to me that he was performing manoeuvres that were beyond his skill and experience to do safely and it was only luck that kept him alive. He was particularly anxious to demonstrate his skill to we fighter pilots, especially me and the other 'Four's' Four chaps, and invited us to fly with him for a demonstration.

I took the view that it was only a matter of time before he killed himself and whoever was with him, so I declined his invitation, and strongly advised the chaps to do the same. Most of them did, but John Osborn, who had perhaps more courage than the rest of us, agreed to go with him. They were both killed when they hit the ground.

Egon xxxx was the secretary of the Hunsborn flying club, He was a very nice chap and he and his wife were most hospitable to Sylvia and me. He desperately wanted a trip in a Hunter and it saddened me to have to tell him that there were rules against it.

At one of our get-togethers he started talking again about a Hunter trip and I weakened. I had him go to our quarter which was off station one lunchtime when things were rather quiet, I drove home in my flying suit with another for him. I then drove us to Station Flight where a T7 was ready for us. We strapped in for a thirty minute trip which included a view of his home just west of the Ruhr.

Egon was over the moon! Of course I was wrong to do it – if I had had an incident or accident with him on board there would have been a diplomatic to – do.

But he so wanted it and I so wanted to repay his kind hospitality.

I led the team for the three years of my tour, and as the team members were posted out at the end of their tours they were replaced by Mike French, Johnny Baines, Tony Richardson, and Pete Headley. Every one of them was a first class aviator and a first class man, and they all gave me unstinting support and loyalty. Leading is comparatively easy, but staying 'tucked in' no matter what the leader does takes a high degree of skill and is hard work. It was

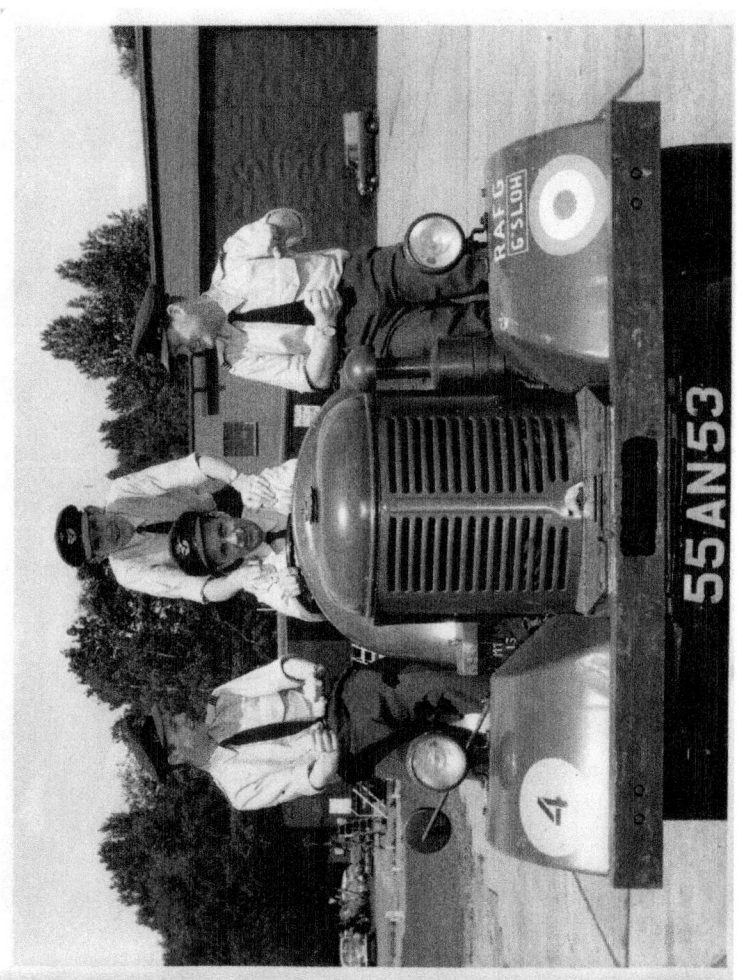

4's 4, My chaps spurned the Hollywood, steely eyed pose for an international brochure. Mike French, Tony Richardson, BM, Barry Stott

a pleasure and a privilege to lead them, and any praise for our performances should go to them.

Pete Headley was very good type and had been one of my cadets at Cranwell. When the list of new cadets came though, his name was misspelt with an M. I am the only Meadley ever to have served in the RAF (if you don't count my Canadian cousin who served in the RCAF) and thought it would be rather nice to keep it that way. So I was not pleased to see Pete until I discovered the mistake.

I was lucky to be born to have the perfect build for a fighter pilot – short and stocky. (A gentleman's tailor might call it 'short portly'). Such a build can withstand two or three more 'g' than a tall thin person. The Vampire and Meteor were limited to 6g that I could tolerate comfortably. The Hunter was restricted to 7g, and we were equipped with g-suits to cope with it. These were suits with built-in air bladders round the legs and stomach which filled with air when we pulled g, thus reducing the blood flow from head to feet, which is the process that causes blacking out. They are uncomfortable and take time to put on. I found that I could easily take 7g without the g-suit, so sometimes if I was in a great hurry, I would leave it off. The g-suit, which is worn under the flying suit, has a hose that connects to the aircraft air system, and this sticks out of the side of the flying suit and shows that the g-suit is being worn. It was against regulations to fly without one, so I had a hose from an old suit that I would tie round my waist to stick out the side to look as if I was properly equipped.

Pete came to my office one day and said that there was something that perhaps I should know, but he was not sure whether he should tell me. I told him to go ahead, and if it were something needing my attention I would take care of it, and if it were something he should not have said, I would tell him so, but that no one else would hear about it from me.

"Then I will tell you", he said. "Someone on the Squadron is not wearing his g-suit."

"How do you know?" I asked.

"I found this on the floor of the locker room!"

He produced my hose with the strap.

The 'box man' pulled out to take this picture of my blood-shot eyes.

"You did right to tell me, Pete. Leave it with me. And don't worry, no one will ever know that you told me."

I told Pete the truth at a reunion some years later. We had a jolly good laugh together.

RAF transport aircraft regularly flew along the air corridors to Berlin, which by agreement they were entitled to do. In times of political tension, Russian fighters would 'buzz' them. Some situation arose which led to every flight being 'buzzed'. The Commander in Chief wanted to know if the Russian fighters were making 'threatening manoeuvres' or just flying nearby, and so this question was asked at debriefing. The transport crews were unable to answer because they were not versed in fighter operations and tactics, and could not differentiate between a curve of pursuit and a lurching swerve. So somebody in high places conceived the wheeze of putting a fighter pilot in the transport aircraft as a passenger with the sole duty of observing the Russian fighters and determining whether or not they were manoeuvring into a firing position.

There were no instructions concerning what action we were to take in the event that the fighters made a live attack, and I suggested to the WingCo Flying that we would be more effective if we flew escort in our Hunters so that we could engage the Russians if we deemed that they were about to attack. That suggestion was firmly refused. I think I was the first on the Squadron to fly in a transport. I did not see any Russian aircraft at all, but I did see the most impressive and enormous military concentrations on the ground. If the Russians had come over the border, they would have done so in very great strength. We had a short break at RAF Gatow, (my first visit to Berlin) then flew back down the corridor. Again I did not see any fighters, which was rather an anticlimax. Shortly after that, the politicos came to some arrangement and the 'buzzing' stopped.

Once a year the recce forces in NATO took part in a recce competition with the name of 'Royal Flush'. In our training for war, we used to fly as low and as fast as we could, just as we would have in the real thing. Even then I doubt that many of us would have survived a conflict with the Russians. In the Royal Flush competitions and practices, pilots would slow right down to 200 knots and climb to 500 or even a 1,000 feet to get a good result. So I took the view that the competition was of very little value in our training. Senior officers, however were obsessed with it, because a good score (or even better, a victory) would bring them credit. When they tried to enthuse me about it, however, I used to explain its shortcomings and advocate that it be discontinued, but I was unable to persuade them.

At this time, the Rhodesians, whose country was a colony, were clamouring for independence, but the British government would not grant it unless they handed it over to the majority black population. Their leader, Ian Smith, who had a distinguished record as a Spitfire pilot in WW2, refused to do this in case someone like Mugabe took over. How prescient he was!

The impasse was resolved (temporarily) by Ian Smith's UDI (Unilateral declaration of independence).

The government considered taking military action against the 'rebels', and there was much discussion in the RAF about what we should all do in that event. How could we fire on people with names like 'Smith' or 'Jones'? How could we fire on people who had suffered more losses per capita in WW2 than any other nation in the Commonwealth? How could we fire on people who were trying to maintain civilisation? I was as keen as ever to fire upon the Queen's enemies, but these people were not enemies. On the contrary, they were the staunchest of friends.

The Ministry of Defence asked its middle ranking officers to make discreet, informal, off-the-record enquiries among the junior officers as to their attitude. My Wing Commander approached me during a 'happy hour' and asked about the chaps on the Squadron.

I informed him that I for one, and I thought that all of the Squadron thought the same, would go, of course, if ordered, but that our air-to-ground scores would suddenly fall to zero. We would go, but would be totally ineffective. I think that the same view was expressed throughout the Service.

So we heard no more about going. A squadron of Javelin night-fighters was deployed to Lusaka, where it could not serve any conceivable military function. But it was a comfort to politicians and other people who have no conception of the real world.

One of my secondary duties at that time was Bar Officer in the Officers' mess. The duties were not onerous – I did an unannounced check of stock and accounts about once a week, checked that the bar and its equipment was up to scale and clean, and took whatever steps were necessary if there were a complaint. We had a first class staff and there were hardly any complaints.

Every Christmas, the officers paid for a staff party for all the mess employees. The bar staff attended and we used to employ temporary staff from an agency for the occasion. These would turn up in the afternoon to be briefed on their duties by the head barman. On the day of the party I went to the mess before opening time to make sure that there was no hitch in the arrangements. The agency people had not turned up and our stalwarts, Ernst and Willy, were preparing to open as usual.

"But where are the agency people?"

"They have not come, so we will run the bar as usual."

"But you can't miss the annual party! Go at once and you will not be very late."

"But, sir, who will run the bar?"

"I will. Now off to the party with you!"

My duties had made me familiar with the procedures and routines, and I had the bar open on time. I press-ganged the first person to come in to be my assistant and that duty was performed by many officers that evening. The word seemed to get round, and many people came in that evening who had not planned to do so. Everyone who came in wanted to stand me a drink, and I considered that it would have been churlish to refuse, and I do try not to be a churl. It was not long before a terrific party was going on.

The non-stop toil and the weight of responsibility must have been greater than I had anticipated, because about half way through the evening, I felt tired and found it difficult to concentrate. In particular, if someone ordered three or four different drinks, I could not remember the details. I solved that problem by supplying the right number of drinks, but all the same as the first one ordered. This resulted in lots of people having drinks they did not expect or indeed had ever had before. This seemed to add to the merriment of the occasion.

Unfortunately the Commander-in-Chief had chosen that day to pay an informal visit to the station, and was staying with the Station Commander. After dinner in the latter's quarters, they strolled down to the mess for a night-cap. They were served by one of my 'assistants' with two drinks that had been prepared for someone else. They did not stay long. But everyone else did.

In the morning I stood in best blue with my heels together, in front of my Station Commander while he forcibly explained that he regretted and indeed resented that I had turned a quiet postprandial drink into a fiasco. He also pointed out at some length that both he and the C-in-C were very disappointed in me.

I thought that the interview was over when he said: "And now dismiss." But I was wrong. I reached the door and heard him say: "Brian!" I stopped and turned. He now had a smile on his face and said: "It was very good of you to be concerned for the staff. We'll have a drink together at cease flying!" It was easy to take a reprimand from such a man.

I regret to admit that at about this time I became a heavy smoker. I knew it was not good for me (though the overwhelming medical evidence was not available in those days) and tried unsuccessfully to give it up several times. My annual medical examination became due and I reported to Doc Davies for it.

He listened to my chest through his stethoscope (I think it is) and asked how many cigarettes I smoked per day.

"Oh, about twenty."

"This is a serious question!"

"Well, perhaps thirty."

He listened in again.

"I think you had better tell me the truth!"

"Well, sometimes sixty."

"And sometimes more than that?"

"Well, yes, Doctor. Does it show up on your machine?"

"I'll say it does. Your lungs are not in good shape, and it looks to me that you sometimes go over the hundred."

Though I did not admit it, that was true.

"Is it serious, Doctor?"

"It certainly is."

"What should I do?"

"If you stop smoking completely right now, there is a chance that your lungs will recover. If you do not…"

He left the sentence unfinished.

From that moment on, I never smoked again.

When I had finished my tour and was being dined out, Doc Davies got me a drink and said his farewell.

"I am very glad you found my problem in time, Doc, and I want to thank you for that advice, which seems to have done the trick."

He grinned. "There was nothing wrong with you. You were as fit as fiddle."

"Then why did you say what you did?"

"I overheard you in the bar one evening holding forth about how you would like to give up smoking but couldn't. I just gave you a helping hand, that's all."

Good old Doc. If you should happen to read this, sir, my grateful thanks again.

Nowadays, his trick would be considered a breach of human rights for smokers or some such twaddle. It is not everything that changes for the better.

One of our young bachelors, Flying Officer YZ, who lived in the mess, was a very good chap and very good pilot and a very good party-goer. He did not appear at met. briefing one morning, and I asked the other living-in chaps where he was. They were reluctant to answer, but after a bit of bullying they said that he had had a late party the night before, had not made breakfast, and they thought he was still in bed.

I dispatched two of them to the mess with orders to get him up, get him dressed and bring him to the ops room.

They brought him in and he certainly looked the worse for wear. I told him to go and put his flying kit on and report back to me. When he was kitted out I ordered him to go to the aircraft that was waiting outside and get airborne. He was to do one circuit, and land.

"But", he complained, "I am giddy and the room is spinning round. I don't think I could keep the wings level. I think I would spear in."

"Listen YZ. You know the rules, you can drink and party as much as you like but you must be fit for duty in the morning. I would rather lose an aircraft and a pilot than be in an air force that would allow this sort of behaviour. I am sorry about the aircraft, but a pilot like you would not be a great loss in your present state. If you don't take off in the next ten minutes, I shall put you under arrest, and have you court-martialled."

He got into the aircraft, started up, taxied out and took off. He flew one circuit and landed safely.

He was never unfit for duty again. And he never realized that I did not have the authority to send him for court-marshal!

About three weeks later he came to me in a quiet moment and said that he was sorry about his behaviour, and thanked me for not taking the matter further, and said that he now thought that I had done the right thing.

We remained firm friends.

The Dutch Air Force Wing at RNAF Leeuwarden was equipped with the Lockheed F104 – a hot ship and a complicated one too. The airframe manufacturer, Lockheed, had a technical representative there and so did General Electric, the makers of the engines. Their job was to take care of any technical problems that were beyond the capacity of the RNAF. During one of the parties that the Dutchmen threw for us, I got chatting with the GE man – a nice fellow. He said that he would very much like to meet our engine tech. rep.

It was my pleasure to answer: "We don't need a tech. rep. We have Rolls-Royce engines!"

Before getting their 104s, the Leeuwarden wing had been equipped with the Hunter. Now, on a plinth by the guard-room, was a Hunter. It was a nice piece of RNAF history, but rather embarrassing for those of us still operating the type.

We were about to conclude our attachment and return to base. One of our aircraft had a faulty hydraulic pump and our ground crew could not get a spare in time to have it ready for departure. It would have to be left behind and a working party would have to come back and fix it later. We liked to arrive home in one piece, so to speak, and leave no loose ends, but it seemed that there was no choice this time.

In the morning, Mr McBride, our splendid technical Warrant Officer reported all aircraft serviceable and ready to depart.

"But where did you get the pump?"

"You don't want to know sir!"

I found out later that he and one of our 'chiefies' had gone to the guard-room memorial Hunter late at night and taken the hydraulic pump from it and replaced it with our duff one!

Mr McBride and his kind were the salt of the Earth, and the backbone of the RAF. If you should happen to read this, Mr McBride, my very best wishes to you and Mrs McBride.

Day fighter pilots consider that night flying is an unnatural activity that is done during bar opening hours, and is best performed by night fighter pilots and such people. But they have to be proficient at it because a TOT (time on target) of dawn requires a night take-off, and a TOT of dusk requires a night landing. So once per month we would do a stint of it – a short fairly easy cross-country and a few circuits and bumps. The cross-country navigation exercise was usually a triangular route and I was half way along the second leg one night when I had the most extraordinary feeling that I was not alone in the aircraft. I checked the oxygen supply and connections and they were all good. Of course there was absolutely no way that a stowaway was on board – there simply was not room. But I still shone my torch behind me to make sure! If there was no room for a human, it would have to be......?

I went direct from that position straight back to base and landed, and as I put the safety pin into the top of the ejector seat, I had a really good look behind it. Of course there was nothing there. I said nothing to anyone about it, in case they sent for the men in white coats.

I must admit that I was a bit apprehensive about the night flying session the next month, but determined to do the whole cross country course come what may. I did, and the experience was not repeated and never was again. I never knew what it was, or could even guess what it might have been!

NATO had a rotation system whereby the various air forces would operate with each other for a few days. This was to ensure that aircraft fuel couplings, electrical connections and such were compatible and 'NATO standard', and also so that we could get to know each other and so make a more cohesive force. So it was that I led six pilots to operate for a week with the German Air Force Eggebeck wing. The wing was equipped with the RF-84F – the Thunderflash – and because the runways at Eggebeck were being worked on, they were temporarily based at Sylt.

They made us most welcome and threw a party for us the first evening. I made friends with one of the squadron commanders, a Major Kriegs. (A most apt name for a German warrior!) After a few beers he asserted that he could do more press-ups than I could. My chaps dissented. So he got down and did twenty. Amid hoots of encouragement from my chaps, showing more enthusiasm than discipline, I did twenty one. (I really was very fit in those days). Kriegs was delighted and got us more beer. He then announced that he could drink a litre of beer faster than I could. My chaps, showing more exuberance than prudence announced that he could not. Two litres were produced, and I beat him by a short head. (It was not that difficult – I had had lots of practice that evening!) Kriegs was again delighted and got us more beer. Then he said that I may be able to do these things but could not fly an RF-84F.

"Let me have one in the morning and I'll show you I can!"

He cheerfully agreed.

So next morning he strapped me in to one. It all looked very strange and it had something called an A and B system hydraulics that I did not comprehend, but Kreigs said I did not need to know about it. I mentioned that I had no idea what the various limits were. He replied that it would not help if I did, because the gauges were all metric. He assured me that if I pulled the stick back, the houses would get smaller just like in any other aeroplane. He leaned into the cockpit and started the engine, and off I went, with him flying 'chase' in another 84. It was a strange beast to

After my trip in the German Air Force RF-84F Thunderflash.

fly at first, but I soon got the hang of it, and I managed to 'lose' him in a tail-chase.

We could hardly leave it there, so after my trip, I sent him off in a Hunter. I was, after all, the senior RAF officer present, and no one from base would know, I hoped. But to be on the safe side, I did not want too much talk about it. But Kreigs insisted on taking photographs of us after the episode.

It was an interesting and enjoyable week and we became familiar with their methods of operating and tactics and briefing and debriefing, and they learned something of our methods. Naturally, we thought we did it better! In particular, the German pilots were not allowed as much discretion as we were used to, especially by air traffic control.

We were taxiing out to fly home when the controller asked if I was ready for the clearance. I said I was, expecting him to say that we were cleared to line up on the runway. He said something like: "After take off, climb to 1,000 feet on runway heading and at 10 miles turn left onto 140, climb to 5,000 feet at not above 250 knots, and cross the ABC radio beacon not before time 22 then increase speed to 350 knots, turn right onto 160 and climb to cruise altitude."

"Roger."

"Read back the clearance!"

"I can't read it back, I didn't get any of it!"

Years later, when I was an airline pilot, this type of clearance was routine and necessary. But the RAF never used it for fighter operations.

He transmitted the same rigmarole and ordered me to read it back.

"If you don't mind, we would like to take off, do a low pass over the airfield, then RTB (return to base)."

Pause. Then: "Roger, Royal Air Force."

Back at base, the WingCo Flying and the Station Commander came to the crew room for coffee and chat to welcome us back. The Station Commander asked me what the RF-84F was like to fly and I gave him my impressions of it. He did not say anything about Kreigs flying the Hunter but if he knew about the 84, he must have known about it.

I thought I saw the suggestion of a smile on his face.

Another trip I did as part of the rotation system was to lead a four-ship to a French Air Force base (I forget which). The language of aviation is English and the language of NATO is also English. But some French service men insisted on speaking in French. Pride in country is a fine thing, but can be a nuisance to others. We landed and turned off the runway and proceeded down the taxi way. I did not know where they wanted us to park so I asked the tower for taxi instructions. They answered in French, which I did not understand, so I asked again, only to receive the reply in French again.

We were approaching the tower, so I turned off of the main taxi way and stopped as close to it as I could get. Then I gave the order: "Brakes on", followed by: "Set full power!"

Four Avon engines at full power make an ear splitting noise, and I again asked for taxi instructions. I could barely hear their response because now, as well as the noise I could hear direct, it was being transmitted to my ear-phones as well. But I could just make it out – it was taxi instructions in English.

My time on the Squadron came to an end. I had greatly enjoyed it, but it was time to move on. We went back to UK to take up my next appointment as an instructor on the staff at Chivenor.

I was allocated to No. 63 Squadron. My friend Ernie had served on it when it was a front line squadron. It was now a reserve outfit with the task of training new boys, but if need be could easily revert to operational status.

They needed an instrument rating examiner (IRE) on 63, and as I had been one in Training Command, I was sent on the course to be qualified in Fighter Command too. The only other student on the course was Sandy Wilson from No. 2. He and I have the same type of sense of humour and we got on well together. Some years later, I ran into him again by chance at a party at RAF Benson. (The station with the narrow runway!) He had just been appointed to the command of No. 2 Squadron, which was about to re-equip from the Phantom to the Jaguar. He promised me that if I turned up at RAF Laarbruch, in Germany, he would give me a trip in a Jaguar. An official handing over ceremony/party was held and Sylvia and I went to it. Sandy greeted us and said that he was pleased we had made the tedious journey. I replied that it was well worth it for a trip in a Jaguar. He explained that the new aircraft was suffering many teething problems, and that many of his aircraft were under repair or modification, and that Jaguar hours were like gold dust and his chaps were lucky to get ten hours a month. They would not have been very pleased with their Boss if he gave time to a visitor like me. "But", he said, "A promise is a promise."

"But, Sandy, I won't hold you to your promise in this situation."

"You cannot release me from my own promise. Only I can do that."

"In that case, Sandy, I simply refuse to get into the aircraft!"

He grinned at me, shook my hand, and said simply: "Thanks mate."

Sandy went on to achieve very high rank, as indeed he should have. But he is a great chap and does not allow the great gulf between our ranks to interfere with our friendship.

As well as training new fighter boys, the OCU also trained forward air controllers (FACs). These are usually front line soldiers (occasionally RAF men) whose job is to direct (from the ground) ground attack aircraft on to their targets just beyond the front line. It is not an easy task to accomplish when the aircraft, doing over 400 knots and is in sight for only a few seconds. But it can be done with training and practice, using the correct techniques. We needed another FAC instructor, and so I was sent on the course at the School of Land/Air Warfare at Old Sarum to get the qualification.

I found it a most interesting diversion to teach this difficult art. We conducted the course first in the class room, then in the field demonstrating to the students and then inviting them to try it. If there were spare aircraft we also took them up in the T7 and showed them what it was like from the other side, so to speak.

If the power controls of the Hunter fail, it is still possible to fly it 'in manual'. The controls are extremely heavy, and it takes two hands to move the stick a small amount in any direction. It is an uncomfortable experience, because the pilot barely has control of the aircraft. We all practiced it, of course, and students had to show that they could cope with a landing in manual. Before I was checked out to instruct at Chivenor, I had to demonstrate that I could also take off and do aerobatics in manual. It is surprising what you can do if you try!

The course for the Hunter students was done in phases. First they had to learn to fly the aircraft. As a QFI, I was kept busy then. Then they had to learn to fly it on instruments and get their instrument rating. That too kept me active. I was also a tactics instructor so took part in that phase too. When they started doing low flying and low level navigation, my fighter recce background gave me plenty of flying again. I was not qualified as a weapons instructor, so when they did air to air and air to ground firing, I took a back seat, but was able to take any empty 'slots' on the programme to keep myself in practice.

So the fighter instruction and the occasional FAC course gave us an intensive job that was enjoyable and rewarding.

The Hunter had its 'press to transmit' button on the end of the throttle lever, and the rocket firing switch was one of the switches on the top of the control column, or 'stick'.

At about this time, someone at higher authority, for reasons never revealed, decided that these two switches should be reversed, and so a programme was started to carry out the necessary re-wiring.

The first aircraft with the new lay-out was ready and was allocated to a ground attack exercise using rockets. The range procedure required that the pilot would make a radio call to the range officer just before his final turn-in and state 'turning in live' or 'turning in dummy', so that the range officer would know what to expect. The pilot called 'turning in live' and forgot that the switches had been changed and fired off two rockets in the general direction of Cardiff. He realised at once his mistake, and pressed the button again and transmitted: "Oh! I am terribly sorry!" thereby sending two more rockets towards Cardiff. The programme was halted, and the switches put back to their original (and correct) position.

The Royal Saudi Air Force was about to equip with Hunters, and they sent some of their pilots to Chivenor to learn to fly and operate the type. I flew with one of them, Ahmed xxx one day in rather bad weather. We entered cloud soon after take off, and as we went through about twenty thousand feet, still in cloud, the engine failed. No one would have blamed me if we had ejected in those conditions, and I did consider that option. But my student did not look very happy, and I wondered if he would pull the blind to eject, so I decided to attempt a '1 in 1' approach. The name comes from the fact that the Hunter, with gear down and flaps up, will glide one mile for each thousand feet lost. With the gear up, it will glide one mile for the loss of only six or seven hundred feet. So the ground controller gives headings to steer for base, and the pilot flies at the lower rate of descent. The controller is constantly checking distance against height and when the distance equals the height in thousands of feet, he calls '1 in 1', at which point the pilot drops his gear, and maintains the 1 in 1 till the runway is in sight, and when landing is assured, drops his flaps. It takes a high degree of confidence in the controller to do this in cloud, and we had never been out of cloud! We broke out at about five hundred feet, on the runway centre line but much too high. (The controller told me later that he had planned a few extra feet to be on the safe side!). I did a steep S bend each way to use up the excess height, and we landed safely, and even managed to turn off the end of the runway on to the taxiway so as not to block the runway. Phew!

It was nearly beer time anyway, and we celebrated our continued existence that evening in the standard fashion.

I have since regretted that I decided not to eject. In hindsight, I had time to talk my student through the ejection process. I had a perfectly good reason, and by not taking the opportunity, I missed adding another experience to my memories.

I was approaching my 38th birthday, at which point the RAF gives its officers the option of leaving the Service on the minimum pension, or staying in till the age of 55. It was time for me to review the situation.

My motivation for joining the Service had been to fly and fight the Queen's enemies. I had not accomplished the second part, and as I got older, the prospects of doing so could only get worse. Also, as I got older, there was an ever greater chance of being sent to fly heavies – bombers or coastal or transport. Or a desk!

It did not look as if the RAF intended to promote me – if they did, it would have happened already. And some of my erstwhile juniors had become my seniors. They were all most courteous and considerate to me, but even so......

So, somewhat sadly, I decided that the time had come, and I put in my papers to leave.

In the army, captains after six (or is it eight?) years service are automatically promoted to major. In the navy, lieutenants automatically become lieutenant commanders after the same time. But in the RAF, promotion to the equivalent rank of squadron leader is not automatic but by selection. I think that to be fair, flight lieutenants who are not selected should be promoted the day before they leave, so that in retirement, they can share similar status and pension with their contemporaries from the other Services.

Regulars leaving the Service are entitled to go on a re-settlement course. This is to learn a subject which might help in getting a civilian job. Several of my colleagues studied for their civil flying licences this way. (I did mine by correspondence course.)

I had an ambition to build our own house, and so I applied to go on a house maintenance course. The RAF did not run such a course, but the Army did, and I was lucky enough to get a place on it. I was the only Air Force man among about 100 army retirees, two of whom were generals. For practical work, we were divided into small syndicates of about eight. The generals insisted upon my being in their group, and when I asked why was told: "I had a lot to do with the Air Force in the war. My experience was that the Air Force always knows what to do, and always does it. We are counting on you to take care of us here." Thereafter they addressed me as 'Air Force'. They were most agreeable and we got along together very well.

In one lesson we had to prepare brick foundations for a garden shed, and one of the points made was that if the spirit level is not long enough, if B is level with A, and C is level with B, then A is level with C. One of the generals had a problem with this and asked me to explain it again. I did.

"Yes, yes, I understand the theory, but how do you know if A is level with B?"

"The spirit level tells you."

"That's the point. How does it tell you?"

"It's level when the bubble is between the marks."

"Bless my soul! Is that bubble supposed to be there?"

"Of course! It would not work without it."

"I thought there was a leak or something."

"General, are you telling me that you have never used a spirit level?"

"Now look here, Air Force. Gunners and technical people and trades people and such might very well be familiar with this, but you should not expect a chap from a decent regiment to know about it."

Another lesson was about plastering a wall. First was a lecture, then a demonstration, then we tried it ourselves. My General simply could not cope with this. The plaster went up his arm, down his trousers and on to his erstwhile very shiny boots. All the time he was muttering: "Damned stuff! Damned stuff!"

Then he got me to do his bit of wall before the instructor came round to examine our work.

"You see! I knew you would look after us!"

After classes, we sometimes had a drink and dinner together. They were delightful company and I greatly enjoyed teaming up with them.

I got my diploma, and the course helped me no end when we did, finally, build our own house.

April 1st 1968 was the 50th birthday of the RAF, and the Wing Commander Flying, Nigel Price, ex 56 Entry, (see what I mean about my juniors becoming my seniors?) decided to get the whole wing airborne and do a fly past of neighbouring towns and airfields. I approached him and asked for a place in the formation.

He replied that of course I could not take part, because by then I would be out of the RAF.

"Only just! And I would so much like to do it!"

He grinned at me and said that he would fit me in, (see what I mean about their being considerate?).

So my last trip in a Hunter, and in the RAF, was in a large formation to celebrate the RAF's birthday. It was a very fitting end to a wonderful experience that I would not have missed for the World.

Chapter 7

BUSH PILOT

When I left the Service, I was sure that I wanted to continue flying rather than take up some other profession. But I was not keen to become an airline pilot because they seemed to me to fly straight and level for hours on end, and never got a chance to point their feet at the sun. I wanted something a bit more stimulating, perhaps flying military aircraft somehow or becoming a bush pilot.

Before I left the RAF, I was contacted by a man in the MoD Resettlement Branch. This was a small department that on request would try to put retiring officers in touch with prospective employers.

"I've been talking to a chap from Kenya. He is a farmer with his own airstrip and a couple of aircraft and is thinking of starting an air charter business. He wants to meet someone who is just leaving the RAF and might be interested in joining him. I thought it was right up your street."

It sounded interesting, and so I met Tony Lutyens, the farmer, who was on a trip to England. He was an extremely nice man. He gave me lunch and explained his situation, and warned me that he was a long way from actually starting up and could give me no dates. We agreed to keep in touch and he said he would let me know when there were any developments. He also said that if I were to go to Kenya, he would be pleased to meet me and show me around. I thought that if there were other nice people like him in Kenya, it must be a very good place. I found out that there were and it was.

I do not know if my flame out landing with Ahmed had anything to do with it, but Airwork – the company that had the contract to train the Saudi Air Force – offered me a job as a civilian instructor at the OCU at Dharan, flying Hunters, Lightnings, and Sabres, with a view to taking over as chief flying instructor. That sounded attractive. The untaxed salary was £10,000 pa, which in 1968 was considerable. They promised that a married quarter would be available immediately. After much discussion with Sylvia, I accepted and went out to Dharan.

I was met and welcomed and given a room in the mess. Next day I was shown over the hangar and operations room, and the aircraft line. I had to convert on to the Lightning and Sabre, and would fly them both for the first time solo. Super! And I had to learn to find my way around the desert, and a new air force way of doing things.

I said: "This is going to be a big job, and I cannot get my teeth into it until my domestic arrangements are sorted out. Please can we look at my married quarter?"

"But there is no married quarter for you."

"But I was promised one!"

"Not only is there no quarter for you, there are no married quarters at all!"

I went to see the chief Airwork man at Dharan and told him about the promise.

"Yes, old boy, we have to promise that or no one would come out. But you'll soon settle down. Have a trip in the Lightning and you will soon feel better."

"I am not going anywhere near the hangars till I have a married quarter!"

"But, old boy, that might get you the sack."

"You'll have to be quick to do that before I quit."

They flew me up to Riyadh to see the chief Airwork man in Saudi Arabia. I had a pleasant evening there with my old friend Paddy King, ex 54 Entry. He was instructing on Cessnas at the Military Academy.

My conversation with the big boss was fruitless, so I returned to Dharan and told the boss there that I was leaving.

"Yes, old boy. Lots of people say that, but they never do."

It was necessary to obtain an exit visa to leave Saudi Arabia, which takes a few days to get, so I put in an application. Perhaps to humour me, the company processed the application. It came through and I bought a one-way ticket on Pakistan Airways to Nairobi in Kenya.

I was in the line walking from the waiting room across the tarmac to the aeroplane when one of the admin. fellows rushed up to me.

"The top Boss man says that if you stay, he will do whatever it takes to get you a married quarter this month!"

I considered his offer for a second.

"Tell him he's too late!"

I presented myself to the immigration officer at Nairobi airport. He demanded to see my return ticket. I explained that I had arrived on a one-way ticket. He answered that no one was permitted to enter Kenya unless they had a return ticket.

"Why is that?"

"So that they cannot become a burden on the State."

"So I will have to leave, or get a ticket?"

"Ndio."

"So either way, I will have to go to a ticket office."

"Ndio."

"So you will have to let me through so that I can."

"No one is allowed in unless they have a return ticket."

I went back into the arrival hall to consider my next move, and I noticed that the baggage handlers were moving bags on trolleys through swing doors that appeared to lead to the other side of the barrier. I followed them and found myself in the outer hall. The nearest country was Ethiopia, so I went to the Ethiopian Airways office and bought a ticket to Addis Ababa. Armed with this, I went back though the swing doors and presented myself again to the same immigration officer. Now that I had a ticket out, he was happy to allow me to enter the country, this time legally. He showed no curiosity about how I had got the ticket. It was then easy to go back to Ethiopian and get my money back. The games we have to play to satisfy the admin. wallahs!

Tony Lutyens kindly came to the airport, and after welcoming me, suggested that we go to his place for two or three days. I expected him to take me to the car park but we went to air-side again, got into his Cherokee 6, and flew to his farm which was on the far side of the Great Rift Valley at Mau Narok. The scenery was stunning and I enjoyed the trip immensely. He had a charming wife and family who quickly put me at my ease, and made me feel at home.

Next day he suggested that we fly to Nakuru for lunch, and he invited me to do the flying. I knew the theory of high density altitude operations; now I had to put it into practice. His farm was at 11,200 feet above sea level, so for a start there was the oxygen consideration. In the RAF, flying above 10,000 feet without oxygen is forbidden. This allows for a safety margin, and anyway, it is possible to go higher for short time periods. After a few weeks of living at high altitude, the body grows more white (or is it red?) corpuscles, which enables one to go higher safely. But I had just arrived, and was short of breath all the time. Tony lived there, so if need be, he could take over. I planned that after take off I would find an area where I could descend.

At sea level the engine mixture control is set at fully rich for maximum power for take-off. Fully rich at that height would probably cause a rich mixture cut on take off, and engine failure. Even if it kept going, it would not be producing its maximum possible power, which itself is much less than sea level power. So the engine has to be run up to about 2,000 rpm and the mixture control adjusted to produce maximum rpm.

The take off was noticeably long, but we got off safely, and I was soon descending into the Rift Valley towards Nakuru. The Rift is an awesome sight, especially when seen from the air. There was a pleasant flying club at Nakuru and I was introduced to some of the members. There was a shortage of experienced pilots in Kenya at that time, and when the chairman found that I had just left the RAF, he offered me the job of full time professional flying instructor, on the spot. I promised to consider it.

On the following day, we flew to the Kenya coast to meet Tony's prospective partner in the air charter company. The scenery was again magical, and included my first sight of Mount Kilimanjaro. There were areas of forest, others of scrub, Massai herding their cattle, the mud and straw dwellings of the local people, and occasionally, big game – elephant, giraffe, wildebeest and even a rhino. Europe is full of radio navigation aids, but the RAF fighters I flew were not equipped to use them. Here the reverse was true – Tony's aircraft had several radio aid receivers, but in Kenya there were very few such aids. So to find Kilifi, I would have to use pilot navigation methods that I was familiar with. I was already beginning to think that this would be a good place to live and fly.

We landed at Kilifi and stayed with the partner in his holiday house. The partner was another agreeable man and I was really getting to like this place. While I was taught water-skiing, the two partners had a business meeting and decided that they could not start their air charter business for at least another year. This was disappointing, but I quite understood – Tony had made no promises.

From there, we flew to Wilson Airport, the general aviation field in Nairobi. I took the controls again and was getting familiar with it all and enjoying it greatly. The pilot-navigation (as distinct from guidance by a qualified navigator) I was doing was similar to the method we used in fighters at low level – with a map on the knee and a good look-out. But I was used to reaching features very much quicker than I was doing now, so had to slow down my anticipation. The essence of good navigating is to hold an accurate heading. A fighter at over 400 knots will hold its heading unless a definite action is taken to change it, whereas a light aircraft will change heading in a moment if attention is relaxed. And wind speed is such a small fraction of jet-aircraft speed, that wind drift can be ignored, whereas in a light aircraft it is a significant fraction and must be assessed and corrected. So to fly accurately in a light aircraft took as much attention as flying in a high speed aircraft.

I decided that if I were offered a job here, I would take it. Tony took me round the airport and introduced me to the chief pilots of the three main air charter companies. Because of the pilot shortage, each one offered me a job.

Then Tony took me to the Aero Club and introduced me to a chap called John xxx who had just left one of the charter companies to start up on his own and was looking for someone to help him. John had been a fighter pilot in the war and had been shot down in the Western Desert. He had been waiting his turn to go down the tunnel during the Great Escape when the Germans discovered it and he had to go back to his hut. He offered me a job too.

I talked it over with Tony, and decided to accept the one with John. I sent a telegram to Sylvia telling her to pack up and come to Kenya, and joined Kenya Air Charters. My title was Chief Pilot. My selection was not difficult – I was also the only one!

One of our most distinguished fighter pilots during the war was the South African Piet Hugo. He had shot down twenty four German aircraft, had won a DSO the three DFCs and ended the war as a group captain.

I had arranged to meet John the next day at tea time in the Aero Club. There was only one other member taking tea and we introduced ourselves. He was a quiet modest sort of chap but was very welcoming to me as a new club member. He said his name was Piet Hugo. He asked where I had come from and I told him that I had recently left the RAF.

He stirred his tea and mentioned that some time ago he too had been in the RAF. "But I was in it for only a few years".

When I met John later I told him about my meeting and mentioned that it was a rather unusual name and that it was odd that two Hugos had been in the Service. John smiled and said that there were not two - the man I met was THE Piet Hugo

I am glad that I have had the pleasure and privilege of shaking the hand of that Great Man.

John had acquired premises on the apron at Wilson and had bought a brand new Cessna 206C. This was six seater (including the pilot), but the seats could be removed and freight could be loaded through the wide cargo doors. I was checked out in it by Alan Herd, a super pilot, super aircraft engineer and super chap who was our chief engineer. He and his wife, Beverly, became good chums. I had not flown such a thing before – it was rather heavy on the controls, but not excessively so. The more I flew it, the more I liked it.

Our first customer arrived by taxi from Embakasi, the international airport, having missed the daily scheduled flight to Mogadishu in

Somalia, He wanted to be flown there ASAP. I quickly worked out the distance and the price, which did not seem to matter to him, the aircraft was just outside and ready to go, and we were airborne in under ten minutes. Wilson airport closed at 20:00 hrs, and if I came back after that I would have to go to Embakasi which would incur costs and be inconvenient. So I needed a quick turn round.

When I got within radio range of Mogadishu, I called them and asked them to have Shell standing by to refuel me without delay. Then I dictated my return flight plan and asked them to process it. That would save about ten minutes.

When I taxied in, there was no sign of the Shell truck, so I went to the tower to find out why.

"Shell is on the far side of the airport."

"Then telephone them!"

"The telephones do not work."

"Then send someone on a bike!"

"It is too hot to pedal."

"Have you put the flight plan in?"

"No, sir."

"Who did I speak to on the radio?"

A miserable looking wretch admitted that it was he.

"Did you copy down my flight plan?"

"No, sir."

"Why not?"

"I cannot write, sir."

I firmly told them all in no uncertain terms that this was by far the most inefficient airfield I had ever been to. (It was true then, I had only just left the RAF!) While I was delivering this rebuke, a man dressed in a suit and collar and tie came in and asked if he could be of help.

The man, whom I took to be the airport manager, quickly arranged the fuel and the flight plan. I thanked him, but added that this was a shambles of a place and ought to be bulldozed into the sea with the staff in it. He apologized and left.

The illiterate wretch then asked me if I knew whom I had been talking to.

I replied that I did not know his name, but presumed he was the airport manager.

"That", the wretch said, "Was the Prime Minister!"

I found that difficult to believe, but the wretch bade me look out of the window, and I saw the PM (for it really was he) greeting a visiting Head of State, guard of honour, brass band, red carpet and all.

I was sorry to hear, a few weeks later, that he had been assassinated in a coup.

And that was the first and last time that I ever rebuked such a dignitary, though there have been times, when watching the political news, that I wished I had another chance!

I was flying an American senator and his wife and daughters on a trip around several game lodges, staying at a different one each night. He was a nice man and we got on well; he liked to have a 'sun-downer' with me "before all those women arrive". He was very fond of dry martinis, but would not allow the barman to mix it for him. He would order a gin in one glass and a vermouth in another and, balancing one arm against the other, would carefully pour one drop of vermouth into the gin.

"Some bartenders are sloppy", he explained, "And they allow two drops to go in. Once in Cincinnati, a bartender put three drops in!"

We were having our drinks one evening when Arthur P. (whom I knew slightly, having met him in the Aero Club) came in. Arthur was known as the 'flying green-grocer' because he had a farm on the slopes of Kilimanjaro where, among other things, he grew high quality vegetables and fruit that he flew in his own aircraft to the game lodges. It was a lucrative business. He told me that his aeroplane was grounded and it was essential for him to get back to his farm in the morning, and asked if I could take him. I explained that I was under charter to the Senator and not free to do so.

The Senator said that as he and his family were doing a game run in the morning, then having breakfast and a leisurely departure, they would not want to take off until about ten o'clock, and if I could be back in time, he had no objection to my helping Arthur out.

We were airborne at dawn, and to reach Arthur's farm it was

necessary to cross the saddle between Mount Kilimanjaro and Mount Meru. As we did so, the ground mist got thicker and thicker till I had my wheels in the weeds, to use an RAF expression. Arthur (a fairly new pilot) said that he had never seen that kind of flying before, and had no idea that it could be done.

The flying instructor in me surfaced. "Arthur, the Queen spent a great deal of time and money training us to do this. Don't even think of doing it yourself until you have a good deal more experience. Besides, if all else fails, you have to pull up into cloud and fly on instruments, so you have to learn instrument flying too."

A couple of weeks later, I heard in the Aero Club that Arthur had been killed in an aircraft accident. He had been flying over that same saddle in bad weather and had hit trees. Perhaps I had not made my point strongly enough?

I was waiting at a coast hotel for my passengers. I filled in the time by taking a book and the crossword to a sunbed in the garden by the beach. A few yards away was another man doing the same.

He did not acknowledge my wave so I did not intrude on him further.

After a while a light aircraft - a Piper Cub - approached and landed on the beach. This was often done and is quite safe provided that the pilot touches down just the right distance from the water's edge where the sand is firm.

Either he did not see or decided to ignore, a clump of seaweed and taxied over it. Unfortunately the weeds hid a rock and he hit it with his propeller. The engine and the aircraft stopped abruptly. The stranger in the other lounger began to take an interest.

When a propeller hits something under power, the regulations require that the engine be stripped down and the crankshaft checked for distortion which can cause undue vibration and engine failure. The aircraft has to be taken to a suitable facility which in this case would need the wings to be taken off and the whole lot trucked out. Even if the shaft is still straight it is a very expensive process.

The pilot took the propeller off, laid it on a rock and proceeded to bash it with another rock. Much to my surprise he bashed it almost back to the right shape. Then he put it back on the aircraft. At this point the stranger, who was now down on the beach asked what he planned to do next. "I was planning to stay a couple of days but now I am going to fly to Mombasa airport and have it checked".

"I don't think so" said the man, "This aircraft is grounded and when I report this, don't be surprised if you are grounded too".

The stranger was an inspector with the DCA (Directorate of Civil Aviation).

The moral of the story: If you bash a propeller on the beach, be careful who is watching!

It was a normal practice in East Africa to catch wild animals and send them off to zoos anywhere in the World. Unusually, some zoologists were setting up a 'natural zoo' on one of the islands in Lake Victoria. It was to have no fences or cages, and the animals could be observed in a really natural environment. To stock it with animals, they bought some from zoos and transported them there.

So we had a request from them to pick up a gorilla at the international airport whence it had been flown in from America. John asked me to do the job in the C206. I drove over to Embakasi to look at the creature. It was in a cage, which, I measured, would just go in the back of the 206 if we took the back four seats out. But the gorilla could put his arms through the bars of the cage. The freight people had tried putting a wooden wall on one side of the cage, but the animal had very quickly torn it to pieces. So the beast could very easily reach through the bars and get me by the throat.

It was against the law to carry a firearm in a civil aircraft, but I spoke nicely to the airport police and they lent me a revolver, fortunately one I was familiar with from my service days. I did the trip with gun at the ready, but the gorilla was content and peaceful throughout.

But I could not help musing that if something had upset him and he had got me round the neck and caused us to crash, the accident report would have been most unusual: Cause of crash – pilot strangled by gorilla.

I had the task of flying a party of clerics to several remote spots. There was bishop, a dean, and two junior officer types. They had been out from UK the previous year to spread their holy benevolence among the locals and were now back to see the results.

The first place was a village situated on both sides of a river. Moving from one side to the other meant wading through deep water, and so the Church had paid for a prefabricated bridge to be built and delivered. All the locals had to do was assemble it rather like a giant Meccano set. We landed at the nearby strip and a local priest met us with a Land Rover to take to the village. There, the bridge parts were in a heap exactly where they had been dumped, and were now starting to go rusty, and were partly covered by bush.

"But why have you not assembled the bridge?" asked the Bishop.

"The women are so busy with fetching the water and working the crops, that they have not had time", the Chief Man explained.

"Then why didn't the men build it?"

"It's not work for men", the Chief replied in an offended tone.

At the next place, they had had delivered equipment for boring a well so that the women would not have to walk a mile to carry water back on their heads. The equipment was in a heap where it had been dropped, and an identical conversation took place.

Finally we flew to a place where the gear for a water purification plant had been dropped. Once again the gear was in a heap and the same conversation was repeated.

The clerics were very disappointed, though the Bishop, who liked to fly in the front right seat next to me, assured me that The Good Lord must have had a reason for making those chaps lazy. I asked him what it was. He replied that The Lord worked in mysterious ways.

When we landed back in Nairobi, I got my maps and things together and started to get out of the aeroplane. The Bishop asked me to please stay seated while he gave thanks to The Almighty for their safe journey. I politely complied. While we were walking from the aircraft to the office I jested to the Bishop that he ought perhaps have given thanks to me for their safe journey.

"Ah my son. You were simply The Good Lord's instrument."

And that is one of the few times that I have been called upon to perform a Holy Duty, the others being flying the Pope from Rome to Nairobi, and flying the Aga Khan from Nairobi to Bombay.

I have a touching faith that on the Day of Judgment, these Holy Trips will be weighed in the balance against my miserable transgressions.

Two Indians came into the office one morning and asked if they could charter an aircraft to take them to Mwanza on Lake Victoria. They were brothers and were on a business trip to Nairobi with their father. Unfortunately, the father had died that morning, and in accordance with their custom, they wanted to take him home to be buried that day.

Alan quickly had the three right hand seats removed, and I and the two sons occupied the three left hand seats, and we laid the deceased in his body bag on the right side of the floor and secured him with the normal lap straps that were still anchored to the floor.

As we approached Mwanza, I did the approach checks and turned round and asked my pax to tighten their lap straps. They did so, and I was touched to see them, without a word, lean down and tighten Dad's straps too.

The Duke of Edinburgh was coming to Kenya on a bird shooting trip. He was to fly by Queen's Flight to Lodwar and go by road to Eleye Springs on the shore of Lake Rudolf. There was a very primitive fishing camp there, and we got the job of flying in to the primitive airstrip at Eleye with supplies and aids to gracious living like knives and forks. The place is almost overwhelmed by flying insects of one sort and another, and so a tent-making company in Nairobi was commissioned to make a huge mosquito net that would fill the mess tent. I got it in the back of the 206 somehow and flew it up there and helped them erect it.

The day before the arrival I got my aircraft ready to go and arranged for the ice cream man to come onto the tarmac. We loaded a good supply of ice cream into the pannier underneath the fuselage, and I took off at once and climbed to the cool air at 10,000 feet. The Land Rover was waiting when I landed and we quickly raced the ice cream to the gas-operated refrigerator.

After the visit I went up to bring some of the gear back.

"I hope the Duke was impressed with the mosquito net?"

"He said that he hated the things and asked to dine out in the open."

"I hope he enjoyed the ice cream?"

"He did not want any."

I went to Eleye several times after that. I enjoyed insect free meals, and there was always plenty of ice cream.

I took a party of people to Kisumu on Lake Victoria, and based there, did a number of side trips in that area, ending up with a night stop in a hotel in town.

Bush pilots are well aware that if they inadvertently leave the battery switch on, they will find a flat battery in the morning. I had adopted their trick of leaving the rotating beacon switched on, so that if the battery switch were also left on, the beacon would proclaim the fact. So I know that I did not leave it on. In the morning, the battery was, nevertheless, quite flat.

I always took jump leads, just in case, and all I needed now was a vehicle with a battery. There was not a single vehicle on the airfield. I commandeered a bike and pedalled into town to find something suitable. Still no vehicle until I noticed the fire station and the fire engine standing outside.

"Can you drive the fire engine to the airport?"

"No, bwana. I cannot drive."

"Where is the driver?"

"There is no driver."

"Is there anybody who can drive it?"

"No bwana."

"There is now!"

We found the keys somewhere and I drove the appliance back to the airfield and to my aircraft. The leads were just long enough, but it was necessary to start with the propeller inches from the bonnet. The engine started and I carefully backed the vehicle away, and parked it near what had once been the tower.

"Bwana, can you drive the fire engine back to the station before you go?"

"No, I'm sorry, but I cannot possibly leave the aircraft with the engine running."

"Then how can I get it back?"

"You really must learn to drive it yourself."

"But Bwana, I have tried and I really cannot do it."

"Then it really does not matter where the fire engine is, does it?"

Some time later, I had to land at Kisumu to refuel. The fire engine was exactly where I had left it. I sent word to the fireman that I could bring his appliance back now if he wanted me to. The word came back that there was no point in taking the trouble. It is still where I left it, as far as I know.

A naturalist photographer came in one day and said that he had been commissioned to take a movie picture of the banks of the River Omo which flows in to the North end of Lake Rudolf from Ethiopia. I suggested that we remove the cargo doors completely from the C206 and the rear right seat, so that he could strap into the rear left seat, and have floor space in front of him and an open gap in front of him. He looked at that and pronounced that it would be a perfect platform for his work.

We flew up to Eleye Springs at the South end of Lake Rudolf (where they had an insect free dining room and plenty of ice cream!) and I removed the doors and seat. He got his equipment together and we took off. He wanted me to fly as low and as close to the trees as I could, so I did not have much chance to look round to see how he was doing. The river twists and turns and it was full time job manoeuvring the aircraft to follow it. This involved doing steep turns, first one way then the other. I remember hoping that my man would not become air-sick.

We reached one of the rare clearings and for a few seconds I was not near any obstruction, and so I took the opportunity to look round to check on my photographer. He had undone his straps and was sitting on the floor with his legs out in space. He was holding his camera in both hands and so was not even holding on! This would have been very dangerous if we had been flying straight and level, but with the sort of flying I had been doing, it was a miracle that he had not fallen out. I started a gentle climb with a constant bank to the left so that if he fell, he would fall inside. When we were too high for him to get good pictures, he came forward to ask why I was climbing. I told him, and said that if he did not strap in, I would return to Eleye. He insisted that it was perfectly safe to do what he had been doing, so I returned to Eleye. On the ground there, he would not listen to reason, so I put the doors back on and the seat in.

"I'm going back to Nairobi. You can come with me, or stay here. Your choice!"

He came back.

I have heard that in a service business, the customer is always right. I know of at least one exception to that rule!

One of our clients was a Brazilian senator who had a secondary activity in making short travel documentaries for Brazilian tv. His entourage consisted of his lady friend, a camera man and a sound man. He was now about to make a movie about Kenya, and I flew them to one of the game lodges for that purpose. He invited me to go along with them and watch the process.

They found a suitable location, and set everything up. I took post by the photographer in a clearing. The Senator came through the bush and into the clearing looking like an intrepid explorer in the heart of the bush (the camera did not show the lodge about 50 yards away) uttering his spiel as he walked. The photographer started shooting, and the Senator's words, which were transmitted via a radio on his back, were received by the sound man, who had a radio receiver on his back, and recorded on the recording apparatus. This was before the days of micro chips, miniature this and digital that, and this equipment used valves and condensers and such, and very large and heavy dry cell batteries, and the back packs were so heavy that they were difficult to lift. The heaviest pack was the Senator's.

At coffee break time the Senator went off somewhere with the lady, and I stayed with the technicians.

The sound man asked me what I thought of the set-up.

"It's none of my business", I replied, "But since you ask, wouldn't it be easier for the Senator to carry the recording equipment on his back instead of the heavier radio, and record direct?"

"Of course it would", he replied, "But he has not thought of that. Please do not suggest it to him, because that would put me be out of a job!"

The bush pilot community I had joined contained a variety of people – good pilots, not so good. good workers and not so good and a few eccentrics. One company, let's call it cox, had a rather odd chief pilot. The company had operated light aircraft with fixed undercarriages successfully for several years, It then enlarged by getting a twin engined aircraft with a retractable undercarriage. The chief pilot opined that the new aircraft was too complicated and difficult for his pilots so decreed that all trips in it would be flown only by him.

A charter request came in for which the new aircraft was just right. The Boss got his pax on board and took off, flew all the way from A to B with his gear down and just before landing put it up and landed on his belly! And he was the best pilot in the company!

Bing Crosby was a keen big game hunter and we heard that he had a trophy room that got ever fuller and more comprehensive. He came to Kenya most years to add to his collection looking for ever rarer species. His white hunter was Terry Matthews, perhaps the best in the business, and he used us, so I got to fly Bing.

Terry set out with his convoy of trucks (including a grader) a few days before Bing, his wife and two friends arrived. He set up camp at a remote spot where he knew that there were a few lesser-spotted whatnots, and with his grader carved out a bush airstrip. I collected Bing and his party and flew them to the map reference given me by Terry. There were no radio navigation aids and the maps of that area are not very accurate, so map reading was not easy. It was even more difficult for Terry, map reading at ground level. But the camp was where it was supposed to be, and the runway, though it would not have passed a CAA inspection, was perfectly adequate.

I stayed in the camp for two days and lived in luxury. Each camper had his own comfortably furnished tent which was a bedroom and en suite full bath room with hot and cold running water. What was called the lounge tent had a thick carpet, very nice arm-chairs, polished occasional tables and high quality lamps. The bar tent had every drink I had ever heard of (and some I had not) and lots of ice, and the library had a wide variety of books and magazines. The dining table had whiter than white table linen, silver cutlery and cut-glassware. At dinner, which was superb, every diner had an immaculately clad waiter standing behind him to cater to his every whim.

Bing bagged his lesser spotted whatnot, and it was then my job to fly the party to the Mount Kenya Safari Club, a very nice hotel on the foothills of Mount Kenya at Nanyuki. The strip, if I recall correctly, was over 11,000 feet AMSL. I had not had the 206 that high before; the take off and landing distances were noticeably longer but no real problem. I had lived in Kenya for some months and so could safely fly to 15,000 feet without oxygen.

Meanwhile, Terry moved his whole outfit about 100 miles across country to a place where Bing could shoot his desired greater reticulated what-have-you. I flew back to Nanyuki, collected the party, and flew them to the new map reference. Once again, Terry, who as well as being a very nice man was a highly competent one, was exactly where he said he would be – the runway was as level and smooth as the first one and the camp looked as if it had never been disturbed.

I had another two days of luxury and when Bing got his trophy, I flew them straight to Embakasi to catch their flight back to the USA.

Bing was a quiet, modest and very friendly fellow who soon had us on first name terms. It was a pleasure to make his acquaintance.

The bush flying I did in Kenya was most enjoyable and rewarding, and I would not have missed it for anything. But there were snags concerning our life style. I never got a day off, let alone a week-end. And I was often required to be airborne as the sun came up (we were only a few miles from the equator and dawn and dusk were about 06:30 and 18:30 throughout the year) which meant getting up at 05:00 hrs. Sometimes I would not get back to base till night-fall, which got me home at 20:00. So we had little free time and so not much social life. The pay was not very good either. We had been there just over a year, and it was time to visit UK to see family and friends, but the cost of tickets would have made a large dent in my meagre salary.

On one of my rare early finishes, I was sitting on the terrace discussing these things with Sylvia, when one of our neighbours walked up and joined us. He was a super chap called Alan Birkett who was a VC10 captain with East African Airways based at Embakasi.

I mentioned the shortage of time off.

He said that he got a few days off after every trip.

I mentioned the poor pay.

He said that his was double mine.

I mentioned the expense of tickets.

He said that he got free tickets, and as a captain they were first class.

BUT, I said that I had wonderful flying.

He said that airline flying was wonderful too, and I ought to try it.

"Don't you think it's time you came and joined us?"

"I could be tempted."

"Let's go!"

We got into his car and drove to Embakasi where he introduced me to the Chief Pilot. He asked about my flying experience, and then offered me a job. I could join as a direct entry captain on the DC3 or as a first officer on the VC10. Both were highly attractive propositions. Alan advised me to take the F/O job because they would not make me a jet captain if I had not been a jet first officer, and if I went as DC3 captain, that is all I would ever be. I took the advice. I went back to Wilson Airport and gave my stipulated one month notice. And so a new life began.

The Pilot

You are at cruising altitude. The westering sun is pink on the disc. Your eyes flick the gauges. The engines are contented. Another day, another dollar.

You look down at your hands on the wheel. They are veined and hard and brown. Tonight you notice they look a little old. And, by George, they are old.

But how can this be? Only yesterday you were in flying school. Time is a thief! You have been robbed, and what have you got to show for it? A pilot. Forty years a pilot. A senior pilot.

But what of it?

Just a pilot.

The voice of the flight attendant breaks in on your reverie. The flight is running full. Can they begin serving dinner to the passengers? The passengers, oh yes, the passengers. You noticed the line of them coming aboard; The businessmen, the young mothers with their children in tow, the old couples, the two priests, the four dogfaces. A thousand times you have watched them file aboard, and a thousand times disembark. They always seem a little happier after the landing than before the take-off.

Beyond doubt, they are always somewhat apprehensive aloft. But why do they keep coming up here in the dark sky despite their fears? You have often wondered about that.

You look down at your hands again and suddenly it comes to you. They come because they trust you, you, the pilot. They turn over their lives and their loved ones and their hopes and their dreams to you for safekeeping.

To be a pilot means to be one of the trusted.
They pray in the storm that you are skillful and strong and wise.
To be a pilot is to hold life in your hands, to be worthy of faith.
No, you have not been robbed. You aren't just a pilot.
There is no such thing as just a pilot.
Your job is a trust. The years have been a trust.
You have been one of the trusted.

Who could be more?

Author Unknown

Chapter 8

AIRLINE PILOT

I joined the next SVC 10 course held at the ground school at Embakasi. There were about 20 of us – mostly company pilots changing their aircraft fleet or upgrading to captain, and perhaps half a dozen new boys.

The atmosphere was very pleasant, informal and friendly, and the instruction most thorough and professional. I realized later that this is an unusual combination. There are flying organisations that are friendly and informal, and have sloppy standards. Others try to maintain a good standard of operation, but are stuffy and formal which can create a tense environment that is not conducive to good crew work.

We spent five weeks studying the SVC 10 in the classroom before moving on to the simulator where we learned to operate the systems, and the check lists and procedures.

Then at last to the aircraft – we went in small groups with a training captain and did Mach runs, dutch rolling, approach to the stall, steep turns, emergency descents, and circuits and bumps. Once again, the mood was one of friendly guidance, but was still most thorough.

Next was a trip to London and back, sitting on the jump seat and observing the crew members (especially the first officer) doing their stuff. It was eyes and ears open and mouth shut.

We were now ready to start our line training, which was done by sitting in the F/O seat and doing his duties, closely supervised by a line training captain. I was delighted to have Alan Birkett for my first few trips.

Alan was a jolly good egg. Off duty, he was good company and certainly liked a drink. On the flight deck he was a very good pilot and a very good captain. I found out later that the two do not always go together. There are good pilots who are not as good as others at getting the best out the crew. Others, who are not as good, can nevertheless create a good cooperative atmosphere on the flight deck.

Captaincy is called leadership in the armed forces and attempts are made to teach it as a subject. This is done in the classroom with lessons on deportment, demeanour, forms of address and so on. Practically, cadets take their turn leading small groups in escape and evasion exercises, commanding on the parade ground and such like activities. These will help a mediocre officer or NCO to get by, but will not make him a really good leader. A more effective form of training is to observe and follow the example of good leaders and not follow the example of the bad.

But true leaders and captains are born and not made, and the reason that the Services have so many good leaders is that they spend much time and trouble in picking the right entrants in the first place.

In civil aviation, learning captaincy by example is more effective because the potential captain, the first officer, shares a small flight deck with his mentor, the captain, for many hours at a time, with few other distractions. But the reason that good airlines have good captains is that they too appoint the right people in the first place.

There should never be any doubt on the flight deck as to who is in command. If a situation arises that calls for immediate action, the captain should give clear concise orders which the other crew members should obey at once and without question. But if there is time, a good captain would invite ideas and suggestions from the first officer, flight engineer and navigator. This in no way undermines his authority, provided that when he has heard all the comments and made his final decision, there is no further debate. Should the captain make a mistake, by selecting, say, the wrong frequency or altimeter setting, the F/O, whose duty it is to cross-check such things and spot the error, should politely point it out. The captain should accept the correction with good grace and thank the F.O. for his diligence. This all worked very well in EAA, and I never came across, or even heard of, a problem in this regard.

Nowadays, one hears stories of captains who resent being

corrected and will not tolerate such 'interference' and of F/Os who argue the toss with the captain about his decisions. This is a potentially dangerous way to run the flight deck, and so a new subject has been invented to restore order. It is called 'cockpit crew resource management' or some such title. Would-be professional aviators have to study it and pass an exam in it to get their licence. I never had to study it, but I understand that it teaches captains how to handle recalcitrant F/Os and F/Os how to argue successfully with their captain. To my mind, this is only 'papering over the cracks', and I think that the subject should be abolished, and the time and effort spent on it should instead be devoted to the better selection of the suitable and the elimination of the rest. It is not everything that changes for the better.

Alan Birkett had, perhaps, the most professional attitude that I ever saw. We were required to wear full harness (seat belts and shoulder straps) for take off and landing, but above 5,000 feet (I think it was) we were allowed to undo the shoulder straps. Alan never undid his and would go for eight or ten hours tightly strapped in, in case he encountered sudden air turbulence or had to take sudden avoiding action. He never addressed the passengers, but got the F/O or Purser to do it. When I asked him why, he asked what should he do if, during a passenger announcement, a red warning light came on. Ignore it, or tell the passengers that he had to go because of an emergency? He would rather not put himself in that position.

He took me to the capital cities of Africa and Europe and the Eastern routes to Aden, Karachi, Bombay, Bangkok and Hong Kong. He demonstrated the landings then invited me to attempt them. The SVC10 was by far the biggest aeroplane that I had ever flown, but I soon got used to it. As a fighter jock, I had scoffed at such aircraft but was now surprised to find that I enjoyed it! But then, I was nearly forty years old! I was soon glad that I had joined as a F/O – I had so much to learn about civil flying. In the RAF, all I knew about airways was how to avoid them – now I had to learn how to fly along them. Fighters had no radio navigation or landing aids (if you don't count the ADF in the Hunter, which nobody ever used). Now we had two VORs, two ILSs, two ADFs two DMEs a Doppler and a radar scope. On fighters we had to memorize the check lists, now we had much longer lists which had to be read off a card. Radio procedures and clearances took time and practice to master.

The company quite rightly did not want its trainees to fly with only one instructor, so I did some trips with Nick Methley. He is a South African and a super pilot, super captain, super instructor and a very nice man. I took to him at once. On the flight deck he is very relaxed, but does not miss a thing, and in the nicest possible way, insists that everything be done absolutely correctly, and I learned a great deal from him. He has a great sense of humour too. There was an occasion when, due to weather and technical problems three EAA SVC10s were departing London at about the same time. The first two were fully laden, but Nick's, the third, had very few pax. At top of climb, when starting the cruise, we were supposed to talk to the pax and tell them about the route, weather and so forth. Nick's cabin address that evening was somewhat shorter: "Good evening, ladies and gentlemen. There are not enough of you to make my usual spiel worthwhile. Talk among yourselves!"

He and his wife Helen are still good friends of ours.

There must be something about Africa, because that description would equally fit Chris Noon and Pat Connington and Dicky Knight, who were born and raised in Kenya, and John Winson, a Rhodesian. This is not to criticise the others – the standards throughout EAA were as good as they get; it is just that the African born fellows seem to have that slight edge.

I found that the SVC10 was an easy aircraft to land, and with a little practice it was possible to guarantee a landing that would be so smooth that people would not know that they were on the ground. This, I am told, is because the tips of the crescent wing descend smoothly into ground effect and provide an increasing cushion effect. All that is necessary is not to waggle the stick about. After some practice, I found that easing the stick slightly forward just before touch down, would reduce the rate of descent of the main wheels (which are a long way behind the centre of gravity) and produce an even smoother touch down. There were four pitot heads (which provide air pressure readings) on the aircraft and they are heated to prevent their icing up and in flight, the current is 8 amps. On landing, a switch in the undercarriage reduced that load to 4 amps to prevent their overheating on the ground. The flight engineer had an ammeter for each one. Some of the F/Es would say after a very nice landing: "Four amps" to imply that there was no other way to tell that you were on the ground.

I was checked out as a line F/O, initially restricted to operating with experienced captains only. Later I was upgraded to operate with any captain, including new ones who might sometimes need a little help themselves.

Flying the routes was most enjoyable. I got to fly with nearly all the captains, nearly all of whom were first class. As an RAF pensioner, I was somewhat older than the average F/O, and all the captains treated me with courtesy and consideration. We were

Home from a trip with East African Airways.

on first name terms on the flight deck, but I always made a point of addressing the captain as 'sir' or 'captain' a couple of times at the beginning of a trip, to make sure that they knew that I knew who was the boss.

In an airliner, the captain occupies the left hand seat and has complete control of the aircraft from there. The F/O has the right hand seat, with his own set of controls and instruments, and it is sometimes forgotten that his primary function is to take over in the event of the captain's incapacity. But since he is there, he makes himself useful by handling the communications, setting the radio aids, running the check lists, looking after the maps, and generally assisting the captain. If the captain 'gives him the leg', he flies the aeroplane and the captain does the F/O's normal duties, whilst still being in command and responsible for it all.

There is no regulation that requires a captain to 'give a leg', but most reasonable ones do. In EAA it was normal to do 'leg and leg about'. Some captains even used to ask me if there was any particular leg that I wanted to do.

One captain, however, Captain xxx, never gave away a leg. Tim and Linda Hudson were good friends of ours, and Tim was rostered to do a London with Captain xxx. The routing would have been something like Nairobi – Entebbe – Rome – night stop – London – night stop – Athens – Nairobi. Tim never handled the controls. After a couple of days off, he was rostered for London again and again with Captain xxx. Once more, Tim was not allowed to touch the controls. Back in the ops room in Nairobi, they finished their paperwork and were preparing to go home.

xxx:	"You live in Langata, don't you?"
Tim:	"Yes, I do."
xxx:	"I have a car problem, can you give me a lift home?"
Tim:	"No, sorry."
xxx:	"If you have some chores to do here, I'm quite happy to wait."
Tim:	"No, it's not that."
xxx:	"If you have to pop into town or somewhere on route, I don't mind."
Tim:	"No, it's not that."

xxx: "Then why can't you take me home?"
Tim: "I don't want to sit next to you any more!"

EAA was the perfect size for a happy airline. Not so small that you flew with the same people all the time, and not so large that most people were strangers. After a few months, I got to know everyone, and what a great bunch they were.

If we were to fly with someone we did not know, we would introduce ourselves in the ops. room when we checked in for our flight. One of the captains was Tony Trent, who had done his national service in the Navy. A new first officer had recently left the Navy after 20 years of service and came into the ops. room and introduced himself.

"Good morning, Captain, I understand that I am to be your first officer today." He offered his hand: "Lieutenant Commander yyy."

"Welcome aboard", said Tony, taking the proffered hand: "Able Seaman Trent."

While I was on the fleet, the Commonwealth Games were held in Christchurch, New Zealand, and EAA was chartered to take the East African (Kenya, Uganda, and Tanganyika) teams there and bring them back. We did not operate anywhere near there and no one knew anything about the area. I was very lucky to be one of the first officers on the crews involved.

One crew operated Nairobi – Mauritius, then another crew took the aircraft on to Perth, in Western Australia, then my crew, which had positioned two days before, took the aircraft on to Christchurch. The weather was perfect and we had wonderful views of South Australia, Melbourne, Sydney, and the Tasman Sea. We came back a similar way, and after a few days off, we went all the way back again to get the teams back.

We had night stops in Mauritius, Perth and Christchurch – the only times I have been to those delightful cities. A truly memorable trip.

When we were on a night-stop (lay-over in American parlance) in London, the company accommodated us in the Skyway Hotel.

A couple of enterprising British Airways stewards had set up a club in the hotel for aircrew. The prices were reasonable, and one could always find a kindred spirit there, from one of the many airlines that operated to Heathrow. It became very popular.

I was in there one day when a British Airways F/O came in, in uniform, and ordered a beer. That annoyed me for a start – in a reputable airline, like EAA, we never drank in uniform, even in private. He then announced that he had just finished a terrible trip to Barcelona and back, and that in Barcelona the cross-wind was right on limits, and that his captain had invited him to do the landing.

"How did it go?" I asked.

"Of course I refused to do it. If I had messed it up that would not have helped my career would it?"

I said: "So your captain took the responsibility of allowing you to have a chance to improve your skills and you turned it down?"

"Too right I did, mate!"

I put my beer down and said: "You are in the wrong club. This club is for aviators. You are not an aviator, you are a snivelling wretch who flies aeroplanes only for the money. Why don't you find a club that caters for snivelling wretches?"

The room went quiet, as much because of my outrageous behaviour (which, I submit, was due to fatigue after a long trip in bad weather) as the wretch's lack of credentials.

He put his beer down and walked out. I never found out if he was able to find a club for snivelling wretches.

At about this time, some of the pilots were complaining that our pay had not kept up with inflation. It was by no means prodigious, but it was sufficient to enable us all to live a very agreeable life style. Most chaps did not complain or even think about it. The AGM of the KPA (Kenya Pilots' Association) came around, and when 'any other business' was reached, somebody proposed that we go on strike for higher pay. After some informal discussion our Chairman, Richard Cairns called for a vote. The phrase 'higher pay' sounded attractive and without much serious thought, nearly everybody voted to strike. I was one of the very few to vote against.

Richard invited me to explain why I dissented. I stood up and pointed out that I had signed a contract with the company, that is, I had given my word, that if I fly such and such hours, they would give me such and such pay. I fly such and such hours, and they do give me the agreed pay, and so I have no dispute with the company.

Somebody behind me said that other airlines get regular pay increases. I replied that if I could get a better job elsewhere, taking into account all factors, I would give the thirty days notice required by the contract, and go to it. I suggested that they all would too. There was a murmur of agreement.

I went on to say that more important than that was the fact that I did not want to cause financial difficulties for the company that paid my salary, in case I made it impossible for it to do so.

At this point, conversation broke out all over the room, and Richard wisely made no attempt to control it from the chair for a few minutes. Then the hubbub died down and I sensed a different mood in the room. Richard then called for another vote, and the motion to strike was defeated by a large majority.

It was certainly not any eloquence of mine that changed their minds – their minds were not changed because most had no opinion either way to begin with. But my words did get them to think about it, and when they did that, they came to the same simple conclusion that I had.

And it took no great courage to make my stand. We were such a happy united group that even if I had remained in a minority of one, there would certainly have been no hard feelings. But if instead of being in a pilots' union I had been in, say, a miners' or a dockers', where dissent would lead to a headache caused by a crushed skull, I would certainly have kept my views to myself!

I grew to really enjoy flying large heavy a/c but I did not lose my pleasure in flying small ones as well. So I continued to do instruction at Wilson, I would check pilots out in their own aircraft or train them for a night rating or a commercial licence or a twin rating, I did not take a fee for this. Instead I asked if I could occasionally borrow their a/c. They were always happy with that and I soon had access to several types. Several flight engineers and navigators from the airline were hoping to change seats and become pilots and I helped those as well. When the airline collapsed a few years later one of them got a pilot job before I did!

Soon after we arrived in Kenya our good friends Ernie and Pat Constable from RAF days visited us there. They took to Kenya at once and came out every year, I could always get a few days off and borrow an aircraft and we used to fly to the coast and various game parks in Kenya, Uganda and TAnganyika. Pat wanted Ernie to leave BA and join EAA but he had accrued time for his seniority and pension in BA which he would not surrender, So he continued the drudgery of the A30 to Heathrow for the rest of his flying life. Better him than me!

One of my favourite captains was Peter Brumby – we flew together many times. We were on a night stop in Bombay staying at the Taj Mahal hotel, and we went to lunch in the 'salon' dining room. This boasted a three-piece orchestra comprising a violinist, cellist, and pianist. They all wore dinner jackets that had seen better days, and the violin and cello were off key (I think it is called) and produced a sort of wailing, scratching noise, and the piano was out of tune. The pianist, who appeared to be the flight commander, sent a waiter across to us with a message asking if 'the English gentlemen' had any requests we would like them to play. Peter said that he knew nothing about music and suggested that I request something. I wrote a title and sent the message back. The flight commander looked at it, nodded, stopped what they were playing in mid-stream and struck up 'Rule Britannia'. Peter and I stood to attention, and table by table, the other diners shuffled to their feet. The music was excruciating, and the scenario preposterous. It was difficult to do, but we kept straight faces.

Peter was, in fact, the epitome of an Irish gentleman. Once, he was on a night stop in Rome and went out to dinner with his crew as was our normal practice. In the morning he telephoned the ops room and told our man in Rome that his F/O was unfit to continue, and that he had better call out the stand-by F/O.

"Certainly Capitano. And what is the problem with your regular F.O.?"

"He is sick, and you had better get a doctor for him."

"Certainly Capitano. And what is he suffering from?"

"You had better make it a psycho doctor. He has gone mad!"

"Oh! Capitano! What makes you think he had gone mad?"

"Last night at dinner, he argued with me!"

I served as one of the KPA (Kenya Pilots Association) representatives on the joint Management/KPA Seniority and Qualifications Committee. The other, and senior, representative was the much liked and respected Eric Molberg. Our task was to consider and recommend (or not) promotions from one fleet to the next and from right seat to left. There was very little disagreement at our regular meetings, because neither side wanted a promotion to be made unless the candidate was qualified and suitable in every way.

I tried, unsuccessfully, to introduce the idea of a Fleet Commodore. I envisaged that there would be only one at one time and the holder would wear not four gold bars but one thick one. He need not be the Chief Pilot or the most senior pilot, but a suitably dignified captain with an impressive presence, deportment and demeanour. He could be selected by a committee of senior captains, or elected by KPA.

Nearly all the current titles were invented by Pan American Airways years ago. It was Pan Am that changed the title of 'pilot' to 'captain', and 'second pilot' to 'first officer' and 'chief steward' to 'purser'. And it was Pan Am that first gave their captains four gold bars. These titles are now in world-wide use. Wouldn't it be nice, I thought, if EAA introduced a title which became universally used?

The person I had in mind for our first incumbent was Peter Brumby, and had it been introduced and had I had a vote, it would certainly have gone to him. But neither management nor KPA were much interested, and the idea was never taken up.

Another captain I enjoyed flying with was Jerry Sirley. He was without a doubt a very fine pilot, but there were a few crewmembers who were reluctant to be in his crew because he simply would not allow second best performance and criticised anyone who did a sloppy job. But if you applied yourself and did a good trip, he was as nice as they come.

We did a daylight to London on one occasion and arrived at about 9 p.m. local time. We would normally shower and change before going out for a drink and supper, but on this occasion the pubs would be closing soon, so we took off our coats and braid and went straight to the pub. So we were wearing white shirts and black trousers and black shoes. This is a fairly common dress around airport hostelries the world over, and the wearers are recently off duty airline crews (or off duty waiters!).

The pub we chose was on the River Thames, and there were several such attires in the bar. Two such worthies were next to us at the bar, and we soon got into conversation. General small talk such as: "Have you had a good day?" produced non-committal but plausible replies. An aviator's remark such as: "The weather was better than forecast today", also produced a comment that seemed to confirm the assumption that they were two other aviators. We quickly became friendly and got each other several drinks. Then the guv'nor shouted: "Time gentlemen please!" (Those were the days when the law required that bars close at a certain time).

I used to keep a car at our regular hotel, and Jerry and I had arrived in it. I offered our new-found friends a lift, but they politely declined, explaining that they had their own transport. Then one of them, Charlie, asked us if we had ever driven a police boat, and when we admitted that we had not, he offered us a chance to do so now. They were not off-duty airline pilots or waiters at all, but members of the River Police. They were not even off-duty, but preferred an evening in the bar to patrolling up and down the river, and their patrol boat was tied up at the jetty at the back of the pub.

Jerry and I both had a go at it – it was a new experience for us both. We got to their station and by then their duty period was over, and they invited us into the staff bar for a few more drinks. When the time finally came to go, I explained that my car was still at the pub, so we were driven there in a police car. When I mentioned that I was a little concerned about driving back to the hotel after my few extra drinks, the nice driver told me to drive carefully and he drove behind as escort with his light flashing to make sure that we were not molested by a policeman who was not in our 'circle'.

Nowadays, we would be flung into jail if we even thought of driving after a half-pint of beer. It is not everything that changes for the better.

Pat Connington was an EAA stalwart who followed the usual path and eventually was checked out as a SVC10 captain. For his first trip in command, I don't doubt that he asked for one of the more experienced and able first officers. I can imagine his disappointment when he found that I was assigned to the trip. But he is one of the few natural pilots I have ever met, and he flew a flawless trip, and would have, whoever had been first officer. He deemed that the satisfactory conclusion of the trip called for a celebration and it was my great pleasure to assist him in that undertaking. We, and the other crew-members, ended up at our house in the early hours. He and his wife Liz became good friends.

The other natural pilot I met was Chris Noon. He flew the aircraft, be it a light sport or four-jet airliner, precisely and effortlessly and made it look easy. A very fine chap, too. I remember one trip to Bombay with him when he had been briefed by his wife Doreen to search the city for a certain type of tile for the kitchen (or was it bathroom?). We spent the day looking and finally found the coveted articles. When we got home, the company transport took us to his house first and I went in with him briefly to say hello to Doreen. After the usual greetings, she asked: "Well, did you find the tiles?"

"Yes we did."

"Well, where are they?"

"We left them in a pub, but can't remember which one!"

Chris's brother-in-law was a white hunter and he invited Chris and me with our wives to visit his safari camp in the Rift Valley. Chris borrowed a Minerva which is a small four seat low wing French aircraft. Neither of us had flown one before but it was a very simple type and so we did not need a check out. Chris flew the first leg to the camp and we had a very pleasant two day stay there living like very wealthy clients. Then it was my turn to fly it back. After a few miles the engine started to splutter and fail and we started descending, Chris looked at me with a smile and asked me what I was going to do now. I replied that I was going to land in that open space over there.

"Good idea," he said. The descent continued until we had lost about 2000 feet and then the engine picked up again and we climbed back up to our original height. Fifteen minutes later it failed again and we went through the same procedure. It did this five times but we did eventually get back to Wilson Airport.

The most likely cause was failure to set the mixture correctly for the altitude, but this aircraft had an alcor instrument which made it possible to set the mixture precisely right at any altitude so that was not the problem. A while later I asked Chris if the engineers had found the cause, He said that they had checked thoroughly but could not find anything wrong. Gemlins??

When I joined EAA, I did not sever my links with Wilson airport. I kept my membership of the Aero Club of East Africa, and did a little part time instructing there, Safari Air, and Caspair. I also did some private instruction with people on their own aeroplanes, in particular converting pilots who had been trained on nose-wheels (which ought to be illegal!) to tail wheels.

I did not do a great deal of instructing at the ACEA – they preferred to maintain a 'club atmosphere' by having private pilot instructors rather than professionals. But they did sometimes ask me to check out a visiting airline captain who wanted to rent an aircraft. It is a surprising fact that many airline captains do not maintain their proficiency in light aircraft – it is only the true aviators who do. And so I often had to refuse to sign them off, or to suggest three or four hours of circuits and bumps if they were really keen. One chap, I think he was from Lufthansa, was most offended when I told him he was not capable of handling the aircraft.

"You can't talk to me like that – I'm an airline captain!"

"Yes I can. I'm an airline captain too!"

Which is, perhaps, why they liked me to do those check rides.

Once a year, the ACEA held a 'Flying Safari', in which thirty or forty aircraft would take part. Take off times were staggered in accordance with a handicapping system, and the clues for the routing were handed to the pilot immediately before he was waved off. There was a refuelling stop somewhere, and the day ended with a landing at some agreeable place at the coast. Then the party began. Next day was similar, finishing at Nairobi and another party in the Aero Club. I entered it one year with Jock Hay, an ex RAF navigator, now with EAA, in a Rheims Rocket (a souped-up Cessna 172) that I borrowed from Safari Air. Jock did a super job and everything went well until the lunch-time refuelling stop. The afternoon leg started well, but half way to Malindi – our night-stop location – I noticed that our fuel consumption was inexplicably increasing. But we had plenty so it was not a problem and we continued with the Safari. About forty miles from Malindi, the fuel consumption increased again, and I figured that we would just make it. Malindi was the nearest place with fuel anyway, so there was no choice but to continue. We were over the Gedi Forest, with nothing but trees in every direction. I considered heading for the coast road in case we ran out of fuel, but if I did that we certainly would not have enough to reach our destination.

With about twenty miles to go the engine stopped. I had eased up to 3,000 feet just in case this happened, so had a few minutes to get ready. I now did head for the coast in order to land as near the road as possible. I made a 'mayday' call to Malindi explaining that we going down and gave them our position and asked them to send transport to pick us up. It must have been a new chap in the tower because his reply was: "What is your ETA Malindi?"

I answered: "It depends how long your driver takes to find us!"

Several other pilots had heard our transmission and made the pick up arrangements.

On the way down I said to Jock: "I've just said a prayer."

"What did you pray for?"

"I asked the Almighty to arrange that if one of us is be hurt, it's you and not me!"

Pause. Then: "I've just sent a counter prayer!"

I was not aware (and am still not) of any Service or civilian flying manual that gives guidance on how to land in trees. It is a routine

My very good friend Nick Methley and me having won a lesser prize in the East African Flying Safari. Sylvia gazes at us with admiration and awe.

hazard for crop spraying pilots though, and I remember discussing it with a few of them in the Aero Club. Their agreed view was that just before hitting the trees, it is best to drop one wing to hit a tree with it. This will turn the aircraft and use up some of the kinetic energy before the fuselage hits. (It is the dissipation of the kinetic energy that causes the damage.) It made sense to me and I decided to do it that way. It worked! We came to rest in the tree tops and neither of us had a scratch. I wrenched the compass off its mounting and we climbed down about 25 feet to the ground and set a compass course to the road where we were picked up by some of our ACEA chums. The beer tasted good that evening, as we celebrated our continued existence.

The Safari Air engineers cut a road to the site, recovered the aircraft, and because there was so little damage, had it flying again in three weeks. They found a crack in the fuel pipe, which they were sure was not caused by the crash. This was leaking fuel and accounts for the high consumption. The accident could have been far worse. The leaking fuel close to the hot engine could so easily have caused a fire. But we were lucky (again!).

The following year, Jock flew in the Safari again with another pilot in a Cherokee. They were crossing the saddle in the middle of the Aberdaires when they found that the ground was rising faster than they were. The rising ground was smooth grass-land and free of obstructions, and at full power they did a nice landing! I don't think Jock took part in any more 'Flying Safaris'.

Nick Methley and I and two other chaps bought an aeroplane between us. It was a Piper PA 22 Tripacer, 5Y-KKX. Now we could go flying in a light aircraft any time we liked. Sylvia and I or Nick and I, or all four of us (with Nick's wife Helen) did many enjoyable trips in it, mainly to the coast. Nick and I also used it in the Flying Safari.

We had some old friends from the RAF staying with us, and we decided to take them to the coast in our new aeroplane. We enjoyed a very nice weekend but when we flew back the weather at Nairobi was below limits.I tried to creep into Wilson Airport at very low level but the cloud was right down to the deck and I had to turn back to the Rift Valley and try again slightly further to the North. This was also impossible and so I decided to divert to Lake Magadi .

This is a very salty leak about 30 miles south of Nairobi and there is a plant there which extracts the salt commercially. At the plant are a few houses and what looked like a clubhouse and there is also a runway. I had seen it from the air many times but had never landed there.

When I was set on my new course I looked round to check the ladies on the back seat. Sylvia, who had flown with me many times, smiled and gave me a 'thumbs up', but Anne had her eyes closed, her palms together and lips moving in earnest prayer.

As we flew South, the wx improved rapidly. Ann's prayers were answered and I saw Magagi and its runway clearly.

After landing we learned that the workers had finished for the day and the manager and his wife were on leave leaving these two bachelors to run the place.They gave us lots of drinks and invited the ladies to help themselves to the kitchen and larder. This was right up Sylvia's street and she produced a splendid dinner for six. In the morning I tried to pay for the guest rooms and dinner but the club had a tradition that everything was on the house for stranded aviators.

If we had not had bad weather we never would have met these new friends and their delightful club.

The Aero Club held an open day once a year which had fly-pasts, parachute jumping, formation flying, aerobatic shows, and the like. Its finale was the Aerial Derby, and of course, Nick and I entered it with the Tripacer. The course was three times round a triangular circuit starting and ending at the ACEA. The aircraft were handicapped and took off when signalled, and if the handicappers had done a perfect job, we would all have crossed the finishing line together. The first off was the powered glider, and the last the Learjet. We were somewhere in the middle. The aim was to fly faster than the handicap speed, but if that speed were exceeded by 5%, the aircraft was disqualified. Nick wanted me to do the flying so that he could monitor the speed. We worked out a most elaborate table of corrections so that if we were too fast or too slow at the end of each leg, the table would indicate what speed we needed and hence what power to set. I took off and after we passed the first turning point I asked: "How are we doing?"

"Er um."

"Well, are we fast or slow?"

"Um."

"Come on, Nick, how many seconds for the first leg?"

"I forgot to start the stop watch!"

The whole aircraft must have shaken with our laughter.

That Tripacer gave us a lot of pleasure, but I always regretted that we had a nose wheel, and would much have preferred a Pacer, the tail wheel version.

When EAA collapsed and we were selling up and moving on, we tried to sell KKX. Aeroplanes never sell like hot cakes, and we were having trouble finding a buyer. Then there was freak tornado, which hit, out of the millions of square miles in Africa, the apron at Wilson airport. It destroyed over twenty aircraft and damaged many more. KKX was lifted up and thrown on its back and destroyed. The insurance company paid us out in full and our financial problem was solved, but it was a very sad sight to behold in such a state. I am glad that someone bought it and restored it to flying condition.

Soon after I started SVC10 route flying, the long awaited Boeing 747 came into service and we were all looking forward to seeing one.

After a night stop in Rome, as we walked towards our aircraft for our next leg, an Air France 747 was parked next to it. We had plenty of time so I walked up the steps to go inside, I asked where the captain was and was told that he was upstairs. Upstairs in an aeroplane? I went upstairs to pay the usual courtesy and saw him and the other crew members and some cabin staff sitting at the big table enjoying a bottle of wine.

"Good morning, captain, I have never seen one of these before. Do you mind if I look around"?

"No, of course not. When you have seen it all come and join us".

After a good look around I returned to the upper deck and thanked the captain for allowing it., He invited me to join them and have a glass of wine.

Jock Hay (left) and me with the Rheims Rocket that we entered in the E.A. Flying Safari and crashed into trees.

"Thank you but I can't because I am just about to go on service,"

With a winning smile he replied: "But so are we".

There are airlines and airlines!

We had generous off time and leave and we could get free or 90% discount tickets on EAA. And other companies like Alitalia, Olympic, and SAS were very liberal with their tickets. So for the first time in our lives, Sylvia and I could travel to anywhere in the world that we pleased. On our vacations we took full advantage of it, and when we had only a few days off between trips we could easily get to the coast. It was wonderful!

The Director of Flight Operations sent for me one day and told me that I was to get my command and was to start a course on the Fokker F27 Friendship the next week.

"Thank you very much, Trevor, but I don't want to miss the DC3. Could I go on them first?"

"No, you are on a fast track back to the VC10."

"I'd still hate to miss the Dak."

"I'll think about it. Come and see me tomorrow."

I went back tomorrow.

"I've decided to grant your request. You can go on Daks."

"Super! Thank you so much."

"One thing, though. You'll stay on Daks as long as you are with us. You'll never get another promotion! Do you still want it?"

"Well, in that case I suppose not."

He grinned: "The F27 course starts next week."

I completed the course and Jerry Clemmow, the very able chief instructor of the fleet, checked me out and presented me with my first set of four gold bars. It was a proud moment.

John Hudson was the only European F/O on the F27 fleet. He was perfectly happy in that position and had no desire to move onto a larger aircraft or to get his command. He had more F27 hours than most of the captains put together. Most of the other F/Os were low time local lads.

I asked Jerry if he could arrange for me to have John as my F/O on my first trip in command. He said he would.

Refuelling our Tripacer. I do the work while Nick gives moral support.

When I checked in for it, there was no sign of John. Instead a young man introducing himself as Njorogi said that he was my F/O.

"How long ago were you checked out, Njorogi?"

"This is my first trip since check-out."

"Me too! Let's go!"

Some of the most challenging civil flying I ever did was taking the F27 from Nairobi to Entebbe (the airport of the capital of Uganda, Kampala) and back in the rainy seasons. The route crossed the Great Rift Valley, the Mau Escarpment, and the Kenya Highlands, and there were nearly always heavy thunderstorms the whole way. The F27 would not go much over 16,000 feet, so there was no way of going over the weather, and the high ground made it impossible to go below it. The storms extended too far north and south to go round them, so it was necessary to go right through them. In daylight it was possible to avoid the worst of it visually by flying through gaps, if there were any. At night, we would use the weather radar to pick our way. But it was not possible to avoid it all and we (and the passengers) just had to put up with an hour of extreme turbulence. We kept the seat belt signs on the whole time, and the cabin staff too stayed strapped in – there was no question of any cabin service. The turbulence would keep disconnecting the auto pilot, and so most of the leg was 'hand-flown'. I never gave those legs away, but I don't think the young F/Os considered me a Captain xxx, because they were quite happy to just sit there and pray, and I always made it up to them on subsequent trips.

Leigh Allison and his wife May were friends of ours. Leigh had flown DC3s in one of the Middle East countries, and joined us a direct entry captain on them. Leigh's father, many years before, had also been a DC3 captain with EAA, now Leigh was flying the same aircraft – not just the same type, but the same actual aircraft.

I was on a night-stop in Dar and having a drink before dinner with Leigh in the bar of the Kilimanjaro Hotel – our night stop hotel. I mentioned to Leigh that I much regretted missing my turn on the DC3.

"What time are you operating in the morning?" he asked.

"Late. Not till 10:30."

"How about doing the 07:00 Zanzibar and back with me tomorrow?"

I agreed immediately, and he picked up the phone on the bar and called his F/O and told him not to report for the first two legs in the morning.

Leigh put me in the left hand seat, and he took the right, with much help and coaching from him, I managed to do the two legs without his having to take the aircraft from me, although he nearly had to a couple of times. There was nothing risky about this. As well as being a highly competent pilot and instructor, Leigh was an EAA base and line training captain, and he flew the aircraft with 'new boys' all the time. I found the aircraft quite a hand full, and regretted even more that I had not had the chance to really master it.

Dodoma is a small sleepy town in central Tanganyika, and was adequately catered for by two DC3 services a week. Then the government decided to move the capital there from Dar-es-Salaam, and so EAA put the F27 on the route to cater for the expected extra traffic.

I went in to work one morning to do a Nairobi–Dar, and was told that I was to do the inaugural flight of Nairobi–Dodoma–Dar. I looked it up in the charts and saw that it had a short narrow runway and was hot and high. The F27 could certainly be operated there, but at nowhere near normal maximum weights. I mentioned this to the operations staff, but was told not to worry – the planning staff had calculated that I would have ample capacity.

We took off and set course, reached top of climb, and settled in the cruise. Here the workload decreases, and I did the normal routine, which is to calculate the landing weight, then the take off weight, and hence the maximum joining load I could accept. This was to be radioed ahead so that the traffic staff at Dodoma could make their preparations. I was surprised at the figures. I did the sums again and got the same result. The F/O checked them and agreed. So I called EAA and told them that if I landed at Dodoma as planned, not only could I not take on any more payload, but I would have to off load four of my present pax in order to take off again. Did they still want me to land there? After the usual 'stand by' (I could just imagine the frantic phone calls and people rushing up and down the corridors) I was told to cancel the landing and proceed direct to Dar.

And so I never did do the inaugural. It reinforced my view that pilots should treat with care calculations made by 'inside people'.

I enjoyed the extra duties and responsibilities of being a captain, but I cannot say that the F27 was the most sparkling aircraft I ever flew. So I was quite ready to move on, when after about a year on the fleet, I was moved up to the DC9.

EAA did not have a DC9 simulator, so the training was done under contract by Eastern Airlines based in Miami, Florida. I went there with Willie Kuhne who was as nice a companion as I could wish.

Eastern was a very friendly place with extremely high standards, and in that respect was one of the few companies that resembled EAA. Willie and I had one ground school instructor to ourselves, and then one simulator instructor, both highly motivated and competent. With such teachers we could not fail!

The flying training was done back in Nairobi with company instructors. I greatly enjoyed the DC9, which handled not unlike a two-engined SVC10.

Among our destinations were Kigali in Rwanda and Bujumbura in Burundi. At both places, the air traffic control was not quite the same as elsewhere, there were no VORs and the single badly positioned NDBs were unreliable and inaccurate. So the only safe way to get there was to stay below the cloud base and navigate visually. I was used to doing this in the F 27, but to fly a jet airliner just above the trees was a new experience. Some captains used to complain about the need to do this, but I could not think of anything nicer!

I was on a night-stop in Dar-es-Salaam, and a group of EAA pilots were having drinks before dinner in the bar of the Kilimanjaro Hotel where we stayed. The British foreign secretary (or was he the colonial secretary?) at the time was James ZZZZ, and he was in Dar for some meeting with the Tanzanian government concerning an issue that I now forget but which everyone was talking about at the time. He was staying in the same hotel, and as he made his way to the bar he passed our table. As he did so he bade us a friendly "Good evening." At this, one of our number, who was more interested in politics than most, invited him to join us for a drink, adding that we were in a position to provide him with first hand, reliable and accurate information concerning the local situation.

He replied that no facts in our possession could possibly be of interest to him.

I had long thought that our politicians are generally ignorant of the subjects they are required to deal with. I found out then that they (or he at least) prefer it that way.

At that time, the Frelimo rebels in Mozambique had succeeded in gaining their freedom from the Portuguese, who had departed the country precipitately leaving behind a most confused situation. There was no effective government, and no army or even police force to maintain order. There was a large nest of United Nations people in Nairobi, and they, in their benevolence, considered that they should take a group of 'freedom fighters' from their 'safe' camp over the border in Tanganyika back to the Mozambique capital, Lourenço Marques They chartered an EAA DC9 for this purpose, and I was given the job of flying it.

When I got to the aircraft there were already three UN people on board, apparently to supervise the operation. The bulkhead between the first class and economy sections had been moved forward, and they occupied the now tiny first class section. I tried to get more details about the operation from them, but they were vague about what was required. They were not vague about their catering requirements, and asked anxiously if their special supplies were on board. I checked with the Purser and was told that there were first class meals for each of them. They made it very clear that airline first class meals were simply not good enough for UN staff. Then a catering vehicle arrived and brought the UN goodies. It all looked like Fortnum & Mason's best, and there was a huge quantity of it. They were now happy for us to take off.

We flew to Lindi, which was close to the camp, and as I flew round the circuit, I could see thousands of people filling the apron and parking area like a gigantic football crowd. There seemed to be no control at all, and even if there was an airline traffic staff on duty, they would have been overwhelmed by the numbers. I invited one of the UN people to the flight deck and flew round again for him to see.

"Which 120 people do you want me to pick up out of that lot?"

"I am not trained for this kind of thing. I leave it to you, Captain."

"But this is what you came here to do!"

"I'm sorry, but I must let you handle it."

With which remark he resumed his lobster lunch.

The DC9 has two sets of steps. The forward one from the front left door unfolds and rests on the ground. If there were people on it we could never get them off or move the aircraft. I instructed the Purser not in any circumstances to open either of the front doors. The rear door opens in line with the aircraft and does not quite touch the ground. If need be, I could taxi with it open, so that was the one to use.

I decided that it would be unwise to taxi to the terminal building, and as there was not much wind, and I was light, I landed downwind and at the end of the runway, turned round to take off into wind with the full load. I kept the engines running, and lowered the rear door. As I expected, the crowd started running across the airfield, the fittest ones in the lead. I got the Purser to stand by the door and tell me over the intercom when 100 passengers were on board. When he did that I started moving forward, going ever faster. When he reported that there was no one on the steps, I told him to raise them and I took off, and set course for Lourenço Marques.

The UN people, who were now on their second lobster lunch, seemed pleased with the way things had gone. I invited them to make some sort of welcoming speech to the returning heroes, but they declined to leave their cabin.

When we entered Mozambique air space, there was no air traffic control either at Centre, or at the airfield. As we got closer, I could see another football crowd covering the apron. So after landing I did not taxi to the terminal, but turned the aircraft round on the runway, got the Purser to open the rear door, and let the pax out. They were all out before the crowd running across the airfield arrived, and we closed the door and I took off, light, down-wind.

The UN staffers, who were now eating Russian Caviar by the spoon full straight out of the tins announced that they were pleased with the way things had gone.

It was a pleasure to be able to assist the UN operatives in their humanitarian activities.

My Chief Pilot phoned me and asked how it had gone. When I told him, he cancelled the further planned flights.

I was disappointed to find myself rostered to operate on the day of the ACEA open day. But it was a short trip that got me back to Embakasi at about 2 p.m., so if I got a move on, I could get over to Wilson in time for the Aerial Derby with Nick.

When I checked in, there was a note in my box from the Chief Pilot, asking if I would mind doing a low flypast at the Wilson open day on my way back. It would be my pleasure! The main runway at Wilson had a short narrow strip of asphalt for the first two hundred yards or so, the rest being grass. I decided that if I were careful, I could do a 'touch and go' on the hard runway. Of course it could not support the weight of a DC9, but my residual lift would stop me going through it.

I set up my approach with great care – just the right height, speed, power and rate of descent. Just before the round out I started spooling up the engines, and the extra power enabled me to make a very smooth landing. As I touched, the power was already coming in and the aircraft was already accelerating. I ran along the runway for about 150 yards then lifted off. For once in my life, everything had gone perfectly and I was very pleased with myself. So, I heard later, was the crowd. Even better was the fact that my exuberance would not get me into trouble, because the Chief Pilot had asked me to do it. (Well, sort of.) I believe that that was the only time that an airliner touched down at Wilson.

After landing, I raced across to Wilson and got there in time to hop into the Tripacer and take part in the Derby with Nick – and win!

Kenya was a marvellous place for aviation in those days. Nowadays, 'regulators' and such like beings would fall off their stools or go into a decline at the thought of someone doing something non-standard. It is not everything that changes for the better.

Life was most enjoyable on the DC9 fleet and I was in no hurry to leave it. I was still delighted, though, when after about a year on the fleet, I was put back on the SVC10 fleet as captain.

I was even more delighted to find that Nick was to be my mentor. We were good friends and he is so easy to get along with, but at the same time he is as thorough as they come, and I knew that the training would be first class. We went to all the destinations again, this time with me in the left hand seat. In the cruise, which is normally time for tea or coffee, he would set me one problem after another. If we lost an engine and had to descend 5,000 ft, with the higher fuel consumption, what would be our range? Which airfields are within that range? What is the weather there? What if we have a pressurisation failure and have to descend to 10,000 feet? What if the purser comes in and says that a passenger has a heart attack? Or had died? What if the weather at destination is marginal and the instrument landing system(ILS) is off the air. What if the weather at the nominated alternate airfield goes below limits? What if the French air traffic controllers have just gone on strike? What if...... Of course, I was familiar with these considerations in the F27 and DC9, but the SVC10 was more complicated, and went so much farther that there were more possible problems, factors and options.

One trip we did was Nairobi – Cairo – Rome with Luxor as the alternate. The forecast weather for Cairo was CAVOK (ceiling and visibility okay – a beautiful night). The actual weather as given by the tower was the same, so I started my let down at about 100 miles out as normal. As we got nearer to the town, we should have seen a variety of lights, but there were none. The tower was still giving CAVOK so I commenced my approach. I was flying the approach, looking only at the instruments, and Nick, acting as F/O was looking out for the runway. The navigator and flight engineer were also looking out. Nothing was seen, and when I got to minima (at Cairo, 180 ft cloud base and ¼ mile visibility if I remember) with no sign of the ground there was no choice but to go around.

As I went around, the navigator and flight engineer followed standard procedure and continued to look out of the side windows for lights. If they had seen any, I might have considered making another approach, but they saw nothing and so that possibility was out. The alternate was Luxor that was also giving CAVOK, but if that really was the weather, we would have seen the lights on the way north. But there were no lights at all in that area. There seemed to be something wrong with the Egyptian weather observations and reporting that night. I discussed it with the crew and decided not to go there. If we had, and could not get in, there would have been nowhere else to go.

The nearest other airports were Tel Aviv and Beirut, but there was an Arab/Israeli war going on and if we arrived unexpectedly, we would probably be shot down, so I did not want to go east.

"Nick, if there was ever a time for the training captain to take over, this is it."

"No, you're doing fine. Carry on."

I did a quick mental calculation and figured that we had enough fuel to get to Athens. I set course and asked the navigator to do a more precise calculation. If we could not reach Athens safely, I would go into Crete, but I preferred Athens because I was familiar with it. He did his wizardry and pronounced that we did have just enough fuel.

We landed safely at Athens. Nick was delighted with the whole flight. "I wish all my trainee captains had to handle that sort of situation. Excellent training."

Um.

We went into Copenhagen one winter evening when there was a very strong gusty wind. Nick would not let me use the autopilot "to show me that you can cope if it fails."

There was traffic ahead of us and the tower put us into the hold. This is a race track pattern with a radio beacon at one corner. When 'going down the straight' towards the beacon on the correct track, the drill is to assess the wind drift angle and then apply three times this angle in the opposite direction on the opposite straight. This corrects for the drift on that leg and the two curved ends. My drift was 35′. Three times that is 105′. Anything over 90′ is, of course going backwards! I had never before seen such strong wind or drift.

"If I follow the procedure, I'll be going the wrong way round. What do you want me to do, Nick?"

"Do what you think is best."

Quite apart from the drift problem, it was very hard work fighting the turbulence. I took my eyes off the instruments for a second to glance at Nick. He was cutting off a piece of biltong.

"Would you like a piece of biltong?"

No, I did not want a piece of biltong!

We got round somehow, but it was not a very neat pattern. There were no complaints from the tower, so I suppose that it was not too bad.

Nick was again delighted. "I wish all my trainee captains had to handle that sort of situation. Excellent training!"

Um.

What wouldn't I give to fly like that with Nick again.

I must have got a few things right, because shortly after that, Nick recommended me for my command check out flight with the Chief Pilot. His advice was: "Fly with him the way you fly with me. And make sure you make a good fuel decision."

Nick and his wife Helen are still good friends of ours, and we now sometimes visit them in South Africa. He has now retired from professional flying but is the chief instructor at the local gliding club, and he likes to get me up in one of the gliders. He even let me go solo in one of the high performance gliders. Then, after a good day of gliding we adjourn to the bar for a few beers and a few laughs, and have an evening just like old times.

The fuel decision is made by the captain at check in, after he has studied the flight plan, weather, and notams (notices to airmen). The minimum is fuel for the planned trip plus an extra percentage in case of wind changes, enough for an approach and a go-around, enough to reach the nominated alternate, and another thirty minutes. It is against the law to go with less. But more can be taken at the captain's discretion, if he thinks he will, or might, need it. More fuel adds weight and increases the fuel consumption and so costs the company money, so there has to be a good reason to take more.

This reminds me of a story my friend Bill Hutchins used to tell of his days in Pan Am. He was in the New York ops room, having just arrived from London, and there was a new captain about to make his first trip in command across the Atlantic.

"Hey, Hutch. What was the weather like in London?"

"It was okay when I left, but you never know with London. Take plenty of fuel."

The new captain studied the paperwork, and said to the dispatcher: "I want an extra ten tons of fuel."

"Ten tons?"

"That's right."

"But Captain, I'll have to off-load all the freight."

"Okay, do that."

"But Captain, I'll have to off-load some of the pax!"

"Okay, off load some of the staff passengers."

"But Captain, do you realize what you are costing the company? To carry ten tons of fuel across the Atlantic will increase the fuel burn by a ton!"

"I didn't think of that. Put on another eleven tons!"

I reported in early for my check ride to allow plenty of time to study the paperwork. I took an extra 3,000 lbs of fuel (I think it was). Ted zzz arrived and looked at the papers and asked: "Why are you taking all that extra fuel?"

"Well, Ted, it is autumn, and we are arriving at just after dawn. So there could well be fog, or certainly early morning mist at Heathrow. And all the trans-Atlantic traffic that took off just before the American jet ban will be arriving at the same time. We could be held at Lyde for up to half an hour, and I would prefer not to use my reserve fuel."

"Hum."

We held at Lyde for 25 minutes. It was a great pleasure to be kept waiting!

Everything seemed to go well. I did not make any silly mistakes, or forget to do anything. I could answer all his 'what if' questions, and even managed to do several reasonable landings. In Nairobi, Ted actually said: "Good landing", which from him was praise indeed.

I was now a civil four-jet airline captain. When I was a fighter jockey, I could not think of anything worse. Now, I could not think of anything better. There was great rejoicing in the Aero Club that evening.

One night I took off on a direct London. My F/O and F/E were both local lads who had recently checked out and had very little experience. The undercarriage had been retracted, and just as the flaps came in, there were several warning lights flashing and needles moving rapidly round dials. We had lost the A system hydraulics. The contents were zero as well as the pressure, so we had had a leak, which meant that the system could not be restored.

A further problem with the B system would be serious, and certain electrical malfunctions could render the good system unavailable, so the only safe thing to do was land back in Nairobi. We went out over the Rift Valley and jettisoned enough fuel to get us down to maximum landing weight (and enough for my personal motoring needs for the rest of my life).

The A system powered the gear mechanism, so we had to 'free fall' the undercarriage. This needed the F/E to go down into the forward lower bay and carry out certain procedures in conjunction with the drill being done on the flight deck. I asked the F/E if he was sure that he remembered what to do. He said that he was. So I instructed him to go down there, put on the head-set and get on the intercom. He left his seat and I awaited his voice. No voice. Instead he came back to the flight deck and said that he was afraid to go down there because it was dark!

"But there is a light. All you have to do is switch it on."

"I know, but you have go into the dark to get to the switch."

I turned to F/O. "Do you remember the drills"

"No captain, sorry."

I was beginning to contemplate going down there myself, but was not sure that these two very new chaps could cope with the flight deck side of the drill. Then my navigator, the very fine Jack Broadley, said: "You're not going down there and leaving us up here are you?"

I had another solution: "You two go down together!"

They did that, one with the know-how and the other to hold his hand and keep the evil spirits at bay. The F/E came on the intercom, we pulled the right levers in the correct sequence, gravity took the wheels down, and a little gentle wing rocking engaged the undercarriage locks. Three green lights!

We landed without further incident.

I had been with the company for several years and had been rostered for duty over Christmas every single year. Christmas was coming again and this year we hoped to have the day off so that we could invite friends in for dinner. The roster came out and I was down for a trip that got me back home by about ten p.m. on Christmas evening. We talked it over with our chums and they all kindly said that it would be much better to have dinner at about ten-thirty than any earlier. So we made the plans.

But when I mentioned it to one of my chums, he assured me that the company was very reasonable and if I pointed out that I had never had the day off, they would change the roster.

So I wrote a note to the Chief Pilot.

I soon received an answer from him that said that he had looked up the records, that I had indeed never had the day off, that my trip was cancelled and that I should be ready for a roster change.

It came. It said: "Delete trip ABC on 25 Dec, and insert trip DEF on Dec 26." This trip was a night flight departing on Boxing Day at 02:00 hrs. Which meant reporting in at 00:30. Which meant leaving home at 00:05 which, meant getting up at 23:15, which meant going to bed at 16:15. So instead of arriving late at our dinner, I could not be there at all!

I never tried to change my roster after that incident, which was, perhaps, the intention of the Chief Pilot.

The next Christmas (I think it was) there was a shortage of F/Os and so I was rostered with the Chief Pilot to operate direct to Milan on

Christmas Eve, night stop, then dead head home on Christmas Day. But it was agreed that if there were any empty seats, we could stay on board as the next crew brought the aircraft home. When we got to Milan there were fare-paying passengers for every seat, so we would have to night-stop and try our luck on Christmas Day.

I really did not want yet another Christmas messed up, so I hatched a plan. I told the Chief Pilot that I would not be joining them at the hotel, but would be making my own arrangements.

When they had gone, I gathered together lots of blankets and pillows, and went down into the forward radio bay. It had a corrugated floor and though pressurised did not have much heating, I had a most miserable, uncomfortable and freezing trip back to base. But I got home for Christmas!

On the F27 and DC9 I used to practice 'dead-stick' landings, and now I started to do them on the SVC10. Of course a real dead-stick is done with the engines shut down, but I did these with the engines throttled right back, so they were still available if I judged it badly. It is standard practice in airline operations to throttle right back at top of descent, and power up when joining the landing pattern, so that a stabilised approach with constant power, speed and rate of descent are maintained to the landing flare. In the SVC10, for example, this approach would need about 84% power. For the dead-stick, the engines are left throttled right back till touch down, and judgment is used instead of power. The SVC10 flaps were so large and effective that they reduced the speed very rapidly when the nose was raised for the touch down, so there was no margin for error. And because of the rapid speed reduction, it was necessary to fly at the flap limiting speed and no slower, prior to the flare. I found that by landing with 30 degrees of flap instead of full flap of 40 degrees, the rate of speed reduction was much less. Furthermore, as each flap setting had its own speed limit, the approach could be flown several knots faster. These two factors made it possible to virtually guarantee a good landing. Full flap should be lowered immediately after touchdown and the landing run will not be increased significantly.

I did one of these landings one day with a crew member on board who had not seen it done before. He became agitated.

"You've forgotten your full flap!"

"No I haven't, we only want 30."

"We'll go off the end!"

"No, we have plenty of room."

"Watch your speed, you're right on the flap limiting speed!"

"That's exactly what we want."

"Watch your speed!"

I do not think that he ever grasped what was going on, and some years later he gave a garbled account of the episode to an author who wrote about it in a book, making it seem more like a cowboy trick than the practiced, accurate and safe procedure that it actually was. The author was kind enough to issue a corrected version when the truth was explained to him.

My Chief Pilot once asked me if I thought it was right and proper to practice this procedure with passengers on board. I emphatically believe that it was. All passenger aircraft are required by law to carry a life jacket for every person on board, and enough dinghies to accommodate them all. This is in case a situation arises which requires an unplanned but necessary landing in the sea. What law of man or nature decrees that such a situation could occur only over water? One can land in the sea anywhere, but on land, unless the landing is made on a runway, an airliner would probably break up, with catastrophic results for the passengers. If such a situation arose over land, within gliding distance of an airfield, it would be unpardonable to kill an aircraft load of passengers simply because the captain lacked the training and skill to carry out a dead-stick landing. Besides, the engines were only throttled back, and were available in case of a misjudgment. And if the aircraft is flown properly and smoothly, the passengers do not even know that it is being done.

If the authorities that be take the view that life jackets should be carried in case of a problem arising over the water, they should not only permit, but require, that pilots practice dead-stick landings in case the same problem arises over land.

My Chief Pilot admitted that I had a point, and raised no objection to my continuing the practice. But he still did not require everyone else to do it.

There was an occasion when bad weather forced me to divert from my intended landing at Rome to Milan. The Rome weather was expected to improve shortly, so we kept the pax on board and waited for the improvement. The Purser came to the flight deck and said that one of the pax would like a word with me. I invited him to the flight deck and he said that Milan was his destination, and that his original plan was to change planes in Rome, but now that we were here, could he not just get off? I consulted the traffic man who told me that he certainly could not, because we had no 'traffic rights' that would have permitted it. I took the view that we had not intended to bring the man here and so breach 'traffic rights', and if we let him off, no-one would gain or lose a penny and no precedent would be set. And to make him wait with us for the weather, then fly him to Rome and wait for another aircraft back seemed to me to be preposterous.

I got a clip board from the purser, gave it to the man, and told him to walk next to me as I marched through crew customs, and read items off the list as if he were an official of vast importance. Apart from a cheery 'Bon Giorno' from a policeman, no-one took any notice of us. I escorted him out into the land-side of the terminal, and bade him farewell. He was most grateful, and I was glad of the opportunity to use a little common-sense.

When flying into London, all crew members filled in a document called the 'general declaration' which the captain signed and a customs man would meet the aeroplane, look it over and study the 'general dec.' and clear us through customs, and our transport would then take us straight to the hotel. Very occasionally, either randomly or as a result of 'information received', the crew would be 'rummaged'. This involved going to a customs room with our bags, and spreading them out on a long counter, and opening them for a customs man to examine them. This happened to me soon after I had been made captain.

We all opened our bags and a customs man checked them and found nothing amiss. But one bag was unclaimed and unopened. It had a crew label with no name, but with our flight number and destination shown as London, so it was on the correct aircraft. A customs man forced it open, and I saw for the first (and last) time a suitcase full of drugs. It looked like a lot of dried grass, and was, the customs man said, indeed the drug of that name. They sent for a senior man, and when he arrived he made it clear that he was also an unpleasant man.

He asked who owned the bag. No one claimed it. So he put us in a room and called us out one by one for a hard grilling. Me first.

I told him that I had a fairly good idea how the smuggling was being attempted, and if he would let me help, I was fairly sure we could catch the miscreant, but we must hurry.

He replied in a nasty tone that I could certainly not help him, and that I was one of the suspects, with which he resumed his bullying interrogation. Of course this got him nowhere. He did the same with all the crew, again without success. We had been flying all night, had missed our breakfast, and now it was past lunch-time. I was getting narked with Mr Nasty. I walked into his room and told him that I had ordered my crew not to cooperate with him in any way until we had had some refreshments. With bad grace he had a few plates of sandwiches and drinks brought in. He gave me the bill for this, which I gave back to him.

Then he started his interrogation all over again and I was getting very tired and very fed-up. I demanded the use of a telephone, and called the Company, the Kenya High Commission, and Airline Pilots' Association lawyer.

I never found out if the phone calls accomplished anything, but we were released in mid afternoon. Were we glad to get to bed?

My opinion was that a group of EAA cabin staff were the smugglers. In Nairobi, we all put our bags on the trolley marked 'London', and it would be easy for an employee not operating that night to go to the airport and put a bag on that trolley. If we were not rummaged and went straight to the hotel, our bags would be put on the floor in the hall and we would all tell a porter which was our bag and the porter would chalk our room number on it and we would go to breakfast while our bags were delivered to our rooms. It would be easy for another of the smugglers already in London, to pick up the remaining bag and take it away. This way, if the bag is discovered, none of the smugglers were involved. Simple! I wanted to explain this to the nasty customs man, and urge him to let us go without delay, so that we could pick up whoever took the bag. But the long delay would have made him suspicious, and I am sure that he was not even present when we finally arrived.

I really wanted to 'assist the customs with their inquiries', but they would not let me! Mr Nasty was so incompetent that he should consider a career as a government minister.

The telephone rang when I was in my room at the Taj Mahal Hotel in Bombay getting ready to leave for the airport. A voice that I did not recognise told me that he knew that I was about to operate to Nairobi and that I could make a great deal of money by taking a small package for him.

I told him that I was not interested.

"But Captain. It is so easy. I will hand you the package, and you hand it over to my colleague in Nairobi. You will make several thousand pounds."

"I am absolutely not interested, and I refuse to meet you. And unless you undertake not to call me again, I shall call the police immediately."

(We all knew that it was most important not to come face to face with such people. There had been cases when aircrew who could identify a smuggler had been murdered)

He hung up and I never heard from him again.

And that was as close as I ever came to being a drug runner.

We were on a night-stop in Rome on one occasion and when we arrived at the EAA office to check in, our man there, Bruno, explained that the baggage handlers were on strike, and we would have to carry our bags a long way across the apron to our aircraft. When we had finished our paperwork, Andy, our F/E, and I got a trolley and got the crew to put their bags on it, and we started pushing it towards the aircraft. At this point, one of the strikers (who should not, of course, have been allowed on to the airport), approached us and demanded in good English that we stop using the trolley. With as much patience as I could muster, I pointed out that though he was on strike, we were not, and neither was the trolley, and furthermore the trolley did not belong to him, and please would he get out of the way.

I gave the order and we resumed pushing. At this the striker grabbed my nearest (right) forearm and tried to physically remove it from the push bar. This really was too much, and so my left fist went under my right arm and connected violently with his stomach. He let go of my arm and fell writhing to the ground.

Andy grinned: "I hope for your sake he has not got mafia connections!"

I hadn't thought of that!

The passengers were on board, the ship's papers were in order and as we were about to close the doors and be on our way when there appeared at the flight deck door the aggrieved striker and two policemen, who appeared to be looking for someone. I congratulated the policemen on their diligence, suggested that they put the villain in the cells, and, unless they wanted to go to Nairobi, asked them to leave the aircraft as were about to start engines. They complied with my request, but I thought I heard one of them mutter something about 'non-intelligenta'. I suppose that that is an Italian word, but I do not know what it means.

I never heard any more about it.

On one trip I operated from Nairobi to London, one of the passengers was Mr Jeffery WWWWW, who was the Colonial Secretary (or was it Foreign Secretary?) in Edward Heath's government. He had visited several African capitals in connection with the Rhodesian declaration of independence. He asked if he could visit the flight deck, and I was delighted to invite him so that I could ask him about his strange political views.

He came up and asked a number of inane questions about flying before I could get him to discuss politics, and he then spoke at length about the unreasonableness of Ian Smiths's government in Salisbury, Rhodesia. Then he said that he had an idea that might change the minds of the Rhodesians. "Why don't you whites of Nairobi drive down to Salisbury one Saturday afternoon and explain to the whites of Salisbury the advantages of black rule?"

I started to offer a polite smile at his feeble bon mot, but then realized, to my amazement, that he was deadly serious. It was incredible that the minister responsible had not the slightest idea of the geography of the area, or the facts of the case.

"Because, Minister, that would be a journey of over twelve hundred miles over bad roads, worse roads or no roads at all. It would be a major expedition taking many days and only the most adventurous would consider undertaking it. Even more to the point, no one knows what the advantages of black rule are."

"But the advantages are obvious."

"Mr WWWWW, please explain to me one single advantage."

"But it's fundamental. A majority government must be superior to a minority one."

"If I understand you correctly, Mr WWWWW, you are telling me that her Majesty's government takes the view that a corrupt, incompetent and cruel government is better than an honest, competent and benign one."

"You simply do not understand these things!"

With which remark he returned to the first class section, leaving me with the question: "How do people with such little comprehension of the real world get to be cabinet ministers?"

It was a Saturday evening in autumn when we left Nairobi for Zurich – London. We kept Greenwich time on board, but in Europe that night, at two o'clock in the morning local time, the clocks were put back one hour.

Zurich airport was closed for noise abatement from 20:00 hrs local till 06:00 hrs local. Dave Harris, our navigator, was very good at his job, (as were they all) and he had proposed that we delay our take off by ten minutes, because the scheduled time, with that night's winds, would have got us there just before the airport opened. Of course he had had to convert from Greenwich to local summer time and then convert from summer time to standard time.

My F/O was flying the leg, so I was doing the R/T. We were handed over by the area control to Zurich Approach Control, and I called them and said that we were ready to commence our approach. We were ordered to proceed to such and such beacon and take up the hold.

"How long will be the delay?"

"Approximately 60 minutes."

It looked as if we had goofed and had arrived an hour before the airport opened.

I looked round at Dave and asked one word: "Dave?"

Dave replied that he was quite sure that that was not so. If Dave was sure, then so was I.

"What is the reason for the delay?"

Slight pause. Then: "You will be clear for the approach in 55 minutes."

"Confirm that the airport is open."

Slightly longer pause. Then: "Eastaf 123, you are clear to commence the approach."

"Roger, but what was the reason for the expected delay?"

"Eastaf 123, you are clear to commence the approach."

Good old Dave had not goofed, Zurich had. But the gnomes of Zurich would never admit it!

The international language of air traffic control is English, and one of the advantages of a single common language is that by listening to the directions given to other aircraft, each pilot gets a broad picture of what is going on. This enables him to double check that air traffic is not arranging a possible hazard, like a mid-air collision.

The importance of this was demonstrated some years ago in Karachi.

If an airport traffic pattern is full, there may not be room for a new arrival. It would then be sent to take up the hold. This is a racetrack pattern with a radio facility at the end of one straight.

The aircraft will hold there until called in to start its approach. There may be several aircraft in the same hold but at different levels and when the lowest one leaves it for its landing all the other aircraft descend one level.

That day in Karachi, the radio went like this:

Tower:	Alitalia 123 leave the hold on a heading of 045 and start your approach.
123	Turning onto 045
Tower:	Air France 234 descend to 2000 feet
234	descending to 2000
234	234 is out of 3000
Tower	Roger. Air Maroc 345 descend to 3000 feet

345	Descending to 3000
345	345 is out of 4000 feet
Tower	Roger, Finnair descend to 4000 feet
345	descending to 4000 feet.
Tower	Roger. Speedbird 456 descend to 5000 feet.
Speedbird	I cannot accept that clearance. Finnair has not called out of 5000 yet.
Tower	(pause) Oh my God. Another day like yesterday.

I cannot vouch for the truth of that story. But I can for this episode in Rome because it happened to me.

It was a clear winter night and we were going into Rome. We picked up the lights about 15 miles out. There was an Alitalia aircraft on the frequency, and the tower was talking to him in Italian.

There was a transmission in Italian, and a reply, presumably from the other aircraft. Was he about to be let down to my level? Or was he being cleared to approach at the same time as me? Or was...

I keyed the mike: "Roma, will you please repeat that in English?" They did. No problem.

A few minutes later, the same thing happened, and again I asked for a translation.

When it happened yet again, I was a little irritated.

"Roma, if you transmitted everything in English, the way that you are supposed to, you would not keep having to repeat it, would you?"

One by one the airfield lights went out – taxi way lights, runway lights, approach lights and all, leaving a great area of blackness ahead.

I got the message and transmitted: "Bon Giorno."

And all the lights came back on!

Nick and I bought a Cessna 206 which we leased out to Dicky Knight, an ex EAA captain who now ran Caspair, a charter company at Wilson. He took care of the maintenance and insurance, and paid us for every hour that he operated it, and we now had a very nice aeroplane for our own use. It was an extremely good arrangement. We began to discuss the idea of buying a light twin; if the 206 would pay for itself, why not a Cessna 402? Life was getting luxurious!

Ever since I joined EAA there had been rumours that it was to be closed down. I no longer took any notice of them. We were the airline of the East African Community, comprising Kenya, Uganda and Tanganyika, though for practical purposes we were the Kenya airline. The community also had common Docks and Harbours, Railways, and Postal services. But now the three countries were having more and more disagreements, and there was a school of thought that held that sooner or later the community would break up. If it did, so would its institutions.

I was on a night-stop in Copenhagen when the blow fell. The company man at the airport called me at the hotel, and said that the flight that I was to take out the next day was not coming in and that operations had already ceased. I went to his office and read the messages for myself – it was all too true. He asked what I wanted to do, and I replied that we had to get the crew home. He said that would be difficult. I had anticipated this, so had gone to the airport in uniform. I went into all the airline offices and asked for help to get me and my crew home. The answers were all the same; they would be delighted to help me if I worked for an airline, but as I did not, there was nothing they could do. And my company had folded barely an hour before!

When I got back to the hotel to discuss the situation with my crew, there was a note in my box asking me who was going to pay the hotel charges for my crew.

British Airways was our handling agent in London and I knew most of the people in the ops room. I called them, and they were very good to us. They organised tickets for us to London, and on to Nairobi.

The ACEA was temporarily renamed the rumour control centre, and meetings were held there regularly! EAA was to be restarted. Then it was not. A new Kenya Airways was to be started. Then it was not. A foreign airline would be invited to form a branch in Kenya. Then it would not.

In the fullness of time we had a back pay and compensation package which was very generous indeed. But at the time, salaries were no longer paid, and people living in company accommodation were given notice to quit. Of course, there were no welfare provisions at all in Kenya. So some people were getting financially embarrassed and started to drift off to their home countries. We were not so badly placed as we owned our own house.

Then came the news that British Midland was to operate the air services out of Nairobi, until the new Kenya Airways could be formed. This rumour turned out to be true. So that was that. That wonderful airline came to an end. I am sure that there has never been, or will ever be again, an airline that combines the highest standards with the greatest friendliness and co-operative spirit, and such a super group of people to have as colleagues.

Every few years, there is an EAA reunion. It is always extremely well attended and it is a great pleasure to meet all these old friends again. People come from Australia and New Zealand, from California and South Africa, and all places in between to attend. And thirty-five years after its demise most of us are still in touch with each other.

I considered going back to Wilson and reverting to being a bush pilot again, but flying the 'heavy iron' was now in my blood, and I did not want to give it up. There were very few flying jobs on offer, but Cathay Pacific in Hong Kong was expanding and recruiting, and several of the EAA chaps went there. But they said that it would take at least ten years to get a command, and at my age I might not ever make it, and I did not want to be a F/O for the rest of my flying career.

Nigerian Airways flew me to London for an interview for a direct entry captain job on the F28. I got the job and flew down to Lagos the same day. After two days there, I decided that if this were the only flying job in the world, I would open a pub or post office! I took the next flight out!

Air Malawi then offered me a job on the VC10, and I took it. Malawi is a very nice place, and the local people are delightful. Had I got to Malawi a little sooner, (instead of going to Nigeria)

I would have got the one captain vacancy. But that had already been taken by another captain from EAA, Tony Britchford, so I was left with the F/O position. I did not welcome the idea of going back to being a F/O again, but needs must, and I set myself the target of being the best F/O in the company. I don't suppose that I succeeded, but it gave me something to aim at.

I first had to get a Malawi ALTP. The Authority would convert a Kenya or a UK licence, so there was no real problem. I did all the medical checks except one in the Blantyre hospital. The exception was that they did the hearing test at a local deaf school where, it was said, they had the necessary facilities. Several hundred deaf-mute children attended the school, and I learned that such unfortunate children make a steady humming/moaning sort of noise without being aware that they are doing so. The background noise was rather like being in an underground station as the train comes in. In UK, candidates are put in a soundproof room and have to respond to signals coming over the earphones. Here, they had me sit in an ordinary room with open windows to do the test sitting at a desk, with no relief at all from the noise. I did my best, but scored a miserable few points that would certainly have failed me in the UK.

"But these results are not valid", I complained.

"Why not?"

I explained.

"Oh, don't worry about that. We apply a factor to the results to compensate for the background noise."

"What factor do you use?"

"Whatever it takes to bring you up to the pass mark!"

He was the specialist and I the layman, and I had to admit that his technical know-how was beyond my comprehension.

The next year when I renewed my medical at the hospital, I met a different doctor who was a local man. He put the right ticks and numbers on the form, signed it, and gave it to me.

"But doctor, aren't you going to examine me?"

"I don't think that is necessary."

"Why not?"

"Pilots are always very fit. They would not be pilots if they were not. So you must be fit."

Once again he was the expert, and I thought it would be churlish to argue the point.

It was a small airline and everyone knew everyone. They were all friendly and helpful and we soon settled in.

The Chief Pilot was a super chap called Dudley Barlow, who had flown Lancasters with No. 44 (Rhodesian) Squadron during the war, and had won the DFC. He had flown thousands of hours on piston-engined aircraft and as a result was a little hard of hearing.

He checked me out in the aircraft, with me doing the flying and he acting as F/O. We did all the standard exercises, and then came the landing. At the appropriate moment I said: "20 flap please." There was no reaction. We were going downwind at 200 knots and there was no time to waste. I remembered his deafness and said much louder: "20 flap please, Dudley!" Still no reaction. I was about to select the flap myself when he turned to me and said: "Don't you think it's time we put down some flap?" I had to agree that it was.

One of the captains, XY, was a little over weight, his hair looked as if it been styled with a knife and fork, and out of uniform he dressed in 'informal' attire – vests with silly writings on them and dungarees. I was a member of his crew when we dead-headed (flew as passengers) from Amsterdam to Gatwick. There, the baggage handlers were on strike, and we could not retrieve our bags. I suggested to our company man there that we go to the baggage hall and pick up our own bags. He replied that if we did that all the other unions would go on 'sympathy' strike, and the only people allowed in the baggage hall were loaders. At this, Dave Harris (also former EAA), our navigator, said to XY: "You look like a loader, why don't you go in and get our stuff?"

XY went in and soon came out with a bag in each hand and another under each arm. He looked more like a loader that ever!

The company operated a small fleet of Islanders. This was a small 12 seat aeroplane (6 seats for two with the pilot on the front pair) for taking very small groups of passengers to the remote country air strips. There was no walkway and no toilet. Air Malawi, "The

Friendly Airline" was the only company which catered for such small groups.

The VC10 pilots could, if they wished, also fly the Islanders on the internal services. I volunteered for this extra duty and was soon made a training captain.

One day, I was operating an Islander from Mzuzu to Karonga with a couple sitting behind me. After a while, the man leaned forward and asked how long it would take to reach our destination. I told him that it would be thirty minutes, Soon after he leaned forward again and said that his wife could not wait half an hour. What to do? Ahead I could see a large field with an unobstructed surface and a clump of trees at the far end. The Islander has a fixed undercarriage, renowned for its robustness. I landed straight ahead, taxied to the trees, shut down the starboard engine and opened the starboard door. Then I looked at the lady and pointed to the trees, She got out and disappeared in them.

A few minutes later we were on our way again. I turned around to talk to the man, He leaned forward to hear me.

"You don't get that service with BA!"

He grinned and agreed

The company looked after the President's personal aircraft, a Cessna 341. I was made a Presidents's pilot, and I had to fly that very nice aeroplane once or twice a month to stay current on type. I never did fly the President, but I did get the extra salary!

Luchenza is a very small town about 30 miles south of Blantyre. There is a grass airfield there and a small but very nice Flying Club which, of course, we soon joined and we went there every Saturday and Sunday when I was not down the route somewhere. It had a Piper Cherokee and a Piper J3 Cub for tail wheel work. There was a clubhouse with a bar and a dining room. Not much happened there through the week but at weekends the few enthusiasts gathered there for some laid-back flying training and practise.

Two of the low time private pilots had got their instructor

ratings but there were no instructors with any experience so I was soon appointed chief instructor. There was no flying programme as in most clubs and members who wanted to fly simply put their name on a list on the board and we flew them as in when we could. Everything stopped for lunch which was prepared by members or members' wives and it was always a very pleasant occasion.

One lady member I flew with, Joan X, was a competent and confident pilot. She told me one day that it was her ambition to get her night rating. I gave her the necessary instrument flying training first and she coped with that very well. She did the same with the night flying. We reached the point where I said that I was getting out to send her solo. She said that she knew she could do it but did not have the nerve. I assured her that I wouldn't be sending her unless I was sure she could do it, but she still hesitated. I then undid my straps to get out and told her that she could now either taxi the aeroplane over to the hanger t and shut down or she could turn the other way, taxi down to the runway and do one night circuit . Then I got out. To my very great pleasure she turned the other way, taxied to the runway, took off and did a very nice circuit and a very nice landing. We were both very pleased with each other!

I flew a trip to Europe as F/O to Captain Martin Gee. Martin was a very competent aviator and a very nice chap too. Coming back to Blantyre, via Nairobi, the forecast weather for Nairobi was way above limits, so we would have an easy trip. We made our approach, but in fact the weather was way below limits, and we had to go around. As we did so, the navigator and flight engineer could not see anything at all, so there was no point in making another approach, and Martin decided to go to the alternate, which was Mombasa. When we landed there, we had used all our legal duty time, so we would have to go off duty and take our legal rest period. But it was Easter week-end and there was not a hotel room to be had anywhere on the coast, and the law prohibits crew from resting in the aircraft, even if it is on the ground with no passengers on board. Martin had a problem! Whatever he did would be illegal! The only help I could give him was to assure him that I would give him all my backing at the subsequent 'court-martial'.

He decided to off-load his few Nairobi pax, and have Kenya Airways take them to Nairobi, while we with the majority Blantyre pax would carry on to base. At least the weather in Blantyre was good. They said! On route we got the latest Blantyre weather and it had gone below limits. So Martin diverted to Dar-es-Salaam. When we got there we were way over our max duty time, and should certainly have gone off duty, but Dar had the same hotel problems as Mombasa at Easter. Martin asked how we all felt, and the engineer said that he could hardly keep his eyes open, the navigator said he could continue, and I said that I could go on and keep an eye on the engineer's panel too. So we waited until the weather at base improved, and then finally got home. I think we were on duty for over thirty hours, which would make a UK CAA civil servant fall off his stool.

Of course, we should really have gone off duty at Mombasa, and waited in the aircraft (which would not have counted as rest time) while the company flew another crew there. But it was a small company and that would have caused considerable disruption to other services, delayed our pax even more, and been very expensive for the company.

There was no court-martial – in fact we all got nice letters from the company thanking us for our efforts.

I got a phone call one day from Ron Minault. Ron had been a navigator with EAA, and had studied and trained for his pilot licences, and had changed seats to become a F/O on the SVC10. He was now flying in the right hand seat of a DC3 based at Wilson Airport Nairobi. He and his captain, whose name I cannot recall after all these years, had landed at Blantyre en route to South Africa. They wanted my help in doing the paperwork for the next leg of the trip. The paperwork was always tedious and difficult when going from a Black African county to White South Africa (as it then was).

Nick and Helen Methley and their daughters were staying with us at the time for Christmas and Nick and I went to the Blantyre airport, Chileka, to meet Ron and his captain.

I presented the captain with a choice.

"If you let me take the DC3 round the circuit once, I will take care of your paperwork and have you on your way today. Or you do not let me take the aircraft and you do your own clearances and be off next Friday."

"How much time do you have on Daks?"

"I haven't any to speak of, but my friend Nick here has many thousands of hours."

The captain decided that giving us the trip was the easiest thing to do so somewhat reluctantly he agreed.

"Come on, Nick! Let's go."

I sat in the left hand seat, and Nick reminded me of a few points especially about locking and unlocking the tail wheel. He started the engines and set the flap and said: "Do not move the gear or the flaps at all. And don't forget what I said about the tail wheel."

"Okay, but if I do, you can always remind me, can't you?"

"You don't think I'm coming, do you?"

With which remark he left the aircraft.

I did one circuit. I left the gear down and did not change the flap setting, which Nick said was suitable for take-off and landing. It seemed to go well and the landing was better than the ones I had done with Leigh. So I was very pleased with myself.

Later I mentioned to Nick that I had thought that he was coming.

"I knew you would get a kick out of doing it by yourself."

And that is how I got my third trip in the coveted Dak.

I completed their paperwork in time for them to continue the same day. But they elected to delay their departure till the next morning, so that Ron and Nick and I could have a mini EAA reunion.

I was promoted from the VC10 and was made up to captain on the HS748 fleet. That aircraft is an ungainly twin turbo prop thing, vaguely similar to F27. They made me a training captain on it. The aircraft is too simple to warrant having a simulator, but nevertheless, there is one in the World. Indian Airlines have one at their training base in Hyderabad, and one of my new duties was to take trainee F/Os out there for training on it. I had qualified as a Hunter simulator instructor at Chivenor, so it was not difficult to check out as a HS748 simulator instructor, which I did with the Indian Airlines training staff.

I was hoping that I would soon get back to a jet command on the BAC111, and eventually back to the VC10, but the Company announced that the VC10 was not earning its keep, so to speak, and they were going to take it out of service. Its crews were to revert to the BAC111, and so it would be years before I could hope for a vacancy. Life was agreeable in Malawi, but...

Saudia, the Saudi-Arabian Airline, was expanding and was looking for direct entry captains on the Boeing 737. A direct entry jet command is a rare thing, and after talking it over with Sylvia, I applied for a position and was offered a job.

The Saudi aviation authorities did not recognize the British airline transport pilot licence (ALTP), but would issue their own ALTP based on an American FAA one. If a candidate did not have a US licence, Saudia undertook to arrange the flight tests for it, but required him to have passed the ground written exams. I got in touch with my old buddy, Tony Richardson, ex 4's 4 and now with Western Airlines in Seattle, and he arranged a crash course for me at Seattle. A group of us studied intensively from a Monday morning to the Friday evening, and took the exam on the Saturday morning. It is an interesting contrast that it took me longer than that just to write the exam for the British equivalent!

We did 737 ground school at the Saudia training centre at Jeddah, and then went to the United Airlines training centre in Denver, Colorado for simulator and base training in the aeroplane.

Eastern Air Lines training on the DC9 had been absolutely first class. Let's just say that United was a different airline. My check flight with the FAA examiner was a long one because I had to pass all the flight tests for the issue of my FAA ATPL, (normally done in a small training aircraft) then all the exercises for the issue of a 737 type rating on that licence. Most the exercises were the same, but could not be counted twice! An item on the type rating test was an emergency descent. This is performed for real when an aircraft has a pressurisation failure at altitude, in order to get the passengers and crew down to 10,000 feet as quickly as possible.

There are two schools of thought on how this should be done; one holds that the nose should be lowered with the wings level. The other school argues that this might cause a collision with another aircraft at a lower level on the same airway and that therefore the aircraft should be turned off the airway as it descends. The first school argues that in bad weather or at night or in turbulence it would be easy to over bank and end up in a spiral dive from which recovery would be difficult if not impossible, and anyway, aircraft on an airway are rarely precisely on the centre line, so turning off could still cause a collision.

My instructor (who also acted as my F/O on the check ride) was firmly of the opinion that the wings should be kept level throughout the manoeuvre, and this is how I did it on the test. After the test, the FAA examiner told me that I had achieved a partial pass. He said that he was very satisfied with all my flying except the emergency decent, in which I failed to make a turn off the airway. He said that he was confident that I could do it, but could not sign me off until I had demonstrated that I could. So we would have to do another trip, straight up to 35,000 feet and then a 'proper' emergency descent, and land.

At this point my instructor, who was present at the debrief, interrupted: "Now, Charlie, you know better than that! I taught you all you know about the 737, including how to do a descent."

"I know that, but I am in the FAA, and it takes the view that a turn should be made."

"They are wrong!"

"Maybe so, but I will not sign this candidate off unless he does it the FAA way."

So I said: "It looks as if we had better do it their way."

One cannot just go to an FAA examiner and ask for a check ride. One has to be recommended by a recognised instructor.

My instructor said to me: "Unless you agree to do the descent my way, I will refuse to put you up for the test."

To which the FAA man replied: "And if you do, I will fail you again."

Most pilots are a bit stressed on a check ride, and I am no exception. I could do without all this!

So I told my instructor that I would do it his way and got the recommendation, but decided that when the time came I would do it the FAA man's way.

We got to 35,000 feet and the FAA man shouted: "Pressurisation failure!" I started the procedure and my instructor must have guessed my intention, because he put his knee under his yoke to stop me applying bank. I was determined to please the FAA man, and I was more heavily built than my instructor. I applied such pressure to the yoke that my instructor, with a cry of pain moved his knee, and I was able to perform to the examiner's satisfaction. My instructor then folded his arms and took no further interest in the proceedings. On the ground, the FAA man, with a strange half knowing, half embarrassed smile signed the papers.

What a performance!

Then back to Saudi Arabia for line training, before being let loose as a line captain.

The Saudi training captains had an unusual way of instructing. They would shout, scream, abuse and ridicule and maintain a constant barrage of invective. We found this very distracting and our performance suffered accordingly. Two former East African captains and one Air Malawi captain whom I knew to be highly competent aviators failed the course and were fired. I passed by the skin of my teeth.

We had a simulator check every six months and had to endure this treatment repeatedly.

One check, I had a new instructor, He was a pleasant young man who had been educated in England and had an English wife. He conducted my check ride in the orthodox way, and I did my best ride ever in Saudia. He congratulated me on a good check and that emboldened me to asked why the other checkers did what they did.

He explained that Saudia had been set up by the American TWA and that was how they did it because, they thought, if a pilot can cope under bullying, he would be able to cope in an emergency. And he supposed that that was true.

I asked him if he had ever been in an emergency, He had not, I explained that I had several times been in a situation where I knew that if I did not get everything right in the next few minutes

I would end up in the morgue. I explained that that stress sharpened the mind and wits, reduced reaction time and clarified the options which was exactly the opposite of the effect of the Saudi training method.

He seemed convinced and I hoped that he would spread the word. But the Saudi ways prevailed!

Our routes were within the Kingdom, and to the neighbouring countries. The weather was usually good, but visibility was very bad in a sand storm and for some time after. There were not many thunderstorms, but the worse one I ever encountered was right over Jeddah.

Nearly all the F/Os on the 737 fleet were local lads, mostly of limited experience, on their first job with the airline. So I spent a lot of time in the company of young Saudis, both on the flight deck and at the hotel during layovers.

Most of them liked to chat, and I learned about the Moslem way of doing things, and explained to some of them the Christian way. Others did not want to talk about off-duty matters at all.

I remember doing one trip with a nice young lad, and as I had a car problem at the time, I asked him if he would be kind enough to drive me home. This he was more than happy to do, and when we got there I invited him in to have some tea or coffee.

"Is your wife there?"

"Yes, and I am sure that she would like to meet you."

"But she will not be veiled, will she?"

"Well no. that is not our custom."

"Then I cannot come in. It's not that I disapprove or anything – it's just that I have never been in the same room as an adult lady without her veil, and I would be so embarrassed that I would not know what to do."

I found it most interesting to learn something of their customs.

Another young lad came from a family of nomads, and he described to me the wonderful free and simple life of moving about the desert. This was his last trip before going on leave, and I bade him a nice holiday. A few weeks later, I happened to see him in the ops. room.

"Did you have a nice leave?"

"Well, yes. Sort of. Thank you."

"And how is your family?"
"I don't know. I couldn't find them."

While I was there, Saudi Arabia hosted a major Islamic Conference, which was attended by several Heads of State, and many VIPs. As part of Arab hospitality, each delegate was told that he could fly anywhere at any time at any notice. To cater for this, several crews, including me, were moved into comfortable, temporary accommodation at the airport, and we had to be ready to fly anywhere at a moments notice. We had maps to cover the world, and our flight planning charts and tables instantly available. We were there for a week, living in great comfort with superb catering. In the event, I was not called to go anywhere, and I don't think any of us were. But I still have the gold watch that the Company presented to each of us to commemorate the fact that we were ready, willing and able.

I took off one day with a trainee captain, and had an unusual incident. Both engines ran up to take-off power in the normal way, but after take-off, with gear and flaps up at a safe height and speed, when I pulled the throttles back for climb power, one engine did not respond. It was stuck at take-off power. Every manual tells you what to do in the case of an engine failure, but not what to do if the engine does the opposite. Of course I had to shut the engine down and land on one. Jet engines should be shut down from idle, and there is a risk of fire if they are shut down from full throttle, so I got to a position down wind from which I could land very quickly if there was a fire. But there was no fire, and I was lucky (again!). I have done single engine landings for training many times, and when I was on Meteors, twice with actual failures. But this was the only time that I ever did an asymmetric landing with over a hundred passengers in the back. I was quite confident that I could do it successfully, and was glad that my RAF training had been so thorough. As we used to say, 'if they stick with me, they will be all right!"

Saudi flight law was based on the American, and included similar flight time limitations. But they did not enforce them very stringently. Our pay system was based on American practice, that is, we were paid so much per flying hour but with a guaranteed minimum of sixty hours per month. If we flew over sixty hours we were paid for the time in what amounted to overtime. I was preparing for retirement and accepted all the flying I could get. One day, I completed a six leg tour of duty and I was just getting ready to leave the aircraft when ops. called and asked if I would do a further four legs. I asked my crew, and replied that I was able to, but they would have to find me another F/O and a complete cabin staff. I completed the extra four legs with the new crew, and as I was getting ready to leave the aircraft, ops called again to ask if I could do a Dharan and back. I consulted the crew and replied that I could go on but they would have to find me yet another F/O and a complete cabin staff. They did, and I did the extra legs. I think I was on duty for thirty-four hours, having worn out three crews. I was reminded of my long trip with Air Malawi and Martin. I did not get a letter of thanks from the company, but the pay cheque that month more than made up for that!

One of our destinations was Abha, a town in the mountains to the South not far from the Yemeni border. Thus it was hot and high, both of which affect aircraft performance, in particular the maximum take off weight. Part of our procedure was get the temperature from the control tower, and apply it to the various other factors and so calculate the max t/o weight, and thus the maximum joining load we could accept. Sometimes this was so limited that some pay-load had to be left behind for the next aircraft to take. Traffic staff are just as keen as anyone else to get the job done, and they like to get their pax and freight away as promptly as possible. One day there, the stated temperature seemed to me to be unusually low. I suspected a possible reason, so the next time I went, I made a note of the temperatures every hour. As expected, they got higher as the sun came up, dropped at mid-day, (when they should have been even hotter, but when we were about to take off) then got hotter again till late afternoon. It seemed that the traffic man was doing the same calculations that we were but backwards. He knew how much joining load he wanted us to take, then calculated the temperature required to make that possible, then told the tower to give us that temperature when we asked for it. After that, I estimated the temperature based on the morning trend. I think the company found out and moved the zealous traffic man to other duties. We were lucky (again!) and did not have any engine failures there, but had we lost an engine on take-off in the over weight condition we would not have been able to maintain height and must have hit the ground. I wonder if in that event, the accident investigation people would ever have identified the cause.

I was operating a service out of one of the Northern airports to Jeddah, and the government had blocked off thirty-six seats for official use. When we commenced boarding, I could see through the flight deck window eighteen policemen each shackled to a prisoner, walking to the aircraft. A few minutes later the No. 4 hostess (who served the rear section) came to the flight deck in tears. I made her sit down on the jump seat (the spare seat on the flight deck) gave her my handkerchief, and got the Purser to bring her a glass of water. When she regained her composure, I asked what was upsetting her.

"Oh! Those poor men! They are all being taken to Jeddah for execution!"

I gave it some thought before replying: "Now, my dear, those men need some friendly help more than any of the other pax. Give them all some refreshment, and try to give each one a very special smile. Remember that you are the last pretty thing that they are going to see in this World."

I heard later from the Purser that she had done just that. A brave girl.

After several years in Saudi Arabia the summer heat was beginning to get to us. And we never really enjoyed the life style. We were saving money for our retirement at a more than satisfactory rate, and I remember a conversation with one of the American captains who pointed out that 'they' have got more money than we have got time, and that when we have enough, it is the time to go. Besides, for many years I had had the weird desire to fulfil my DIY hobby by building a house from scratch, and if I left the project much longer, I might be too old to undertake all the manual work involved. So the time had come to move on, and open the next chapter in our lives.

Chapter 9

GENERAL AVIATION PILOT

I have always been a do-it-yourself enthusiast, having tackled electrics, plumbing, carpentry, brick laying, cement work and so on. I had had an ambition to build our own house from scratch for a long time, and now that I had the time and the money we were going to do it.

Years before, when I left the RAF, I had been offered jobs instructing at the two main civilian flying schools, Hamble and Oxford. We preferred the Hamble area, and we found a suitable site for the house building project, but when I discussed the idea with the town planning people, they made such preposterous difficulties that we abandoned the whole thing.

Now we were going to do it in Florida, on a very nice lakefront piece of land that we had bought on one of our vacations. The planning people were most helpful, and we started the work within a couple of weeks of arriving. First we installed a mobile home on the property to live in whilst building, then proceeded with the house.

The project was every bit as interesting and absorbing as I thought it would be. I expected it to take a year, and it did, and it cost about what I thought it would. It was a thing I had always wanted to do, and I am glad that I did it, but I would not want to do it again.

When we were in Kenya, I was approached by two fellows called Roger Harris and Peter Austin who asked me if I would convert them from nose wheel to tail wheel flying. They had bought a Piper Pacer between them, but had been trained on nose wheels. They both took about five hours for this, which is normal. I did not take any payment but they allowed me use of the aircraft.

I was busy on the house one day, when Peter called me. He was in the States, and had bought a Piper Aztec in Texas and wanted to fly it to Florida. He had just completed his multi-engine rating, but had very few hours on twins, and would I go and help him. I would be delighted. I flew commercial to Houston and met him. He was a business man with very wide interests, was doing rather well, and had bought an island in the Bahamas. The Aztec was to go between it and Florida.

We flew the aircraft from Houston to our local airport at Lake Placid, and he and his girl friend stayed the night with us, with a view to going on to Fort Lauderdale in the morning, and then on to his island so that I could check out his strip. We had a nice dinner at home with much reminiscing about Kenya, before an early night ready for a busy day ahead.

I was up early, but when I went into the kitchen he was already there and talking on the phone. He said that one of his companies in Europe was in difficulties and he had to go there at once. He had already booked a flight out of Orlando International, and would I fly him there right now in the Aztec. We flew up there, and as he was getting out, I asked: "Peter, what do you want me to do with the aeroplane?"

"Oh, just regard it as your own till you hear from me!"

And that's how I was, temporarily, the proud owner of twin-engined aircraft.

Many weeks later, he called and asked me to deliver it to an FBO in Fort Lauderdale. That I did. I never did get to his island.

A neighbour on our side of the lake was a chap called Bill Hutchins. Bill had flown 'the hump' during the war, that most hazardous supply line from Burma to China over the Himalayas in DC3s and C46s. After the war, he became a crop sprayer before joining Pan American, from which he was now a retired captain. We often got together for a beer and a chat about aviation. He owned a Bucker Jungmeister, a powered glider, a Piper Vagabond and an interesting biplane ultra light called a Hyperlite. Bill let me fly them all except the Jungmeister, because nobody, but nobody, flew that but him.

The house was finished and we were very pleased with it. I had looked forward to the project for many years, and now it was done. I had never really thought that this time would come one day, and so had made no plans for it. We decided to go to England to visit family and friends. While there, I called John Milner, my ex Boss on No. 4 who was now running the AA Learjet operation out of Coventry, and suggested that we got together for a few beers. He told me that he was desperately short of pilots, and asked if I could go and help him out. I had never flown an executive jet, so it was an attractive offer and we went to Coventry right away.

He operated British registered Lears (G numbers), and American ones (N numbers). British law requires both pilots to have the type rating on their licences, which I did not yet have. But American law does not require that the F/O has a type rating, so I could fly the N aircraft in the right hand seat next morning. And did! John checked me out and I started flying at once. Over the next two or three weeks, I studied and passed the ground exams, and John, being an examiner, did my flight tests to put the type on my British licence so that I could now fly either seat in the G aircraft. I never did get it on my American licence, so could not fly the N aircraft from the left hand seat.

It was a new experience, and I enjoyed flying the Lear immensely. Its speed and ceiling compared with the Meteor and Vampire, though it was not aerobatic, and was limited in the g that could be pulled. But I cannot say that I enjoyed the life style. The clients paid a great deal of money for their transportation, and understandably expected the pilots to be totally flexible. So, for example, I might fly a business man to Paris early for a day of meetings, hang about the airport all day, expecting to take him home in the early evening only to find that instead of his coming back to Le Bourget at six, he comes back at ten, and he does not now want to go back to London, but to Rome. I used to take two spare shirts just in case, and that was not always enough!

On the list of the ten most luxurious hotels in the world is the Cipriani in Venice. I was taking a client to Venice one day, and I asked the ops chap where we were staying that night. (The client paid for the pilots' accommodation.)

"He's putting you in the Cipriani."

"That's generous of him!"

"Not really. He does own it!"

(Three other hotels on the list are the King George V in Paris, the Atlantis in Zurich, and the Taj Mahal in Bombay. I have stayed at all three, courtesy of EAA.)

On another occasion, I flew a lady and her girl friend to Nice for about two hours. The lady had a holiday home there, and wanted to show her friend the new curtains she had had installed there. At £1,000 per hour for the aeroplane plus expenses, landing fees and so on, it cost her at least £6,000 to show off her new curtains!

One trip was to fly Prince and Princess Michael of Kent from Biarritz to London. After landing, the Princess thanked us in a most charming way for a nice trip as she left the aircraft, but the Prince put his head in the door of the flight deck to ask a few questions about the aeroplane. The flight deck of the Lear is very cramped and the roof panel low. I struggled to stand up but could not do so.

The Prince said: "You look uncomfortable. Have you got cramp or something?"

"No, Sir. I am simply trying to stand up in front of you."

"How very nice of you, old boy! But please sit and relax."

As he said that, he put his hand on my shoulder as if to hold me down. That is the only time that I have been man-handled by Royalty. He asked a number of thoughtful questions and was very interested in the operation.

He is a natural gentleman and it was a privilege and a pleasure to meet him.

Another regular client used to insist that only Dom Perignon champagne be served. He was about an hour into a flight to Gibraltar, when he asked for a glass of champagne and was served some other type. He demanded that the aircraft turn around, go back to base, and get the correct type. He was told that that would add at least £2,000 to his bill. They still turned round! It came out later that the client, a financier, was using his clients' money, and he ended up in prison, where, I suppose, any kind of champagne will have to do.

An extremely nice passenger was Nigel Mansell, the racing driver. He was most considerate to the pilots, and would usually have dinner with us. He did not drink during the racing season, but he expected us to, and insisted that we put everything we ordered on his tab. He used to take us to the pits on practice days, but on the race day, we had to be in the Lear all ready to go, because as soon as the race was over he wanted to get away at once. If he had to drop out of the race, he would not even stay to see the end. He used to buy a number of Lear hours per year from the owner, but he told me one day that he was thinking of buying his own aircraft, and he asked me if I would be interested in leaving the AA and becoming his pilot. I think it was more thinking aloud than a serious offer. But he lived in the Isle of Man, where the climate in summer is barely tolerable, and in winter must be insufferable, so I politely declined his offer.

After several months of flying that exhilarating aircraft, the day came when John hired another regular pilot, followed by one of his aircraft going off to some other operator, so he no longer needed me. And winter was approaching, so Sylvia and I returned to the warmth of Florida.

In the New Year, we began to consider how to spend the summer. I had heard that Aurigny Airlines was a sharp, slick and happy operation, and I wondered if there might be an opening there for me. It is the Channel Islands airline based in Alderney (Aurigny is the Roman word for Alderney), and it operates to Jersey, Guernsey, Southampton, Hurn, Cherbourg and Dinard, and is equipped with Trilanders. The Channel Islands are a very popular tourist attraction, so I wrote to the Chief Pilot to ask if he needed extra pilots for the summer schedule. I got a very nice letter back from Bill Bailey, the excellent Chief Pilot, stating that they did need two more pilots for the season, and we agreed that I would get in touch when we got to England.

When we got there, I saw an ad. in 'Flight' magazine saying that Air M... was looking for direct entry captains on the B737. I called the number and it was the Chief Pilot.

"Have you got over 3,000 hours in command?"

I had.

"Have you got over 1,000 hours in command on type?"

I had.

"Are you available immediately?"

I was.

I caught the next Air M.... flight from Heathrow, and the Chief Pilot met me, and drove me to his office. On the way we found that we had several friends and acquaintances in common. When we got there, he said that we had to sort out uniforms, licences, a place to stay...

"Won't I need to be interviewed first?"

"We did that in the car."

It all seemed easy until he said: "Now, you have got over 3,000 hours in command?"

"Easily."

"And 1,000 hours in command on type?"

"Easily."

"And 50 hours in command on type in the last three months?"

"Well, no. You did not mention that on the phone."

"No, I forgot to. How many hours have you done in the last three months?"

"None, on type."

He looked out of the window for a while, then said: "I have a number of things to attend to. I have to go to the hangar to see the engineers and then to the roster room. I'll be gone about an hour. Make yourself at home here in my office. Feel free to use my desk – there are writing materials and stuff."

Then he was gone. His meaning was clear – he was inviting me to falsify my log book.

It is not impossible that one day I will become a bank robber. Or a serial murderer. But I could never falsify my log book. He was disappointed but said that he quite understood. They put me up in a nice hotel and flew me back to London next morning.

I called Bill Bailey in Alderney and arranged to fly there from Southampton next day. He and the CEO met me and took me to lunch, which was a nice informal way to interview me. I caught the odd nod and wink between them and then one of them said the job was mine if I wanted it. "But", Bill added, "If you think this is a back door to a regular job here, you will be disappointed."

Bill took me to the airport to catch my flight back to the mainland, and when we got there he said that we had a little time before my flight came in, and there is a spare Trilander, and would I like to fly it to see what it is like. I would. I had flown Islanders in Air Malawi, and this was just a bit wider, a bit longer and had another engine on the tail. He let me do the take-off, and as the nose wheel left the ground he chopped one engine. I managed to keep it straight, and did what checks I could remember from my Islander days. He seemed happy with that, and told me to complete the circuit and land on two engines. There were no passengers or freight on board so the aircraft was light and the flying simple. I considered it a little naughty to give me a check ride unannounced like that. But it got it over with.

Aurigny had pilots based in all three islands and they wanted me on Alderney. Sylvia and I moved into a rented cottage and I began my line training, mostly with Bill. The flying was some of the most intensive I have encountered. Bill was in the right hand seat, but when (if?) I was checked out I would be on my own – no F/O and no auto pilot. The sectors between the islands lasted 15 to 20 minutes. In that time, the pilot would take off, complete the after take-off checks, set course, throttle back to climb power, synchronise the engines, calculate time to the next check point, check out with local control and switch to approach control, talk on company frequency with times and payload, reduce to cruise power, resynchronise the engines, make a cabin announcement, tune the radio aids to the destination field, get the weather at the destination, do the approach checks then the landing checks, then land and taxi in.

If piston engines are not synchronised, they produce an unpleasant droning noise. (Sort of a slow wow wow.) It is simple to synch two engines by leaving one rpm alone and moving the other slightly until the drone disappears. But with three engines, there are two superimposed drones and it takes practice to cancel out one drone at a time. We got plenty of practice!

The turn-round time was only 20 minutes and in that time the pilot would calculate how much more fuel was needed and write that figure on a card for the refuelling man, go to the ops room and complete the voyage report and technical log, check the weather for the next leg, study the number of passengers and freight and indicate to the traffic staff how the aircraft is to be loaded (to stay within centre of gravity limits, which are critical on the Trilander), check the load sheet, do a walk-round inspection of the aircraft, get the maps and charts for the next leg ready, tune in the radio aids for the next leg, and complete the pre-start check list. There was certainly no time for a cup of tea!

On the SVC10, some days we did just one sector, say, a Nairobi-London. The most we ever did was four sectors, so we might do 30 sectors a month, half of which were flown by the other pilot. On the DC9 or B737 we often did four and sometimes six sectors in a duty period. On the Trilander we did 10 and 12 sectors, and one stint had 14 sectors in a duty period, and these were done without a break between an early breakfast and a late lunch or an early lunch and supper time. Until one got used to it, it was exhausting. But it was most satisfying to accomplish it.

On the big jets, we would do a landing down to limits – minimum cloud base, minimum visibility – perhaps once per month. The weather in the Channel Islands is such that I once did a 14 sector period with every single landing down to limits. That was even more exhausting, and I fell asleep while having my late lunch soup!

When landing in foggy conditions, the wind is usually light or calm which makes instrument flying easier. When landing in high wind and turbulent conditions, usually below the cloud base the visibility is adequate. But in the Channel Islands, particularly Jersey, they have a 30 knot fog. No doubt the met. man understands why. So there, it is common to approach in very poor visibility and in turbulent conditions at the same time.

We went to all the destinations, some twice, and Bill said that he was happy for me to go off on my own, if I was happy. I was.

"One question though, Bill. If I have a weather or technical

Boarding a Trilander of Aurigny Airline.

problem, do you want me to obey the letter of the law, or get the job done?"

"That's a difficult question for a chief pilot to answer."

"Thank you Bill, you just have."

Bill could hardly say so in so many words, but he expected us to complete our trips if it was humanly possible to do so, even it that meant stretching the law, though he never wanted us to exceed our own limitations.

(Some years later, we were air touring with friends, and were stuck in Dinard due to weather. We were in the coffee shop waiting for the weather to improve when we heard the sound of aircraft engines. We went to the window to see what was happening, and we saw a Trilander taxi in after landing there.

"Good", said my friend, "That means that the weather is now above limits."

"No it doesn't", I replied, "That's Aurigny, and they fly in any weather!")

It was indeed a slick, sharp and happy organisation, and I very much enjoyed my time there.

The traffic staff was distinctly above average, and it was impressive to watch them get all the passengers off and into the terminal and then the next lot of passengers into the seats that I had worked out, all in a few minutes. And they did that all day, rain or shine.

I was coming back from Southampton to Alderney one day and the weather was on limits. As I made my approach, the weather deteriorated, as it often did in the C.I. I went down to limits, then a little below for Bill, but it was no good and I had to go around. Guernsey was still above limits, so I diverted there, and did all the stuff, including telling the passengers where we were going. The same thing happened there, and I had to go around again and this time divert to Jersey. I did all the things again, but there simply was not time to brief the pax. The weather there was right on limits, but we got in. As we taxied in, the lady behind me tapped me on the shoulder and asked politely if I knew that this was Jersey. I made the time to get on the public address to explain what had happened!

On another trip to Southampton, one of our other pilots, Eric xxx had had mechanical trouble and was delayed, so we took off for Alderney at the same time, and we flew south in a sort of wide battle formation. The weather was good and when I saw base, slightly to my left, I called the tower and said that I had the runway in sight and was ready to commence my visual approach. The controller was a new person, and she instructed me to delay my approach and instructed Eric, who was on my right, and so further away, to commence his. This was an unnecessarily complicated way to do it, and I wondered if she was really up to the job. There was no other traffic, so I said one word on the radio: "Switch?" Eric was a sharp ex RAF man and he answered one word: "Oke." So I used his call sign and followed his instructions, and he used my call sign and followed mine. We made seemly and orderly landings, and I suppose that the controller thought that she had done a good job.

On another occasion, I made an approach to Alderney in daylight, but bad weather. At minima, I saw the ground but could not pick up the runway and there was no alternative to going around. As soon as I did, we were back in cloud. But we were so close that I decided to make another approach. I went out to sea and let down until I was below cloud and could see the waves, then approached the Island from the South, and crossed the coast at a place I knew where the cliffs were a little lower. I nearly reached the airfield again, and had I been still working for the Queen, would have pressed on and made it. But though I might bend the odd rule, I would never, of course, put my pax in any jeopardy. So I went around again and went back to Guernsey, explaining to my pax what was happening. There, they were escorted to a waiting room to wait for better weather. Most airline passengers have never experienced a 'go around'. Mine had experienced it twice in one trip, and I suggested to the traffic chap that they would probably cancel their trip or go by boat! The weather improved and the traffic man told the passengers to get ready for boarding. A deputation of passengers then approached him and said to him that they had not enjoyed the previous trip, and that they would go but only if they had the same pilot. I was greatly touched. The Channel Islanders are a loyal breed.

Sylvia and I are fond of fish especially shell-fish, and we both remarked on how nice and fresh the fish and sea-food were that we got from Archie, the fishmonger. This was because, we thought, the fish had been swimming happily just off-shore only a few hours before and had never been frozen or left lying about. This was certainly one of the advantages of spending time in Alderney.

Then I noticed that Archie was nearly always at the airport when I came in from Hurn. I wondered why, so one day I casually strolled in to the freight shed and saw Archie examining boxes of fish packed in ice. I had flown the boxes in from Hurn, and they had arrived there, no doubt, from Hawaii, Alaska, or Cape Town, and the fish had been frozen for days if not weeks.

After that, though we bought the same fish from Archie, it never quite tasted the same.

The single pilot sat in the front left seat, and the front right seat was used at the captain's discretion. Some would allow a passenger to sit there, while others would not. If an off-duty pilot wanted to go somewhere, it was recognised that the seat was his.

We had made friends with a local doctor and his wife, and when he told me that he had to fly to Southampton and asked to sit next to me, I agreed to set it up.

I was doing the paperwork prior to departure when one of the pilots came in and said that he was going to Southampton, that the aircraft was full and he presumed that he could have the FR seat. Regretfully, I told him that I had already promised the seat to someone else.

"But company pilots have priority," he said.

"I'm sorry", I replied, "But as you know the older you get the more frequent the required medical checks." (Pilots under 40 have to take an ECG every two years, over 40 every year, after 50 every six months, and there was talk of a check every three months for pilots over 55.)

I added: "I've reached the age when I have to have a doctor fly in the next seat to me every trip!"

Winter was approaching and it was getting colder and very much windier. The winter schedule would soon be implemented and I would no longer be needed. So I was surprised and flattered when Bill offered me a full time job. I did consider it, but the weather there is barely tolerable in the summer and we could not imagine spending the winter there. Besides, short-term rental places are all right for a temporary job, but not as a permanent life style. I was extremely glad that I had had the delightful time working with the Aurigny folk – great chaps all of them – but was not sorry to flee to Florida before winter struck.

In the New Year, I received a nice letter from Bill Bailey, inviting me back to Aurigny for the summer season. I had enjoyed the previous season and was tempted to accept, but I had been there and done that, and I was hoping for some new challenge. So I made no commitment and Bill would not keep the place for me, but if I found nothing different, and he still had a place, we would talk again.

We went to England to see family and friends in the spring, and one of the people I called was our old friend James Budd. We had met him through Ernie Constable with whom he had served on 43 Squadron. After the RAF he had gone to BA and after that had a post-retirement job with Gibraltar Airways.

James had been waiting for me to call, and he told me that the Viscount which GB used to operate had been pranged, and most of the pilots let go. It was now to be replaced by a Trilander, and he had been appointed Chief Pilot with authority to recruit two others. He invited me to take one of the posts. I thought about it for about 3 seconds then accepted. The other position had been taken up by John Woodward, a very good-egg type stalwart from Aurigny, whom, of course, I knew.

We had already bought an oldish car for use in UK during our visit and Sylvia and I drove it down to Gibraltar. Accommodation in Gibraltar was limited and expensive, and we found that many people who worked there lived in Spain. So we looked there and found that plenty of places were available for rent at a reasonable price, but that in summer, the prices would go up astronomically. So to avoid being ripped off and to settle the matter, we bought a house. Then I decided that our car was really a banger, and not to be relied upon when I had a schedule to keep. So I bought a better car. So here we were, on vacation, with a job, a house and two cars!

The schedule had two services to Tangier in the morning and two in the afternoon, Monday to Friday with the week-end free. Pilot A would do the mornings for a week, pilot B the afternoons and pilot C was free for the week. The following week we would all move up one place. I have never had such an easy job, and we received regular airline captain pay.

There were no RAF squadrons based at Gibraltar any more, but I was based there, and I was ex RAF, so I was made an honorary member of the RAF mess, and we had many happy times there.

One of their nice customs was that on a ladies' guest night, gentlemen escorted in to dinner someone else's lady guest, and on one such occasion it was my pleasure to escort Mrs Hughes. She was the mother of the Roman Catholic Padre, John Hughes who were both very Welsh. She told me how proud she was of her son's achievements and how well he had done at Cranwell. Since my day, the flight cadet training scheme had been shut down, and now all officers, including dentists and padres and store bashers do a short course there to learn such things as which hand to salute with. She explained that he had been subjected to the most rigorous training for three whole weeks and had passed the course. I mentioned that I had been subjected to the most rigorous training there for nearly three years.

"Oh is it!" she replied, "You must have been rather slower than my John to catch on to the training, look you!"

On the side of the aircraft was the company logo 'GibAir'. Many years before, some prankster went out to the aircraft one night and painted the letters YO in front. Everyone thought this a good jape, and now it was company policy to paint it on.

Our destination, Tangier, had a nice runway and adequate navigation and landing aids, but one had to be careful of the controlling. I was approaching there one day, just below the cloud base when a B727 passed by just ahead of me. The tower had not mentioned any conflicting traffic. I called the tower and reported that I had just had a near miss with an aircraft at my position and height that presumably was on a different frequency. They replied that I should take care of my aircraft and they would take care of the traffic. It is not possible to reason with such people.

I had flown Vampires at Gibraltar many years before and knew that the winds could be 'interesting'. Now I was to do so in a light aircraft with passengers in the back. The wind is normally Easterly or Westerly, and the runway is aligned east/west, and the Rock is just south of the centre point. So if the wind is from the East, it hits the Rock and swirls round and over it causing turbulence on the Western side. The landing must be made into wind, that is, to the East, so it is necessary to go through this turbulence on the approach. The same applies in the other direction. Sometimes the turbulence is severe and the Trilander is not noted for its aileron control. If you needed aileron, you needed full aileron, and even then the wing was slow to recover. Rarely, the wind was from the South, and it would go over the Rock and tumble down the other side causing downdraughts and roughness and at the ends it would curl round and produce a tailwind which ever direction one landed.

The Spanish government resents the fact that Gibraltar is British and so causes as much irritation and annoyance as it can. Presumably they take the view that if they cause enough trouble, the Gibraltarians will develop friendly feelings toward them and so hand the place over to them. The reasoning escapes me. One of their ploys is to forbid any aircraft landing at Gibraltar to fly over Spanish territory. This means that the circuit when landing to the East must be tight in order to comply. This takes the aircraft right through the worst of the turbulence. Some days, if the turbulence was very severe, I would deliberately infringe the law and fly to the North over Spain to avoid it. I reasoned that if ever I were hauled before a Spanish Judge and asked why I had violated the law, I would simply explain that I did so for the safety of my aircraft, my passengers and people on the ground at the point of impact. I was convinced that no jury would convict me. But I was never called.

Another method I used to beat the turbulence was to land

downwind, so that I avoided the turbulence. Of course, this increases the landing run, but the runway was so much longer than was needed for the Trilander, that that was not a problem. One very windy and gusty day I landed with a 25 knot tailwind, perfectly safely. But this could be done only if there was no other traffic coming the other way.

There was no VOR, ILS or NDB at Gibraltar, but there was a non-precision radar approach. This was operated by first class RAF controllers, and worked very well.

I was sometimes asked if it was boring doing the same route all the time. It was not, because Gibraltar always had a surprise in store.

One day at Tangier there were scores of executive jets in the parking area, together with several privately owned airliners and two chartered Concords. It seemed that an extremely wealthy man who lived in Tangier (I think his name was Forbes?) was having a birthday party, and had invited the World's richest and most powerful people to it. We laid on extra flights to cope with the large number of newspaper people who were going. Next day I got chatting to the Daily Telegraph man (should I say alleged man?) and said that I thought it a bit odd that the major papers were taking such an interest in a mere party. He replied that all the most important people in the World were there, and if some extremist organisation blew the whole thing up, it would change the course of history, and it was the mass murder of the great and the good that he was there to cover.

"Disappointed it did not happen?" I asked.

He shrugged his shoulders and grinned.

Among the people about to board my aircraft one day was a teenaged English lad wearing only a pair of shorts.

"Have you got shirt and shoes in your rucksack?" I asked.

"What's it to you mate?"

"I would be pleased if you put them on, so that my other passengers do not have to endure your sweaty body."

"Nah! I ain't doing that."

Gibraltar Airways. L to R John Woodward, BM, James Budd.

"If you did, I would be so pleased that I would let you get on my aircraft."

"You can't stop me."

"Charlie", I said to one of the loaders, "Please go and get the airport police."

The wretch immediately put on his shirt and shoes. When I was his age, neither I nor any of my contemporaries would have been that uncouth or that impolite. But then in those days, discipline had not been abolished in British society. It is not everything that changes for the better.

We were at a party one evening, when I was approached by one of the other guests, a restaurateur, whom I knew slightly. He asked if it would be possible to charter the aircraft so that he could take his employees for an end of season treat to Tangier for the day, and go there and come back at times of his choosing.

I arranged for this on a Saturday, when we had no scheduled flights. Sylvia was invited too and they gave us a very nice lunch. We soon made friends with them all. Their own lunch was a very convivial affair with the drinks flowing freely. Several of them encouraged me to take a drink but of course I did not. Rules are for guidance of wise men and the absolute obedience of the others. I obey all rules in spirit, but have broken the letter of the rules many times. I would be prepared to 'bend' any rule, with one exception. I would never under any circumstances have a drink before flying, and would not, even if there were no rule against it.

Going home, there was severe turbulence again on the approach to Gibraltar, and my cabin address to my new found friends was one that I could not deliver on a scheduled flight.

"Ladies and gentlemen, there is severe turbulence on the approach to Gibraltar. So please make sure that your seat belts are tight. If you have brought sandwiches for the flight, the ground staff would be pleased if you put them straight into the sick bags. This will make their cleaning job easier and provide them with a free lunch. The turbulence will last some days, so if you plan to do this trip again tomorrow, please do not buy any sandwiches, but put the money straight into the sick bags."

They were all highly amused at my drollery. Their party

continued in Gibraltar, and they were kind enough to invite us to join them. This we did, and now I could take full advantage of their hospitality.

One day in Tangier the rear engine would not start no matter what I tried. I got the traffic people to take the pax off and put them in the air conditioned waiting room while I tried to solve the problem.

First I requested the duty engineer of RAM (Royal Air Maroc) to come and have a look. He came and looked but admitted that he knew nothing about piston engines.

Then I managed to get through on the telephone to Tom Baines, our ground engineer in Gibraltar. He suggested that I try to turn the propeller to see if the starter was jammed, (a similar problem can occur in a motor-car). I got a trestle from the RAM man and climbed up it to the engine. I was able to turn the engine and there was no sign of a jammed starter. So the engine was good, but there was a problem with the starter itself.

With no pax or freight on board, the aircraft was very light and the Tangier runway is very long. So I taxied out and took off on the two wing engines, and when I had sufficient speed for the tail engine to windmill, I set the controls for fuel and ignition and the engine started at once. I soon had normal rpm and oil pressure and the engine and oil temperatures were increasing normally, thus confirming that the engine was running normally. I landed on three engines and taxied back to the ramp where I shut down the two wing engines but kept the tail one running. I then boarded the pax. – it was perfectly safe to do so because the rear engine is too high for it to be a hazard.

Then I flew back to Gibraltar. An expensive delay was avoided, the schedule was not disrupted, and Tom was now able to find the fault and rectify it, which he did with his customary skill and speed.

It was, I think, the only time that I was glad to be in a Trilander rather than a SVC10.

I used to point out to the pax the landmarks between Gibraltar and Tangier, and on one occasion when the weather was very clear, I finished my spiel by saying that to the North, it was just possible to see the place where the Battle of Trafalgar had been fought.

After landing, two of the passengers were waiting to talk to me as I got out of the aircraft.

"'Ere, mate", one of the young yobs asked, "Oo was we fighting at that battle?"

"It was a combined French and Spanish fleet."

He turned to the other yob: "See, I told ya."

Turning back to me, he went on: "'E sez we only fights Germans."

The other added: "Yeah, I fawt we only fawt the Germans."

"Not always", I assured him.

I do not know how much money was spent on their education, but it seemed to me that it had not been enough.

Our manager in Tangier was a friendly and highly competent Moroccan called YXXX.

Our friends, the Pittmans from Florida, were staying with us and they and Sylvia wanted to visit Tangier and we thought it would be nice if I arranged to fly them there and back on one of my duty trips. A few days before the proposed trip I asked YXXX what the loads were like and what were the chances of staff passengers getting on. (Fare-paying passengers always go first, and staff pax take the remaining empty seats, if any.)

"Don't worry", he replied, "They will get on."

The day before the trip I asked again and got the same answer.

On the day, there was no problem getting seats to Tangier on the early morning flight, but there seemed to be lots of people at the desks waiting to check in for the evening return journey. But Sylvia and Jack and Doris already had their boarding passes. I did not press the point, but got them all on board and started up.

Next day at Tangier I remarked to YXXX that we had been very lucky the day before to have three available seats. YXXX grinned awkwardly.

I said that it had seemed to me that there were so many fare-payers that our friends had no chance of getting on.

YXXX grinned again: "As a matter of fact, there were too many revenue pax, so I had to tell them that the plane was full."

"But YXXX, you know that revenue pax have priority."

"Yes I do know that of course, but the non-revs were friends of yours and the rev. ones were only Moroccans!"

So though it was to our benefit, he had been very much out of line. But I could not criticise him too harshly!

About two weeks later he was out of line even more. It was the captain's job to decide how the aircraft was to be loaded to keep the centre of gravity within limits, which was critical on the Trilander. We used the circular slide rule that had been devised by Aurigny Airline. I did all this one day in Tangier and took off. The aeroplane felt very sluggish and had about the same performance as a Trilander on two engines. I suspected that we were over weight, and so when we landed in Gibraltar, I got our baggage team to weigh all the freight. We were several hundred pounds overweight, and had I lost an engine, we would have ended up in the sea. When I got back to Tangier, I had strong words with YXXX and told him that if ever did that again I would report it to the management.

The aircraft was loaded and I took off. As soon as I left the ground, the nose reared up and it took all my strength to push it down to the correct attitude. Then I got my knee behind the stick, and though that was painful, it kept the aircraft under control. I considered going back into Tangier, but the landing was going to be an exciting affair and I decided to do it at Gibraltar where there was a highly efficient RAF Crash and Rescue team commanded by Brian Higgins who subsequently became a good neighbour of ours.

I kept the rear engine, which produced a nose down trim at 'red-line' and reduced power on the wing engines as much as I could, but that was not much because as well as being out of C of G limits, we were way over weight again as well. And when the speed reduced, the effectiveness of the elevators also reduced and the nose came up again. It was clear that I would have to approach at high power and high speed. Fortunately the one thing in my favour was that the runway was amply long enough.

I told the pax to tighten their straps because of the turbulence on the approach. There really was turbulence on the approach, which did not make my job any easier. I declared an emergency, and the RAF lads were all at their stations and ready to go.

I came in fast, still with my knee behind the stick, and pushing forward as hard as I could. The nose wheel touched down first, followed by the main wheels. I could then progressively reduce the power. We came to a halt, and once again, I had been very lucky.

When we checked the loading, we found that not only was I way over maximum permitted weight, but the heavy freight, which should have been in the nose compartment, had been put in the tail compartment, putting the aircraft way out of centre of gravity limits.

The company operations manager refused to take any action against YXXX because he was a protégé of the company chairman. So I went in to see him, and explained that YXXX should be fired.

"That is rather a harsh step to take, wouldn't you think?"

"Not at all. Not only did he nearly kill us all, he nearly killed me twice in one day!"

"But you are still here."

"By the skin of my teeth."

"YXXX has been with us for many years, and I will not let him go."

There was nothing I could do about that. But I took a much greater interest in the loading of the aircraft in Tangier!

I went in one Monday morning expecting to do my usual trip to Tangier. I was told that we were now operating to Tetuan, and that I was to do the inaugural run. I carried no pax or freight either way. We did the service for a week, and carried not a single passenger or a pound of freight. The company withdrew the service on the Friday. The next Monday, a GibAir publicity campaign hit the media, advertising the new service to Tetuan. Lots of people went to the ticket offices and airport to buy tickets, but alas no flights were available! It must have been something to do with the big picture, which office wallahs claim that mere pilots cannot understand.

My work-load increased one month, when John Woodward had to go for major surgery, and James Budd had to take time off because his wife Carol had died. I started doing three flights per day, but could not do all four, because the duty day would have exceeded legal flight time limitations. I suggested to the traffic manager in head office that if we reduced the time of the mid day break, I would be able to do them all. I was told that mere pilots do not understand the big picture and that when my advice was required it would be asked for.

Meanwhile the back-log of passengers and freight continued to build up, and the airport staff had an increasingly difficult job. I solved the problem for the GibAir airport manager, by cancelling the last scheduled flight, because of duty time limitations, and laying on an 'extra' flight at lunchtime, to clear the back-log. This meant delaying the third scheduled flight slightly. In effect, we had reduced the time of the mid day break. End of problem! Not only do airlines have the problems of weather, technical malfunctions, air traffic strikes and so on, they also have the difficulty of coping with managers.

I checked in for my flight one day, and Roberto, the shift manager, said that there was a Moroccan at the front desk who wanted to see me. I went out and the man told me that his wife in Tangier had had her handbag stolen and had no money and she was at the airport with Yusef, our man in Tangier.

"Would you take this money over and give it to her?"

I said that we could not leave a lady in distress, and agreed to take it. He produced an envelope stuffed with notes.

"Don't you think we ought to count it, so that I can give you a receipt?"

"Oh no sir! You are an English gentleman, there's no need for that!"

It was good to hear that the English are still held in good standing there.

Someone in the CAA considered that when I reached 60, I was no longer competent to fly passengers. I never met the man, so cannot explain why he took that view. So I had to stop. The last time I did a medical in England, the doc asked me what I thought of the compulsory retirement age. I told him that it was outrageous. He was hurt at that because he had been on the panel that approved its retention. He said that there had to be a limit. I asked why. He said that without a limit, it would be necessary to examine each pilot individually. I thumped my fist on his desk: "And what do you think we are doing right now?"

The American captain who landed in the Hudson River, and the one who landed a Lockheed 1011 with virtually no controls available were both close to retirement age. The CAA seems to think that pilots' brains atrophy on a date that the CAA has plucked from the air.

The day came. I taxied in from my last flight, and was met by the RAF station commander and a large crowd of friends. The Station Commander took me off in a wheel chair to his car and we went to the mess to celebrate. After a few beers, I had to go back to the airport because I had laid on a barrel of beer for the loaders and cleaners, and another for the air-traffickers. Then back to the mess. They had taken my car keys, and had booked me a room, and we had a most memorable party.

A new chapter in our lives then began.

CHAPTER 10

ULTRA LIGHT PILOT

While I was With East African Airways the craze of hang gliding was introduced .The hang glider consisted of a very light frame of wings, made of wood and canvas and the user held it up on his shoulders, ran down a slope until he had enough speed to take off. Moving his legs backwards or forwards or sideways gave him a semblance of control.

A dealer set up shop in Nairobi to sell these things. He would let anyone fly them in the hope of making a sale.

I had my first go after a briefing from the dealer. I didn't go very far but greatly enjoyed it. I did several more trips after that and was becoming more familiar with the process until one day I made a mistake in a turn which resulted in my landing downwind. This caused me to land faster than I could run and I ended up covered in cuts and bruises. I rather lost interest in hang gliders after that!

Then came the ultra light (in the USA, micro light in the UK). This had a small lightweight engine and a basic undercarriage. This was more up my street and I looked forward to a trip in one.

While I was building the house, I had noticed a seaplane taking off and landing on the lake several times and it seemed to be based at a house on the far side of the lake. One day we watched it land and taxi in and we drove round the lake and located the house and went in and introduced ourselves. We met Jack Pittman and his wife Doris, who are still good friends of ours. Jack was a most experienced aviator, who, after flying B25s in the Air Force had spent many years flying for Panagra, the South American Airline. His aircraft was a single seat Buccaneer – the ultra light one, not to be confused with the regular aeroplane of that name. When we got to know each other, he was kind enough to let me fly it, and I did so many times.

So, my introduction to ultra lights was on the water version first. Jack decided to become a dealer and bought a two seat Buccaneer. This was an amphibian, my first, so I got Jon Brown to give me a thorough briefing on that type.

Jack had no experience of instructing so he asked me to give his buyers tuition.

One of them was a delightful Italian American called Bob X, He was badly coordinated and perhaps the worse student I ever had,but we persevered and after much more time than is usual he went solo first on wheels then on water, He is the only student that I took from ab initio to solo on sea and land. We became good friends.

I joined the local ultralight club, and the national association, and got to fly many UL types, some of which were of the most unusual designs, The association sent me a membership card which said that my status was member/instructor/examiner. The FAA did not require training or testing for ULs so my titles involved no duties!

The house was coming along nicely, and I decided that I could spare a little more time off for more flying, so I decided to get an ultra light seaplane. The first one I looked at seemed just the thing. I looked it over and then the owner and I strapped in for a flight. The take-off was satisfactory, and so was the climb to about 500 feet, but then it suffered the fate of many ultra lights of that vintage. It was necessary to keep full power on to avoid descending, and the engine got hotter and hotter. As it rose above optimum temperature, it started to lose power, and that slowed it down and that reduced the air cooling, and that increased the temperature even more. Soon, with full power, we were descending and there was not much we could do about it. If it were mine, I would have closed the throttle, lowered the nose and glided back to the water. But I was a guest. The owner landed at full throttle rather heavily, causing several fuselage and wing struts to break. The engine stopped and would not restart, and we had to be towed in. I decided not to buy it.

The next one I looked at was a two place Challenger – the ultra light one, not to be confused with the regular aircraft of that name. We drove to the house where it was for sale, and found the aircraft in the front garden. It looked just the thing, and when I asked the seller if we could fly it, I was surprised that we got in, started the engine, taxied out of the front gate, down the public road, through the gate of a local airstrip, on to the runway and took off. Only in America! I liked it, bought it, and flew it back to the Lake Placid airport. On wheels, it flew quite well with two people on board, but flown solo, its performance was as good as a regular aircraft. I sent off for a pair of amphibious floats, and my friend Charlie Sheldon, who was a pilot and aircraft engineer, helped me fit them on. (It would be more accurate to say that I helped him!). On water it flew fairly well solo, but was rather sluggish with two people. I could then keep it on our beach at the bottom of the garden, fly off the lake, and land anywhere on water or land. It was great fun.

I flew to an airstrip one day for a coffee and a chat, and as I taxied out to come home, the nose wheel leg collapsed, leaving me supported by the two main wheels and the front of the floats. It looked like a big job to fix it, and I thought it would be better to get it home. I reasoned that if I flew it from the rear seat, the centre of gravity would move aft, and I would be able to raise the nose after a very short run on the grass, which should not damage the floats. (There were no fare-paying passengers on board!). I went quite a way, but the nose just would not come up, so I abandoned the take off. I did not succeed in taking off, but I did succeed in wearing long narrow holes on the bottom of the floats, which were made of fibre-glass. I got a friendly chap with a powered lawn mower to tow the aircraft to a ramp on a nearby lake, put the aircraft on the ramp just clear of the water, started the engine, and at full power, got a few friendly locals to push me into the water. I took off straight ahead, and was off the water before the floats had time to fill up and sink us. In flight, the water in them drained out. Back home, I landed pointing to our beach and at the end of the landing run, I ran up onto the sand, again before the floats had time to fill up. An interesting trip! Charlie and I mended the floats in a couple of hours.

On another occasion, I was flying in our local area when I heard a strange noise from the engine, which I could not identify. It is a good rule in that situation not to touch the throttle because that might make it worse. I went back to my home lake (Lake Huntley) and did not reduce the power until I was just above the water before landing. That made the noise even more peculiar. When I was safely on my beach, I closed the throttle and switched the engine off, at which point the whole propeller assembly fell off. It was a 'pusher' prop, and it was only the 'push' that had kept it on. If I had reduced power in flight, it would have come off then, and severely damaged the tail or even chopped it off. It is a good rule to observe good rules!

In the English Summer we took a trip to UK to visit family and friends and I got a full time job flying Learjets as is described in the last chapter. After a pleasant summer it was time to retreat to the sun in Florida.

I had taken the wings off the Challenger and stored it all in the garage. Charlie and I soon had it out and reassembled and airborne.

One morning, I had been flying solo, and the aircraft was on the beach, covers off, engine warm, and all ready to go. While I was having a coffee, a Piper Cub in army colours flew low overhead and did some steep low level turns. It was obvious that he wanted me to chase him and perhaps have a dog fight. I was off the water at once, and it did not take me long to close up to him and get in close echelon formation. I expected a cheery wave and grin and perhaps his pulling away sharply as a challenge to me to me to try to stay with him. Instead, he gave me signals waving me away. Perhaps I was too close for his comfort, so I moved out to a distance of about two wing spans. Even a new boy ought not to be scared by that. But still he waved me off. Somewhat puzzled, I broke away, landed and went back to my beach. As I stepped out, a police car drove over our lawn to the beach.

"You the guy flying next to the Cub?"

"Well, yes. You see…"

"Sir, I must ask you not to do that, you are interfering in a police operation."

"But it's in warbird colours. Surely it's a private owner?"

"It's a police plane, sir, and I have to ask you not to take off until we have finished our mission."

"What is the mission?"

"We're on a man hunt, Sir."

I was reminded of my man hunt at Oakington some years earlier, and hoped that they would have more success then I did. They did – they took a man away in handcuffs about twenty minutes later.

Shortly after that, Jack and I went to a fly-in and there was the aircraft. The pilot was a very nice policeman, and he explained that the police department used its entire annual aviation budget to buy the plane, and in the next financial year planned a paint job. He said that he would have loved to 'tangle with me' that day, but duty is duty. As indeed it is.

I checked out a couple of Jack's customers, coached a few students at the Seaplane Base (more about that in the next chapter), went to a couple of fly-ins with Jack, and had trips in Bill Hutchins' aircraft. And so we passed a pleasant Florida winter.

The following summer we went back to the UK again and I worked for Aurigny, the Channel Islands airline,as is described in the last chapter. It was all most enjoyable but we were glad to get back home again.

Winter in Florida was as agreeable as ever. My Challenger was running nicely, I checked out one of Jack Pittman's customers in the Buccaneer and did some instructing at Jack Brown's.

Jack and I flew our aircraft in formation to an ultra light gathering and when we returned we found a thunderstorm sitting right on Lake Huntley, so we diverted to Placid Lakes airstrip to wait for better weather. On the ground there it was very windy and gusty so we were under our wings holding on to the struts to prevent the aircraft being blown over. There was a terrific sound of thunder and a bright flash of lightning struck a tree a few hundred yards away and set it afire. As it struck, I felt a distinct tingle from my hands, holding the metal strut, to my feet that were grounded. This surprised me, but when I thought about it, I realised that the charge must need some distance to drop from a zillion volts to zero volts.

Jack and I planned to go to the fly-in at Clermont, and take part in the competitions. One of these involved a pilot dropping a tennis ball from his aircraft and his partner on the ground catching it. We practiced this on the local strip with an elementary bomb sight that I had rigged up, and we found that with practice, Jack could catch it every time without moving his feet. We won! On the way home, my engine kept losing power. It did not stop completely, but it did make it impossible to hold my height. I would then set up for a forced landing, only to find that on finals the engine would go to full power again. This happened at least six times, so I had six adrenalin rushes in one trip. The last time it happened I set up to land at Lake Wales airfield, and this time it did not pick up again. There is an ultra light facility there and I parked just by it. They quickly found the trouble and fixed it, and I got home safely.

The next year we decided to sell our house in Florida and make the UK our home. So our Challenger had to go and with some sadness I flew it to its new home on a nearby lake. Soon after that, ULs went out of fashion because they were replaced by the light sport aircraft. They are not seen flying any more and I am glad I flew them when they were extant.

Chapter 11

SEAPLANE PILOT

When I was with Saudia, we went on one vacation to Jack Brown's Seaplane Base at Winter Haven in Florida, so that I could do the seaplane course, a thing that I had long wanted to do. It operated Piper Cubs, the original J3s, on straight floats (that is, not amphibians). My friendly and very able instructor was John Rennie, a young Englishman. I enjoyed flying with him and very quickly took to seaplane flying too. It soon became clear that Jack Brown's was a very special place. It combined friendliness and informality with very high standards, and was almost as much a social centre as a flying school. Everyone and anyone was welcome to drop in for visit and enjoy a coffee and a chat. Jon Brown (Jack's son) and his wife Frances make everyone feel at home and just being at the place is as much a pleasure as flying the seaplanes.

I liked it so much that on our next vacation I persuaded Sylvia that we should go back again so that I could do some more seaplane flying. So we met up with the Browns and John Rennie again. We had not been back in Saudi long before we had a phone call from John, announcing that he was now working in Jeddah and lived not far from us. He visited us often, as our place was the only one that he knew in that dry country where he could get a drink. During one of our chats, I told him about our plans to build our own house in Florida, and he suggested that I might be able to do some instructing for Jon.

We started our building project, and Jon's place was just over an hour's drive away, and as a break from building, I went there two or three times a month. I asked about the possibilities of doing some instructing, and Jon said that he could use me if I got the necessary qualifications. FAA rules are that to hold an instructor rating, it is necessary to hold the appropriate commercial licence, and since I was to instruct on single engine aircraft I had to have a single engine commercial. My only American licence was a multi engine ALTP, so I had to back track, so to speak, and take the written and flying tests to get the commercial. Then, with some coaching from Jon's friend Dennis Kochan, I took the written and flying tests to get my American instructor's rating. Dennis is a building contractor with a great interest in anything to do with aviation, and is a highly competent pilot. I tried a few times to get some advice from him on building problems I had encountered, but he quickly brought the subject back to flying. Once licensed, I did several more hours to get thoroughly familiar with seaplane operations, then Jon welcomed me as a part time CFI. (In British parlance, CFI is Chief Flying Instructor, in American it is Certified Flying Instructor.)

The students already have pilot licenses, and come to the Base to qualify for the seaplane rating. They learn the idle taxi, with the floats acting as boats, the step taxi, with the floats acting as water skis, and the plough turn to turn against the wind. Then they learn normal take off and landing, glassy water take off and landing and rough water operation. They also are taught engine failure procedure and sailing and docking. It takes about five hours flying to complete the syllabus.

I was too busy with the house to go to Brown's very often, but I taught a student for his rating perhaps once per month.

After several hours in the Piper Cub, I began to feel really at home on floats, and under the friendly and expert guidance of John Curtis, I qualified for my multi engine sea rating in Jon's Twin Seabee.

Jon is very careful who he takes on as an instructor, and his care pays off because they are always very competent and dedicated and just right for the job. It was easier for me because I was only a part timer, and Jon has many British students, and likes to have a Brit about the place.

The appointment carries with it a great deal of prestige. I did not realize how much until the next annual seaplane 'splash in', which used to be organised by the Base. The competitions were about to start, but there was no aircraft available for me, so it

Taking Pat Constable for a trip in Jack Pittman's Buccaneer.

looked as if I could not compete. Frances thought this a shame, and introduced me to their friend Mike Fuller who owned an extremely nice Super Cub.

"He hasn't got an aircraft for the competitions", Frances explained.

"Too bad", Mike replied.

"And we do like our instructors to take part."

"You instruct at Jack Brown's?" Mike asked me.

"Well, yes, I do." I did not mention that I was only a part timer with an English advantage.

Mike, whom I had never met before, handed me the keys of his aircraft. "Here, take mine. And Good Luck!" He did not even come to the aircraft with me to make sure that I knew what I was doing.

His Super Cub was a joy to fly, and enabled me to win a couple of prizes.

A few years later, I had as a student Jon Marsh who is an FBI investigator. He is a very capable pilot and a very nice man, and when he got his seaplane rating on the Cub, he asked me to check him out in a Cessna 172 on amphibious floats that belonged to a friend of his. I said I would like to, but his friend did not know me and I would like to get his permission at first hand.

We went to the Oyster Bar (a road house popular in the seaplane community) that evening, and there, quite by chance, was Ned. When we had been introduced, I asked if it was true that I could fly his amphib.

"Of course!"

"But we've never flown together, and you don't even know me."

"You instruct at Jack Brown's don't you, and that's good enough for me!"

Jon owned an American Eagle, a 1928 aircraft with a Kinner engine. It was the only flying one in existence, and worth a great deal of money. Jon said that he would let me fly it 'one day'.

I was working on the house when Jon called me and asked if I could take a student early in the morning. I could. It meant getting up very early to get there in time.

Next morning, as I drove in to the Base, Jon was waiting for me.

Taxiing my Challenger on to our beach in Florida.

"I know you got up early to come all this way, but now the student has cancelled. I don't know what to say."

"I know what you could say."

"What's that?"

"You could say: 'Let's go and fly the Eagle'."

"Let's go and fly the Eagle!"

I flew it for a time and got familiar with it, then Jon said: "Try a landing."

I set up my approach, and asked Jon: "What's a good speed over the hedge?"

"Oh, I don't know. Fly it at a speed that feels right." (Now that's a real aviator talking!)

So I flew at a speed that felt right and pulled off a passable landing.

Jon then said that he had things to do in the office, and if I wanted to fly it anymore, I would have to do so by myself. I flew it solo for about an hour and really enjoyed it. A memorable trip.

Jon also had a very nice Cessna 182 on wheels which we could use whenever we liked. We did many good trips in it sometimes just us and sometimes with another couple We used to fly down the Keys as far as Key West and other nice spots as far away as Georgia.

After leaving Gibraltar Airways, we went back to Florida for the winter.

We thought about our situation long and hard. Because of the biased, outrageous, prejudiced, unreasonable, unjustifiable and ageist attitude of the CAA, I was not going to get another serious flying job. (A few years later they raised the retirement age from 60 to 65, but that was too late for me).

I could continue to fly my Challenger or any aircraft in a private capacity, and I could still instruct. The most satisfying and serious instructing available to me was at Jack Brown's, but that was 1 ½ hours drive each way, and I did not want to do that too often. We had greatly enjoyed the house-building project, but now that it was complete, there were no great attractions in Lake Placid to keep us there.

We had been overseas all our working lives and we thought it was time to try living in UK. We had some reservations about that – the climate was still awful, discipline had long since been abolished in schools, so that many modern Brits were uncouth in comparison with the previous generation, and criminals were no longer effectively punished, so that there was a good deal of crime. There was no effective control over immigration, and so there were large pockets of alien culture and no attempt was made to assimilate them. And even quite a few of the well-mannered and non-criminal people seemed to be left wing, politically correct types, who opined that Britain should be governed by unelected, corrupt foreigners. Even so, we thought, surely there are enough dinosaurs like us to make us feel at home.

So we decided to sell the Florida house, sell the Spanish house, and move to England. But we must give it a fair try, so we would get a nice house in a nice area and get ourselves an aeroplane, and we would go to Jack Brown's once or twice a year, stay in a motel in the vicinity, and do my serious flying there.

We made a good sale of the Spanish place and a very good sale of the Florida one. After a great deal of house hunting we found a place in the West Country at Chard. It was a 4 bed /3 bath /study /double garage /conservatory type of place in a good vicinity and on the other side of the road was a nice open parkland, which, we were told, would never be built on.

Only a few miles away was nice farmer called Brian Anning, and he had a grass airfield, and for a modest rent, it was possible to keep an aircraft in one of his hangars. He put me on to a chap who had an Aeronca Champ for sale. We went to see it and it looked most attractive in a new all yellow paint job. I flew it, liked it, bought it, and flew it to Anning's place.

Brian, among his other farming activities, kept sheep, and he used them to keep the grass cut on the runways, so sometimes we would come back to base and find the runways covered in sheep. I would then fly down the runway at low level, revving the engine and shouting through the open window: "Mint sauce, mint sauce!" This always cleared the runway, but I never found out if this was because the sheep were fleeing the implied culinary arrangements, or because they were frightened by the engine noise.

I slightly preferred the Champ to the Cub. It was roomier, the view out was better, and it was easier to get in and out. In the Cub, if one is sloppy with the rudder, the aircraft still flies reasonably well. But in the Champ, one must operate the rudders correctly all the time or it is all over the sky, so flying it right is a more satisfying feeling. The only snag was that the control cables ran down the fuselage beside the seats, so it was important not to interfere with them with maps or bags. Sylvia liked it too and we had many happy trips in it.

All this took much more time than it takes to tell, and suddenly it was spring. That is a good time for me to go to the seaplane base for two reasons. Sun 'n Fun, the second biggest flying event in the USA takes place then at Lakeland, a few miles from Winterhaven, the location of the SPB. Tens of thousands of aviation enthusiasts attend it, and it takes only a small percentage of them to decide on some seaplane flying for Jon to be inundated with customers. And most years one or two of Jon's regular instructors leave and go to Alaska where the seaplane season is just opening. So the base can always use some extra help at that time.

We made our way to Winter Haven, got a room in a motel, walking distance from the base, and I started some serious teaching. Jon and Frances made us most welcome, and the regular instructors, most of whom were young chaps just coming into aviation, were friendly and helpful. This was something that I could get my teeth into and far superior to going once or twice a month from Lake Placid. I greatly enjoyed it. Working with the youngsters kept me feeling young and I hope I did not make them feel old! We got along very well with two Daves, two Adams, James, Richey, Tristan, Lee, Nick, and many more, and I, at least, did not notice the age or the nationality difference. A month is about as much as we could stand in a motel, so after that time we headed back to England and the Champ. We followed that routine for several years, and were very pleased with the new arrangement.

We flew the Champ to many fly-ins in a variety of places, and we took trips to the Scilly Isles, refuelling at Land's End, and across

Me with Sylvia in the back seat of our Champ, coasting in over Bournemouth, having crossed the Channel.

the Channel several times. The first time was over the shortest crossing, refuelling at Headcorn. Then we became a little more adventurous and went Isle of Wight to Cherbourg. My radio transmission packed up going there, but I could still receive, so I fitted in with the other traffic and landed without any confliction. When I climbed out of the aeroplane, I noticed that the controller in the tower was looking down at me, so I pointed to my mouth and gave a 'thumbs down' and then pointed at my ears and gave a 'thumbs up'. He held his hands out palms upwards and shrugged his shoulders. I expect that is how they won the war.

Going back home over the Channel it was impossible to avoid a rainstorm, and when we landed at Shoreham the leading edges of my propeller looked like firewood. But it got us home, and after a few days of building it up with resin and glass cloth and balancing, it was as good as new. (well, almost!)

One interesting trip was to the Isle of Man.

We wore life jackets for these over water trips, and I would not cross the coastline until we had good radio communication with the appropriate ground station, but I still sometimes ponder the wisdom of crossing water in an old aeroplane with an old engine.

We also went to the Channel Islands a couple of times and I enjoyed retracing the routes I had flown in my happy days with Aurigny.

The longest trip we made was to Oerlinghausen, a small field just north of Gutersloh in Germany, and we had the pleasure of meeting up with some German friends and giving them rides.

I read in one of the flying magazines an article on Lundy Island, in the Bristol Channel. Years before there had been an airstrip there, and there was an aerial photo of the terrain with the old runway marked out. I telephoned the chap who runs the small hotel there and he said that he thought it would be possible to land there. We flew across the straights and I flew down the old runway several times to look at the surface. It appeared usable (just!) and we landed safely. After a pleasant stay in the nice little hotel, I walked the runway and noted rocks and rabbit holes, and made a safe take-off. An interesting trip.

One of the fly-ins we went to was at Popham, and after parking in the line of visiting aircraft, I climbed out of the aircraft. As I did so, a young yob said in a loud voice so that I could hear: "These daft old fools don't know when to give it up. They should be in their rocking chairs."

Just then one of the organisers came up and asked me if I would mind moving my aircraft over there as he wanted to start another line. So I asked the yob if he would swing my prop for me.

"I don't know ah to do it, mate."

"I can quickly show you."

"Is it dangerous?"

"If you do it wrong it will kill you!"

"Nah mate. I ain't goin' near that."

"Okay. I can easily find a daft old fool to swing it for me."

And I did.

Air shows should have special enclosures for yobs to keep them away from the civilised folk.

We flew into Blackbush to visit James and Denise Budd. When we taxied out to go home I found that my right brake had failed. This made control on the ground difficult because the propeller forces tend to turn the aircraft to the left, and to steer with power and rudder would result in a high taxi speed, which is undesirable, particularly with faulty brakes. With the agreement of the tower people, I went down the taxi-way in a series of arcs. When I reached the left edge of the taxi-way, I would go on to the grass and do a sharp left turn right round and back on to the runway and start another long arc. It was rather like gybing a sailboat. At the end of the taxi way I was cleared to enter the runway and hold. I told them that I did not have enough control to do that and asked if they could clear me for take-off from my present position.

They were most cooperative, and did. So using lots of power and rudder I horsed it round on to the runway, and kept going and soon I had sufficient speed to have full control over events.

Taxiing behind me was a shiny new Cessna 402, and up till then the pilot had shown commendable patience at being slowed down by my antics. But now he ran out of it. The weather was not good, and I soon disappeared in the mist. Then I heard the shiny new Cessna 402 on the radio: "I have lost visual contact with that yellow thing, what is his position?"

I replied: "The yellow thing is on the runway centre line, just crossing the airport boundary at 300 feet." Then I added: "And I can fly your aircraft, Charlie, but I bet you couldn't handle this!"

We flew into the Popular Flying Association annual gathering and looking around the ground exhibits, we came across a booth displaying a seaplane school in Florida. And so we met Peter Scott and his wife Louise. Pete owned a farm in Yorkshire, and ran a Cessna 310 charter business. He also had a helicopter for charter and TV news cameras. They had a place at an air park called Eagles' Nest, about 100 miles north of Winter Haven, where they spent the winter months running a one man one aircraft seaplane school with a PA11 Cub Special. Their school was unusual in that they had one or two students at a time, and gave them B and B accommodation in their own house. We arranged that we would visit them there during our next trip over.

Some weeks later, Peter telephoned and told me that he was having great difficulty with his American visa, and at the moment was not allowed to enter the USA till it was sorted out. This would take some time. He already had some bookings for his school and did not want to let his clients down, so would we consider running the place for him?

I called Jon Brown to ask him if he had any objections. My first loyalty was to him and Peter was a competitor. Jon had no objection and it sounded like an interesting idea so we agreed to do it. The other residents at Eagles' Nest were very nice and made us most welcome.

At Brown's we recover the seaplane by parking it with the front of floats on the ramp, and then towing it up the ramp with a tractor, and putting a dolly under it, and hand pulling it into the hangar. Peter had devised a method whereby a trailer, hitched to a jeep, was backed down the ramp and into the water. The seaplane was taxied on to the trailer and secured with straps, and then the jeep, trailer, aircraft and all, were driven up the ramp and in to the hangar. It took a bit of practice to put the seaplane exactly where it had to go on the trailer, and that added to the fun.

I flew with one student to an old sugar mill in a National Park, where it was possible to land and park a seaplane and have a coffee or lunch. There were water-weeds just in front of the beach where we wanted to park, and when we shut the engine down just before beaching, they compressed and then expanded and pushed us back out into the stream. So I restarted the engine, got out onto the float with a rope in my hand and got the student to taxi to the beach as before. I waited for the propeller to stop and then threw the rope over a post to secure us. As I did so, the propeller kicked back and sliced the top of my left hand. But we were secure and we both got ashore and went to the Park Ranger's place. The Ranger had some training in first-aid and as the nearest doctor was miles away, I got him to bind up the wound, which was bleeding profusely. We then flew back to Eagles' Nest, and I went to the doctor in Crescent City. He looked at the hand and asked: "Do you gamble?"

"No, I don't."

"You should. You are a very lucky man. You could easily have lost your hand!"

He did a wonderful job of patching me up, with about twenty internal stitches that eventually dissolved, and about the same number of surface ones, which later had to be removed. He was very concerned about my finger tendons, but managed to avoid any damage to them. The job was finished with a large thick bandage.

I could not use the hand for nearly a week, but I was surprised by what I could do without it. I could do the seaplane launching and recovery and engine starting. I could fly by using my right hand on the throttle whilst holding the stick between my knees. The most difficult job was refuelling the high wing aircraft, but the students were happy to do that for me.

The hand recovered completely, but I still do have a scar on it. I am rather proud of that, and regard it much as, I suppose, a Prussian Officer would have regarded a duelling scar.

We became good friends with one student, TXX, and his wife PXX. Though he held only a PPL, he was a CAA examiner, and was authorised to do check rides on other private pilot licence holders. He showed considerable zeal concerning rules and regulations, and before our first trip he asked about the local restricted, prohibited and danger areas. As usual, I told him that I would take care of all that as he would have enough on his plate coping with the new type of flying. But he insisted, so I showed him the areas on the map. He remarked that we would have to be careful not to infringe a particular one. I repeated that he could leave all that to me, but he still seemed concerned. I feared that his CAA examiner attitude had become ingrained, and devised a wheeze to pry him free of it.

One of the exercises that seaplane students have to master is glassy water landings. It is impossible to judge height above glassy water, so the normal landing flare cannot be done. Instead, a very slow rate of descent is set up before crossing the shore line, and is maintained without reference to the water until the aircraft touches down. I demonstrated one on the St Johns River, and invited him to try one himself.

"But I can't do it here. There are cables across the river ahead."

"Can you quote a rule that says you cannot do a glassy water landing practice if there are cables ahead?"

"Well, no."

"Carry on, then."

He flew a good pattern and set up a very good descent, and as we slowly lost height, the cables got nearer and nearer. Just before we touched down, I gave him another problem.

"We are simulating that a power boat race has just set off and the runway is blocked. Go around."

"I cannot go around – we are too close to the cables."

"The runway is blocked. You have no choice."

"Okay (reluctantly). But I don't think we can clear the cables."

"Then you will have to go under them!"

After passing them, he said: "I've never flown under cables before."

"Welcome to the club."

"Can we do it again, but without the rigmarole of the glassy water landing?"

"Now you're talking."

As I said, we became good chums.

Two of our students were John Ashby and his wife Anne. We had met before when they visited Jack Brown's, and we became good pals. John was a flight engineer by profession and was with Cathay Pacific, and knew many of my old EAA colleagues who had gone there. He was also a highly competent private pilot and greatly enjoyed his piloting. Anne is also a very good pilot and in fact is a QFI.

I enjoyed several trips with them, both on floats and on wheels.

I quite enjoyed running the show and having my own seaplane and school. We got on extremely well with some of the students/lodgers and made some long lasting friends. Then there were the others.

I might well, if the opportunity arose, run another seaplane school, but we will never, ever, run another B and B place.

We did not really settle in England. Now that we were getting older the climate seemed even worse. And though murderers, rapists, republicans, left wing people, perverts, illegal immigrants, expense-fiddling MP's, cabinet ministers, anti-monarchists, over-charging lawyers, supporters of the EU, and bonus grabbing bankers were walking the streets free as the wind, if all a civilised, law-abiding citizen wants to do is go home after a nice dinner out, the police are on to him like a ton of bricks. And the only difference between drunken sailors and the government, was that drunken sailors waste their own money, and the government wastes ours. So taxes were high and that led to everything else being too expensive. We had given it a fair try, but decided to move back to Spain, which we did.

When we went back to Winter Haven the following year, Jon had located a pair of apartments for short-term rent, and we moved into one of them. It was far from luxurious, but a jolly sight better than the motel. We stayed longer, and the next year even longer. The year after that, when I called the owner to make the booking, he told me that it would not be available when we wanted it. That settled it; we decided to buy a place near the Base. We located a trailer, or caravan, or in American parlance, a mobile home, on a lake-front nearby. It was nearly as big as our home house and very comfortable, with all possible amenities. We bought it and moved in and made friends with the neighbours. We made another home there with personal touches like several of Sylvia's paintings, and some of my books and music. Now we go for about four months at a time, and I can really get down to some serious flying. We should have done that years ago!

That year was the fiftieth anniversary of the 54 Entry graduation, and we all tried hard to attend the Old Cranwellian reunion that year. The organisers must have considered that we were old and decrepit, because we were issued with special car passes which led us to park in a particular place where cadets were waiting to escort us to our rooms and carry our bags. In our day, flight cadets were all male and training to be pilots (except for the associated secretarial and equipment branch cadets at nearby Digby) but now there were girl cadets, and all branches did a short course there. The cadet who offered to help me in my dotage was one of the girls and what a charming one she was. She seemed surprised when I would not let her take my bag.

"But, sir, we have orders to carry the bags."

"My dear. Over the years I have often had occasion to carry a lady's bag, but never in my life have I allowed a lady to carry my bag."

"But, sir, I am not a lady, I am an officer cadet."

"Can't you be both?"

"I don't know, sir. We have not got that far with our training."

The reunion was a great success, and it was a great joy to spend an evening with the stalwarts of 54, all of whom, I discovered, had carried their own bags.

The first day that we were back at the Seaplane Base the following year, Jon asked me if I was ready for a student as soon as I walked in. I replied that I would like to run round the pattern with one of the instructors for half an hour to get my eye back in. Jon said that he would arrange that as soon as there was a spare aircraft and instructor. About an hour later, Jon said that he could not spare an instructor – would I mind going on my own? I replied that if

Me with Sylvia in the back of one of Jon Brown's J3 Cubs over Lake Mattie, Florida.

he was happy then so was I. A little later he came in and said that aircraft 123 was available and I could take it now. As I was walking out, Jon said that this chap wanted an introduction to seaplane flying and it would be a shame to waste a seat and would I take him with me? The trip went well – I really did not need a practice run, and of course, Jon had known that all the time!

Now that we were there for longer periods, I decided to attempt my multi-engine instructor rating. Chuck Brown (Jon's brother) was kind enough to fly a couple of trips with me in the 'twin Bee' and impart some of his great knowledge of seaplane flying to me. What Jon and Chuck between them do not know about seaplane flying is not worth knowing.

The Twin Bee is not like any other aircraft I have ever flown. It handles on the ground and in the air as if several of the components were made of elastic, and it wallows and lurches rather than taxies or flies. Some say that if you can get it to the runway you can probably fly it!

Don Grisham was also good enough to give me some coaching. Don has a wealth of flying experience and has done a great deal of instructing, from ab initio students to airline pilots, and is very good at it. He has a particularly pleasant instructional manner, and one of his ways is to put his critiques in the form of a question accompanied by a friendly smile. This is a most effective way of driving a lesson home, and I sometimes now use the method myself. I was most grateful for his help in passing the check ride. He and his wife Pat became good friends of ours.

All floats leak, some more than others, and it is normal procedure to pump them out between flights. We had one that was worse than most and would soon have to go into the hangar for a serious seal job. I was flying it one day, and after landing, the left wing went down alarmingly. I assumed that the float was sinking, and without taking the time for much consideration, put the power on to get some speed to get some lift on the wings to stop us sinking anymore. The left wing came up as I had hoped, thus appearing to confirm my erroneous diagnosis. In fact, one of the bolts holding the strut between the fuselage and the float had broken; the float was not sinking, but the wing was collapsing down towards it. My corrective action worked for that situation too. I flew back to base and landed as close to the ramp as I could. As I taxied in, it started to collapse again, but with some smart recovery work by Jon and a couple of chaps, we got it on to the ramp just as the wing tip was entering the water.

On another occasion, I was flying with a new instructor when we both thought that the engine 'sounded funny'. I could not identify the noise, but better safe than sorry, we decided to return to base. Not knowing the cause of the problem, I did not touch the throttle until we were within gliding distance of our lake. Then, when I did reduce the throttle, the engine started breaking up, making some loud bangs and streaming oil. Some bits of engine were blown off with such force that they came right through the cowling. We landed safely and a friendly fisherman towed us to the ramp.

This episode reminded me of an occasion when I was flying my Challenger over Lake Huntley. I noticed a man in a boat trying repeatedly but unsuccessfully to start his outboard engine. Dusk was falling, and I envisaged the poor chap out in his boat all night. I landed next to him and asked if he needed help. He did. So we tied a rope from his bow to my float spreader bar and I towed him to his dock. Boats sometimes tow seaplanes, but I have never heard any other case of a seaplane towing a boat.

At another time in one of Jon's Cubs, I had an engine failure caused by a broken fuel line. I managed to glide to Lake Lowery and landed there without any further damage. It is possible to 'sail' a seaplane, and we teach our students how to do it. Without engine thrust (or with it in a strong wind) the aircraft goes backwards downwind, but with the right control deflections it can be made to go to the left or right of the exact downwind direction. Using this technique, I sailed the aircraft to Greg Anderson's beach. Greg is a seaplane owner and a friend of Jon's and so it was much more convenient to repair the aircraft there than it would have been in the weeds.

I was teaching a student sailing and docking on Lake Mattie one day, and when we had finished, I swung the prop to start the engine. It would not start. I swung it about a thousand times, and used all the tricks I knew – back turning to get the surplus fuel out of the cylinders, full throttle to give plenty of air to counter act the surplus fuel, starting with the fuel off, and even with the carburettor heat on. I thought that one more swing and my arm would fall off. Just then Richy, one of the other instructors and a very good chap, who happened to be using the same lake, saw that I was in difficulties and taxied up to see if he could help. He swung it about a thousand times, and used all the tricks that I had. It simply would not start, and we agreed that there must be something wrong with the engine. So we tied a rope from his seaplane to mine and towed it across the lake to a spot where there were a few houses and therefore a road. Then we called Jon and told him the story. He and his mechanic, the very able Mark, arrived about a half hour later. While we were waiting, I remarked to Richy that it would be rather embarrassing if Jon started the engine with one swing. I expect you have guessed the rest. Jon set the controls and swung the prop once and the engine burst into life! But Jon is a good man and did not say a word.

One day, three Dutchmen came into the base, they all appeared to enjoy their food and drink and were grossly overweight. The two lightest (if that word is appropriate for people weighing in at 260 pounds) declared that they would like to take a short sight seeing trip. It fell to me to accommodate them. I took each in turn and gave them about 20 minutes in the air. After landing they were overjoyed at the experience and said that it had made their vacation. At this point, the largest, (there is no doubt that that is the appropriate word), who admitted to weighing 320 pounds, but was more like 340, declared that he too would like a trip. I agreed to take him, confident that he would not be able to get into the aircraft. We went out to the ramp and I invited him to get in, thinking that would be the end of the attempt. To my surprise, he managed to get in. I pulled the front stick back, confident that his girth would prevent the stick's full movement which would mean that we could not go but with no loss of 'face'.

Again to my surprise, the stick came fully back. I looked into the rear cockpit and saw that the rear stick was totally enveloped in his vast stomach.

"Doesn't that hurt?"

"Nein, not a bit!"

I was hoist by my own petard! Fortunately, the aircraft had only about three gallons in the tank, and there was a good 10 knot wind to help us off.

I did a circular take-off going round the lake more than once and the second time we came to the in-to-wind heading we lifted off. I did one large pattern (circuit to the British). I never reduced power from maximum until we were back on the water, and the aircraft would not go above 200 feet. Several times on the way round I asked myself why I had put myself in that ridiculous situation. I still do not know the answer.

As I have said, the Seaplane base is almost as much a social centre as a flying school, and many of the students come back to see us and fly again with us, several of them regularly. Sometimes it is many years since they first came, and we have difficulty remembering their names, or sometimes, even their faces. In Sun 'n Fun week there are always a large number of visitors, and one of them was disappointed, hurt even, that I could not recall his name. I was sorry to displease him. Later that day, a chap walked in and smiled at me in a most friendly way, and though I did not recognise him, I naturally assumed that he was also on a return visit, and did not want to disappoint him too, so I decided to hunt for clues.

"Hello", I said, "It's nice to see you again. Was it four or five years ago that you were last here?"

"I've never been here before", he said, with the same smile still on his face.

After flying, there is often a gathering of pilots sitting on the porch, having a few beers, and 'shooting the breeze'. Some amusing stories are told and a true one that I liked concerned a pilot approaching an airfield to land. He called the tower and they gave him the wind and pressure setting and so on. He then asked for priority in landing.

"We already have an aircraft on priority landing, you are Priority 2."

"But I really must get down fast, and request to go Priority 1."

"You can only go ahead of Priority 1 if you declare an emergency."

"Roger. Mayday, mayday, mayday. Aircraft ABC declaring an emergency!"

"Roger, ABC. What is the nature of your emergency?"

"I am very short of fuel."

New Voice: "That still makes you Priority 2, Bud. I haven't got any fuel at all!"

Another (said to be) true story concerned a pilot taxiing to the take off point in a great hurry. As he approached that point, there was an aircraft ahead of him so he called: "Aircraft nearing take off point, will you please pull over and let me pass?"

"Negative. I am No. 1. Wait your turn."

So he called the tower: "Tower, will you please instruct the aircraft ahead of me to pull over so that I can go first?"

The tower people must have thought that he was an important person or something, for they did as he asked, and the aircraft pulled over. As he passed the first aircraft, he transmitted: "How do you like them apples?"

He lined up and started his take off run and just before he lifted off the first pilot put his microphone by the fire bell test and pressed the test button. The second pilot heard the fire warning bell go off, chopped the throttles and stood on the brakes and came to screeching halt at the end of the runway.

At which the first pilot transmitted: "And how do you like THEM apples?"

One of my students was a heart surgeon, and we were having a chat over a beer after flying and he said: "You know, all my working life I have been a heart surgeon and all my life, flying has been my hobby."

I replied: "What a coincidence! All my working life I have been an aviator, and my hobby has been heart surgery."

"I've never heard of that. How do you do it?"

"I belong to a club, and we get together on week ends and do heart surgery on each other."

For several seconds he believed me.

The CEO of one of the major national car hire companies enrolled as a student. He was, it seemed, a better executive that he was a pilot. He had already been to three other seaplane schools and failed to get his rating at each one. Now he was going to try again with us, and Jon, in moment of mental aberration, allocated him to me. Our standard course took five flying hours, and most people completed it in that time. Some went to seven or eight, and the record was fifteen. This chap had about thirty before he started his fourth attempt. I worked very hard with him and eventually got him to a point where he just might make it. A CFI should not recommend a student for a check ride unless he is confident of a pass, but it is possible to overdo the training and then the student's performance starts to deteriorate. This chap was never going to get any better than he was now, so I put him up and he passed. Not a good pass, but a pass. He was over the moon, and kept shaking my hand and telling me how grateful he was and he wished he knew how to thank me. The fourth time he said all this, I said: "May I make a suggestion?"

"Please do."

"You could give me your card and a note, and the next time I need to rent a car from you, perhaps I could get a deal."

His demeanour changed instantly. "I'm not that grateful."

Another student I had was the County Sheriff – a very nice man. When we were doing ground school, we were constantly interrupted by his phone with one sided conversations like:

"Yeah."

"Yeah."

"Take four officers, two with rifles and two with shotguns. If he doesn't surrender at once, open fire."

After a few such calls, I asked him what would happen if he dropped dead.

"My deputy would take over."

"Tell him you're dead!"

He got the point and switched it off. He was a good student and did a good check ride. When we were saying our farewells he gave me his card and said: "Now, if you ever get into trouble with the law, be sure to get in touch with me. If I cannot keep you out of jail, I can make sure that you get a good cell!"

This brings my flying story up to date. The telling has whiled away the dark evenings, which was the main purpose of it, but it has required a great deal of looking back, and I really prefer to look forward. There is much to look forward to. This year, Sylvia and I celebrate our diamond wedding and I hope that we shall get some communication from Her Majesty to mark the occasion.

Also this year is No. 2 Squadron's 100th Birthday, and they are already making plans for it. We shall certainly attend, and I shall be able to brag that I joined the Squadron more than half way back through its history.

In the summer, we shall go to England so that I can attend the Old Cranwellian Association annual reunion dinner. Last year marked the sixtieth anniversary of No. 54 Entry's graduation, and we all made a special effort to attend. I greatly look forward to meeting my old chums again. Regretfully, there are only half of us still on the planet.

But before that, we are going to Florida where Jon has invited me to do another stint of instructing. Jon and Frances are going to meet us at the airport, and have suggested that we stop off for a drink and dinner together on the way home. How nice that will be. Next day, I shall be back in a seaplane.

Next month.

I can hardly wait.

Estepona Spain
February 2012

POSTSCRIPT

After the first edition of this book was published 12 years ago, my Sylvia and I had several idyllic years together Our home in Spain was exactly right for us, we had a nice circle of friends and a happy social life. Our holiday home in Florida was very comfortable and I greatly enjoyed instructing at the Seaplane Base.

Every now and again, Sylvia would say something strange or do something odd, the first signs of her dementia. As time went by these episodes became more frequent, more prolonged and more serious.

As we approached the end of one stay in Florida I realised that by the next year Sylvia would need my full time care and attention. Sadly, I explained to Jon that we would not be able to come back again,

On the morning of our departure, a formation of seaplanes led by Jon, flew over our lake at low level and as they passed our house they dipped their wings in salute. It was the seaplane pilots' farewell. I had great difficulty swallowing the lump in my throat.

The Spanish specialist told me that Sylvia's dementia was quite well advanced and that in about a year she would need care and treatment which would be beyond my capabilities and she would have to go into a home.

I did not want her to go into a Spanish care home so we sold up and moved back to England and found a very nice house in Axminster. The very kind and considerate mental health and welfare nurses visited us every month to check on Sylvia whose behaviour was getting increasingly erratic and even violent. Then one day they took her to the care home.

There, her behaviour got worse and the nurses often had to give her a shot in the arm to calm her down.

Just before the end, she reverted to her normal placid self. On her last day i was sitting by her bed holding her hand, and she was sitting up in bed with her eyes closed and was calm and peaceful and looked almost content Then I was aware – almost felt – her spirit rising up and leaving her earthly frame and I knew that she had gone. We had been married for sixty four golden years.

I found her loss and my grief very hard to bear. My neighbours Pat and Steve were a very great comfort to me at that time with their sympathy and support. I shall always be grateful to them and we became good friends.

It struck me one day that my sorrow had been for Sylvia – for the mental anguish and torment she had had to endure. Now that she was at peace, it could only be for me. That is just weakness and I knew that I had to pull myself together.

First thing was to start flying again. I received a warm welcome at the Base, quickly revalidated my licences and started instructing again. It was good to be back.

Back in the UK I saw Pat and Steve again and I told them about my trip. Steve's interest perked up and he said that he would like to have a trip in a seaplane. So the next year he came over and I gave him his trip. He greatly enjoyed it and back in England he said that he would really like to fly an aeroplane solo. So the following year I arranged access to a Cessna 150 on wheels and we started the RAF standard syllabus for a new pilot. After about ten hours of instruction (very commendable considering that he was much older than most students) I soloed him – the most important trip in an aviator's career.

I had had my very first students, Tony and Guy, sixty five years before and I was still friends with them both. I am pleased that history repeated itself and now Steve, my latest and last student, is also a firm friend.

All my life I have passed pilot medical exams with no problem. But the next time I went to the States I failed the test due to deteriorating eyesight. I had developed macular degeneration and would never be able to hold a pilot's licence again. So after sixty nine years as an active pilot, flying fifteen and a half thousand hours in one hundred and fifty aircraft types, I had to give up flying, I told my friends that I was just getting the hang of it!

We get only one run through this life, Some people have a good one , others are bad with most people somewhere in between. Mine has been a really good run because the two pillars of it – first my darling Sylvia and second my flying career among splendid aviators and aeroplanes – were unmatchable.

I know that to say that I would not change a thing is a cliché but in my case it is a true one,

How wonderful it would be to go back to the beginnings and do it all over again!

Axminster, Devon
October 2024

Printed in Dunstable, United Kingdom